Apparition
at the Moment
of Death

"*Apparitions at the Moment of Death* is a thrilling compilation of crisis after-death communications across time and space. Bourke takes us from ancient Egypt to modern times, shedding light on the phenomenon from many angles—from history and spiritual scholarship to folklore with its legends, lyric, and lore, while not forgetting the views of saints and shamans. These common, beneficial, and comforting experiences, which seem to be inherent to the human condition, point to the possibility of the survival of consciousness. Bourke's meticulous and wide-ranging work supports the assumption that after-death communications are universal and timeless. The time has finally come to normalize these experiences and remove them from the realm of anomaly, where they do not belong. This book provides original, comprehensive, and compelling insights into spontaneous contacts with the deceased, for which the postmaterialist hypothesis offers a convincing explanatory framework. I highly recommend this brilliant book."

EVELYN ELSAESSER, EXPERT ON
AFTER-DEATH COMMUNICATIONS AND
NEAR-DEATH EXPERIENCES AND AUTHOR OF
SPONTANEOUS CONTACTS WITH THE DECEASED

"This extraordinary collection gathers stories of death apparitions ranging from ancient Sumer to today, spanning many cultures and continents. An invaluable sourcebook, its greatest strength is its breadth of coverage. The cross-cultural viewpoint reveals overarching patterns and themes found in sources as diverse as Aboriginal Australian tribal lore, Icelandic sagas, and lives of saints and mystics of many faiths as well as stories from ordinary people bewildered by visits from the dead."

CHRIS WOODYARD, AUTHOR OF *A IS FOR ARSENIC* AND
EDITOR OF *THE VICTORIAN BOOK OF THE DEAD*

Apparitions
at the Moment
of Death

The Living Ghost in Legend, Lyric, and Lore

A Sacred Planet Book

Daniel Bourke

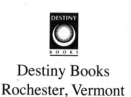

Destiny Books
Rochester, Vermont

Destiny Books
One Park Street
Rochester, Vermont 05767
www.DestinyBooks.com

Destiny Books is a division of Inner Traditions International

Sacred Planet Books are curated by Richard Grossinger, Inner Traditions editorial board member and cofounder and former publisher of North Atlantic Books. The Sacred Planet collection, published under the umbrella of the Inner Traditions family of imprints, includes works on the themes of consciousness, cosmology, alternative medicine, dreams, climate, permaculture, alchemy, shamanic studies, oracles, astrology, crystals, hyperobjects, locutions, and subtle bodies.

Cataloging-in-Publication Data for this title is available from the Library of Congress

ISBN 979-8-88850-056-9 (print)
ISBN 979-8-88850-057-6 (ebook)

Printed and bound in the United States by Lake Book Manufacturing, LLC

10 9 8 7 6 5 4 3 2 1

Text design and layout by Kenleigh Manseau
This book was typeset in Garamond Premier Pro with Big Caslon CC and Classico URW used as display typefaces

To send correspondence to the author of this book, mail a first-class letter to the author c/o Inner Traditions • Bear & Company, One Park Street, Rochester, VT 05767, and we will forward the communication.

For Cosmo ~ Our Best Boy

Contents

)

Foreword

Patricia Pearson

In the modern, secular West, our fear of death has given ghosts a bad name. Culturally and collectively, we associate spectres with the spooky rituals of Halloween, with haunted houses at amusement parks, with chilling supernatural tales. Ghosts are vengeful, or perhaps melancholic, drifting through hallways or rattling chains. They—which is actually to say our fear of death—continually haunt us.

Yet at the same time, as *individuals*, research suggests, we are far more likely to privately encounter spirits in the guise of the people we care about—arguably manifesting themselves to us on a conduit of love. They say goodbye, they reassure, they tend to our concerns.

The appearance of these more personal ghosts may literally be visual, or we might hear a beloved voice or feel the distinctive presence of a parent or spouse. Sometimes the visitation occurs in a striking dream. In all cases, the encounter is typically brief, unembellished, and utterly undeniable. What is most thought-provoking for researchers is that this kind of manifestation can serve as the first intimation that a loved one has died, experiences that, since the late 19th century, have been referred to as *crisis apparitions*.

With this book, Bourke has created a much-needed compendium— drawn from myriad cultures and eras—to emphasize the essential human ordinariness of the crisis apparition and its visionary relatives. While it may be uncommon to speak of aloud, given cultural taboos that are adamantly policed by Darwinian materialists, it *is* most certainly common all over the world. For example, in one household survey of the inhabitants of an Italian city, hallucinations in healthy people pertained almost entirely to death and crisis. Further, 76 percent of those who had the experience took action of some kind in response to their seemingly synchronistic awareness.[1] A study of "second sight" or extra-sensory perception in Scotland revealed that among those who report having had it, 30 percent had a "vision of a person recognized before, at the moment of or after death."[2] A German study of psychic experiences in the general population found that "crisis ESP," defined in this case as experiencing "strange things happening at exactly the same time someone died or had an accident elsewhere," had occurred in 18.7 percent of respondents.[3] And a more recent multinational survey found that, of those who reported an after-death communication to the researchers, 20.7 percent identified their encounter as a "crisis ADC."[4]

While the vocabulary around this experience remains notably unsettled, the experience itself is not, and has remained remarkably stable through the ages, as Bourke will show you. So how do we come to grips with it, beyond rushing to the chalk board to calculate statistical probabilities of coincidence? The first task, it would seem, is to gather the stories and examine them more closely. Oxford biologist Alister Hardy, who collected over three thousand first-hand accounts of spiritual experiences from citizens of the United Kingdom in the mid-twentieth century, argued that "a truly quantitative science of living things was made possible only by the foundations laid down by the observations of the field naturalists."[5] A similar approach should be taken, he believed, with spiritual experiences, first building up a body of reports and then beginning to analyze and classify them. "The specimens we are hunting are shy and delicate ones," he cautioned of this elusive and so often unjustly repudiated field.[6]

At Stanford University in 1970, political scientist Raymond Wolfinger told his graduate students that "the plural of anecdote is data." What he meant was that we can begin with one report of human experience and build out from there until we have a quantitative data set. Remarkably, as physician Bernard Beitman relayed after corresponding with Wolfinger, this off-hand classroom remark somehow evolved into its very opposite in common skeptical parlance, wherein people are warned away from "pseudo-science" by being told, "the plural of anecdote is not data." *Not.* Wolfinger's meaning got flipped on its head.[7]

In fact, everything we know about human subjective experience arises from anecdotal report. There is no blood test for depression or urine sample for envy. We cannot prove, objectively, the differing natures of platonic and parental love, or why we are awed by sunsets but largely unmoved by brick walls. We rely instead on personal observations. When we have enough of them, we arrive at a sort of consensus reality. Roses smell beautiful; music is stirring; loneliness hurts.

By taking a cross-cultural and cross-temporal syncretic approach to gathering accounts of these "living ghosts," Bourke posthumously presents Alister Hardy with an excellent new data set. It behooves other researchers to dig in. He also reminds us of something we are curiously determined to forget in this post-Enlightenment Western corner of the world: that we are deeply connected to one another, and that love is the indelible, enduring thread that binds us.

PATRICIA PEARSON is an award-winning journalist and author of several books, including *Opening Heaven's Door*. Her work has appeared in *The New Yorker*, *The New York Times*, and *Business Week*, among other publications. Her TEDx talk, "Why Ghosts Are Good for You," points to research showing the importance of apparitions in helping people cope with grief. She is based in Toronto, Canada.

Magic and Meaning at the Moment of Death

The imaginal life is central to the human story, and should be central to the writing and teaching of history. The world of imagination nourishes humans and leads them to action. A history without imagination is a mutilated history, a history of the walking dead.

JACQUES LE GOFF

By some magical means, recorded and remembered in all ages, man has demonstrated the strange yet undeniable capacity to receive information regarding the well-being of others, often loved ones, at a distance and at a time when they could not have discovered this information through ordinary channels. Primarily recorded in relation to the discovery of a distant death, these are the "apparitions at the moment of death" of our title, the *crisis apparitions*, so marveled at by their subjects and those who come to know of them, accounts of which fill the following pages. From the most ancient tablets through the celebrated annals of antiquity—surviving the relentlessly didactic pennings of the long Middle Ages, hidden away among the fairy and folklore of all lands, and finally found in the hospices and emergency rooms of the twenty-first century—such experiences have certainly been collected previously,

1

but never from such a wide variety of sources. Here, the crisis apparition as a truly universal phenomenon is brought to light.

The encounters chosen here are most often from ancient, obscure, folkloric, romantic poetic, hagiographic, and cross-cultural sources. While the likes of astronomer Camille Flammarion collected hundreds of accounts, those were predominantly French and European (see Flammarion's *The Unknown or Death and Its Mystery* and similar). The likes of Aniela Jaffe collected many Swiss and other accounts in her *Apparitions and Precognition*. Likewise, Gurney, Myers, and Podmore collected many thousands of accounts in their seminal *Phantasms of the Living* volumes, a primarily British survey. There are other accounts, too, from places such as Hong Kong, Italy, Scotland, Iceland, and more, though again, those are mainly restricted to those regions[1] and while certain cross-cultural references had been made in those and other works, particularly those of Stefan Schouten, who compared British and German accounts,[2] here it is the rule rather than the exception, and the cases will be of a truly varied and worldwide type. This allows us to more clearly appreciate the impressive and surprising stability of the experiences across time, space, and culture. For this reason, too, the chapters have been organized by *type* of experience (i.e. apparitions, visions, symbolic visions, accounts which involve a third party messenger, etc.) rather than the experiences of certain groups or time periods. Whether the shaman, the salesman, the sinner, or the saint, the experience itself, the crisis apparition, is first and foremost a human encounter and does not discriminate in its manifestation. While the chapters will focus primarily on one area, there will be some crossover where it is helpful or otherwise illustrative.

To varying extents, the choices presented here are the result of practicality, some serendipity, and, finally, favor—those that I have personally been drawn to. Perhaps most importantly, though, they are those that illuminate the varying and interconnected ways in which this intriguing phenomenon has manifested through time. Those which, in fact, weave in and out of the human story itself and will bring us as much to the lives of some of history's most well-remembered men and women as to its least-known characters. These curious records, in their number, are a testament to some mysterious faculty that, while fundamentally associated with death and dying, speaks more, in the end, to the love and connections not just between ourselves and our loved ones but between ourselves and our departed forerunners. Those who have gone before.

When the deeply skeptical sixteenth century Protestant theologian Ludwig Lavater wrote confidently that "There have been many times men seen walking on foot or riding on back, being of a fiery shape, known unto diverse men, and such as died not long before,"[3] he could not have known just how widely such encounters had been and would continue to be reported in both the old world and the new. From the ghost-obsessed upper classes of Victorian England to the far remote tribes of Tierra del Fuego, neither geography nor time are factors. These are the stories of the crisis apparitions proper, the so-called *wraiths, swarths, fetches, tasks, tokens, lledriths, presentiments,* and *forerunners,* as they are known in just a small number of different lands, accounts that freely flow from a thousand tongues and fill the pages of the folklorist, the anthropologist, the ethnologist, the hagiographer, and the parapsychologist alike; accounts that are found wherever they are asked for. While their pedigree is impressive and their age and ubiquity noted, they are both more archaically and more widely represented than has yet been compiled.

Just as the romantics, the monks, and the scribes of the Middle Ages and beyond were familiar with these kinds of experiences and, as will be explored, would have seen the value in adopting them for literary use, so too would have been such pre-classical authors and their renowned successors. As we'll see, the works ascribed to Homer, Virgil, and Apuleius, among others, contain references to these very same encounters. What becomes clear is that the "ghost" both inspires and is inspired by literature. This is evident in instances such as that of playwright David Belasco, author of the 1911 Broadway play *The Return of Peter Grimm,* who tells us of his own ghostly encounter which directly inspired his work:

> I went to bed, worn out, in my Newport home, and fell at once into a deep sleep. Almost immediately, however, I was awakened and attempted to rise, but could not, and was then greatly startled to

see my dear mother (whom I knew to be in San Francisco) standing close by me. As I strove to speak and to sit up, she smiled at me a loving, reassuring smile, spoke my name—the name she called me in my boyhood—"Davy, Davy, Davy," then, leaning down, seemed to kiss me; then drew away a little and said: "Do not grieve. All is well and I am happy;" then moved toward the door and vanished.

Belasco's mother, then far distant in San Francisco and speaking those very words at her last, had indeed died that same night.[4]

"The new marvels," wrote Scottish polymath and pioneering compiler of folktales Andrew Lang, in reference to the ancient and widespread phenomenon of ghostly rappings and disturbances associated with distant deaths, "were certainly not stimulated by literary knowledge of the ancient magic."[5] Encounters such as Belasco's, as we'll see, are a testament to those words as they relate to the crisis apparition.

So often, these apparitions have been noted for their relative mundanity. They are "as common as they are dull," wrote Lang.[6] "None of these spirits were the chain-clanking, blood-spattered, terrifying ghosts of fiction," observed University of Wisconsin professor Deborah Blum.[7] Commenting on the work of classical scholar Frederick Myers and psychologist Edmund Gurney, who themselves had been struck by the similarity of the reports they received by the hundreds and compiled in their still unsurpassed collection of accounts in the late nineteenth century, journalist Patricia Pearson importantly noted that "given the wide and rich body of folklore about the supernatural that their subjects had access to in Victorian England, no reports came back of headless horsemen or fairies or spooky castles or Dickensian variations on the ghosts who haunted Scrooge."[8] Regularly, however, and in striking contrast to this common observation, these are potentially paradigm-shifting encounters that, in a moment, might fundamentally reorient the individual in their personal relationship to the very cosmos. "My mother convinced me that the dead come back," wrote Belasco emphatically after his encounter, later deciding to write his play, as he explained, "in terms of what I conceive to be actuality, dealing with the return of the dead."[9] Harriet Hosmer, considered perhaps the most distinguished neoclassical sculptor of her time in America, awoke to the form of a young woman she knew named Rosa at the end of her bed, telling her, "I am well now" around the time she had died at a distance. Hosmer observed that "to me this occurrence is as much of a reality as any experience of my life."[10]

Put simply, unsuspecting individuals report encounters with the apparitional forms of their dead or dying loved ones at times when they could not have been aware of their situation by ordinary means. As noted, these crisis apparitions are a long-recognized phenomenon which occur widely across cultures and time, and the experiences often impel religiosity, personal transformation, and creative endeavors alike. It is this misty and magical continuum of the literal and the literary, the romantic and the real, the very purview of the ghost, with which we are concerned here and through which these pages will travel. It is for this reason that the present study is concerned at least with documenting a certain ancient, widespread, and greatly influential notion while at most offering a firmer indication of just how geographically and temporally ubiquitous these phenomena truly are.

Whether reported or recorded by the shaman, the saint, or the "layman," these apparitions and visions seem also to call us to entertain the possibility that we are more connected to each other and to our world in more fundamental ways than we think. And while this is no scientific study but rather a syncretic and at times speculative one, we should, before setting out, at least be open to the idea that not only are there valid ways of knowing as those lauded and wonderful methods of science, but perhaps, as the experiences in these pages seem to suggest, there are even other, equally valid, ways of knowing still to be discovered, at least by those of us who have yet to touch or be touched by that mysterious and so often inscrutable beyond.

Throughout this book, we will freely and unapologetically traverse the realms of the romantic, the legendary, and the literary, of both memorate and myth alike. Let it be said upfront that these are experiences not to be taken lightly. The apparitions and visions at the moment of death collected here are often seen to impart in the individual what Jeanne Von Bronkhorst, author of *Dreams at the Threshold*, referred to as a "marvelous, wondrous certainty" regarding, among other things, the continuation of the personality beyond death.[11] In this way, the crisis apparition and its relatives have been and continue to be a unique and powerful line of communication between the familiar and that great and mysterious other.

ONE

Apparitions, Ghosts, Death, and Hope

I am convinced that a fundamental reason that spiritual beliefs have been able to resist the enormous social pressures toward secularization is that they are, in part, rationally founded on experience.

DAVID HUFFORD

In the encounters which follow, the individuals involved are mysteriously visited by the recognizable form of those that they love or, more rarely, strangers around the very time at which they had died somewhere far distant. Such visitations are the most common of apparitions, and abundantly found in the legend, lyric, poetry, and lore of almost every age. In this spirit, we begin in ancient Egypt, where communication with the dead was expected, where letters were routinely sent to loved ones long passed, where the soul was long known to separate from the body, and with perhaps the very oldest of all recorded crisis apparitions. The following excerpt is taken from the famed instructions of a royal father, Amenemhat I, the founder of the twelfth dynasty of ancient Egypt, to his son, Senwosret.[1] While rarely if ever cited for this specifically, the inscription, which was written in 1963 BCE, nevertheless contains one of the oldest descriptions of an apparition bringing news of their death at a time when that death was unknown to the "percipient" or subject of the encounter. Long before even the shades of antiquity, the various visions of the sinner and the saint, or the messenger ghosts and wraiths of legend and lore, these accounts had been recorded, and in an entirely familiar form.

In a rather dramatic monologue, the Pharaoh Amenemhat returns as a ghost to explain to his son and loyal followers what had happened during their absence from the palace. Senwosret's father gives a detailed account of his murder during a palace coup. "And see what happened, foul murder," cried the pharaoh's ghost to his son, explaining that they had killed him in the night.[2]

Whether this is interpreted as a literary device, a political commentary, or an account that served an entirely propagandistic function is, for our purposes, unimportant.* The narrative itself, conspicuously reminiscent of the ghost in *Hamlet*, also famously revealing its death to the onlookers, is entirely in line with its equivalents, which millennia later were to be found amongst the forerunners of Eastern Canada, the tokens of North America's shores, and the fetches and wraiths of the Scottish Highlands, and speaks firmly to the perennial nature of the crisis apparition, form notwithstanding. "The mere fact of imitation," wrote Finucane while discussing changing ideas regarding the perception of the ghost through the centuries, "is useful as indicating continuity of expectation and belief across more than a millennium."[3]

While there are many related ways in which the news of these distant deaths are presented, including apparent waking or sleeping visions, the idea that the apparition specifically comes to reveal their fate is a variant by definition older than the written word. While our Egyptian pharaoh Amenemhat lends truth to the antiquity of the idea, the notion that ghosts, in the general sense, may indirectly or directly inform one of their death is older still. A Sumerian tablet (K 2175+) at the Royal Nineveh Library contains advice for people who are being pursued by one of several types of ghosts, one of those being, as it relates to our

---

*For an interesting discussion on these various interpretations, see Goedick, *The Beginning of the Instruction of King Amenemhat*, 15–21.

work, the soul of an unknown murdered man or woman. According to the tablet, the person being pursued can ward off the ghost with this incantation:

> Ghost who has been set on me and pursues me day and night [...] may he accept this as his portion and leave me be![4]

CRISIS APPARITIONS OF ANCIENT GREECE

We will revisit the Near East, but for now, we meet much later in antiquity with the ghost of Creusa from the *Aeneid*, one of the more well-known and celebrated classical apparitions. While the account was put to page in that era, the event itself is placed during the legendary Trojan War (c. 1299 BCE–c. 1100 CE), making this another of the oldest of all recorded crisis apparitions. Furthermore, given the extent to which Virgil's epic drew from older traditions, and in what will become a lesser but important theme here, such encounters in whatever form invariably came and went in much larger numbers than the relative few that we have from that period.

With Troy burning at the hands of the Greeks, the Greco-Roman mythological hero Aeneas notices that his wife, Creusa, is no longer with the fleeing group.[5] Distraught, he returns to Troy to find his home in flames. Searching from house to house, Aeneas is suddenly met by his wife's ghost, who famously and enigmatically notes, "The Great Mother of the Gods detains me on these shores." Creusa then further divines her husband's future, including a wife yet to come and urging Aeneas, just as Belasco's mother urged him, not to live in grief but to continue on as best he can in her absence. Creusa shows her husband in no uncertain terms that her existence has continued, and from this, Aeneas draws comfort and impetus anew.

The extent to which crisis-related apparitions and visions, in all their forms, may assuage grief or either impact or engender belief in the first place has not been greatly explored, particularly as a historical phenomenon. Accounts as old as these, however, are relevant attestations and are connected in this way to those countless encounters that were to come.

We would be remiss not to include the following vision at the outset, even though it is widely known and reproduced. It has particular importance considering the extent to which it was to be representative of those that would follow. The narrative, which Cicero considered in his *On Divination* as being "a clear and direct kind of dream,"[6] comes down to us from the surviving fragments of the work of the Greek philosopher Chrysippus (c. 279–206 BCE). This is one of the most widely referenced of the dreams, and while usually considered in the context of a prophetic dream, the kind then recorded with the most frequency, it has been somewhat underappreciated as a crisis apparition proper.

The account itself involved two friends of Arcadia who came to the Greek city of Megara. Having parted ways, the first one dreamed that the other was in danger, saying that it might still be possible to save him. After awakening and regaining his composure, the man returns to sleep. Again he dreamed, this time that his friend had been put to death, and the form of the man himself told his friend that his body was "at that very moment" being carried to the city gates. Hurrying to the location indicated in the dream, the man found the body of his friend exactly there.[7]

Few authors have noted or thoroughly explored the similarity between accounts from antiquity and those more recent. Regarding this famed account from Megara, scholars such as Morton[8] and Felton[9] disregard it and similar dreams in their own studies, while others, such as classicist Collison-Morley, take a more neutral approach.[10] The issue is simply one of definitions and parameters. Collison-Morley made the specific connection between this account from antiquity and the anecdotes being collected in her own time by those parapsychological researchers as "one of the very few stories from antiquity in which the apparition is seen at or near the moment of death."[11] Both those scholars, along with others like Nadia Sels, note that dreams which coincide with the very event of their contents are rather unusual in classical antiquity,[12] though we will see that those that do exist have been notably influential and, furthermore, that their numbers are greater than have been supposed, particularly when including hagiographic and literary sources.

Although separated by thousands of years, the essential tales are rarely meaningfully dissimilar. Around 2 CE, as relayed by Plutarch, a young Pythagorean named Lysis came to Thebes, died there, and was buried by his friends.[13] In a dream, his ghost appeared to some acquaintances he had left in Italy and who learned of his fate in this way. The Pythagoreans, who, according to British classical scholar and linguist Jane Ellen Harrison, were "more skilled in these matters than modern psychical experts,"[14] had a certain sign by which they knew the apparition of a dead man from one of the living, a fascinating distinction that millennia later was to attain much importance.*

Also overlooked as a clear example of a crisis apparition in antiquity has been the ghost of Polydorus of Troy, who so dramatically announces his fate in the opening paragraphs of Euripides' circa fourth century BCE play *Hecuba*: "Then did my father's friend slay me his helpless guest for the sake of the gold, and thereafter cast me into the swell of the sea, to keep the gold for himself in his house. And there I lie one time upon the strand, another in the salt sea's surge, drifting ever up and down upon the billows, unwept, unburied."[15]

Like the many shades we will meet with from beyond the curated confines of fiction, and indeed far beyond those of the Mediterranean, Polydorus makes it quite clear that he has been slain and, as his folkloric successors would so often do, reveals the location of his body. Polydorus makes it plain too that he has appeared to his mother Hecuba, noting, "For yonder she passeth on her way from the shelter of Agamemnon's tent, terrified at my spectre." This is soon confirmed by Hecuba herself. When she is told after the body is found, she is not surprised and says, "Alas! Alas! I read right the vision I saw in my sleep."

THE FAR EAST AND BACK

We now move many thousands of kilometers and many hundreds of years later to the east, to the 1478 CE crisis apparition of Permalingpa, a Tibetan Buddhist shaman whose visions are said to be the basis for

---

*Professor Hornell Hart in *Six Theories about Apparitions*, 153–239, for example, argued that the fact that apparitions of the living and the dead are "essentially indistinguishable constituted evidence of the survival of personality beyond bodily death." It is interesting to read that the same distinction was made in 2 CE.

many volumes.[16] With a close relationship to the world of dreams and the dead, the shaman was uniquely placed in his receptivity to such experiences and indeed frequently sought them out. Permalingpa dreamed that the "treasure revealer," Ratnalingpa, told him that he was departing for heaven at that moment and encouraged him to bring welfare to the lives of living beings. Permalingpa later came to find out that Ratnalingpa had died that very day.

In a Manipuri folktale from northeastern India, a child awaits the return of her mother and another named Sangkhureima from fishing.[17] Sangkhureima, however, had killed the child's mother and lied to the child, telling her that her mother was still at the lake. That night, the child's mother came to her in a dream and told her in no uncertain terms, "You are waiting for me, but I am no longer alive."

From "a very long time ago" and again in Manipur, a young man was killed and came to a young girl in a dream, telling her, "I have been killed by your father and thrown into a pit in your farm."[18]

A Japanese folktale published in 1908, but also relating to a time "long ago" was told to British naturalist Richard Gordon Smith.[19] The story is of a man named Yoichi, whose closest friend Ichibei agreed with him that they would always come and help each other in times of need. News, however, traveled so slowly in those days that when Yoichi died far away, Ichibei had not heard of it. His shock, then, upon awakening one night to the figure of his best friend standing by his bed, should not be surprising. "Why, Yoichi! I am glad to see you," he said, "but how late at night you have arrived! Why did you not let me know you were coming? I should have been up to receive you, and there would have been a hot meal ready. But never mind. I will call a servant, and everything shall be ready as soon as possible." "I am no longer a living man," answered the ghost of Yoichi. "I am indeed your friend Yoichi's spirit."

A Japanese man named Nagatani and his wife, Makiko, who lived during the Onin War (1467–1477), were separated by the events. While apart, the young woman was stabbed to death by soldiers. When Nagatani returned, he went to his wife's house and found no one. That night, "as in a dream," she appeared, and he asked her what happened.

She explained that she had been caught and killed by the soldiers while they were apart.

Iwasaka gave a later memorate from the village of Hamanakamura in Japan.[20] A man was coming home from a local temple at night when he suddenly met Jin-san, someone who lived back in his village. The moment he attempted to speak to Jin-san, the man disappeared. When he returned to the village, he learned, "to his amazement," that Jin-san had died of a stroke just before they met.

In a Korean folktale recorded by eminent folkorist Kim So-Un, a young hunter traveling to the Kumgang mountains came across a certain young girl.[21] When he asked her for some water, she replied that the souls of both her father-in-law and mother-in-law appeared to her, telling her they had been killed. The same man later came across another stranger, who also told him that his mother-in-law told him in a dream that she had died.

China's incredibly archaic and impressively robust literary tradition regarding the supernatural documents that the belief in ghosts goes back to the dawn of their history. Of interest here are the observations of Professor of Sociology James McClenon that many such *chih-kuai* narratives fit the patterns of modern apparitional cases in the psychical research literature.[22] In any case, a work on the seventh to tenth century Tang dynasty tells us that when P'ei Chung-ling was governor of Kiang-ling, he sent his military commanders T'an Hung-sheu and Wang Chih to the south of the Sierra.[23] After a confrontation with some aggressive birds, T'an Hung-sheu suddenly got a severe headache and could not continue with them. Back in Kiang-ling, Governor P'ei Chung-ling dreamt that T'an Hung-sheu came to him and told him he had been murdered on the way by Wang Chih, the truth of which was discovered ten days later.

Millennia later in China, these crisis apparitions were still being reported in local newspapers, such as the following from a nineteenth century issue of *The China Mail*.[24] A junk ship sailed from Hoifoong for Macao. Having arrived there, the boat was robbed of its cargo, and the captain was killed and thrown overboard. One night the master of the local barracoon dreamed that the ghost of the murdered man was before him, explaining that he had been killed. The guilty pirates' gunboats were later found at the very spot indicated by the ghost.

British student of Chinese folklore Dennys similarly relayed the narrative of two "men of letters" at Nanchang who were very close. The elder one went to his home and suddenly died. The younger man, unaware, went on with his studies at the monastery in the usual way. One night after he had gone to sleep, he saw his old friend open the bed curtains, come to the bed, and put his hand on his shoulder, saying, "Brother, it is only ten days since I parted from you, and now a sudden sickness has carried me off. I am a ghost. I cannot, however, forget our friendship, and so have come to bid adieu."[25]

Turning from China to Cornwall, a man named Joseph headed down to the local cove to see if it was true that oranges had washed ashore after a fruit shipwreck off the coast.[26] When he didn't return, his mother became greatly anxious. Sitting at the window, she exclaimed, "Oh, here he is; now I'll see about the tea." She returned, however, unable to find him at either the front or back doors. Joseph, as it turned out, had been swallowed by the raucous sea after wading out to a rock.

In another British example, from a 1909 issue of the occult and psychically concerned *Light Journal*, Isaac Marsden of Lancashire, England, disappeared from his home, leaving behind a daughter of twenty-five, who later died of consumption. She was greatly distressed, and, after declaring that she had seen her father's form by her bedside, she informed those around her that his body was in the water at Aspen Bridge. An hour or two later, her father's body was removed from the canal at the precise spot she had named.[27]

In 1780, a man in the south of Iceland named Haldor Bjarnason sent his sons away to buy sheep. As they crossed the mountains on their return, they soon found themselves lost.[28] The winter passed with no word of their whereabouts until one of them came to their sister in a dream and said, "No one now can find us here, 'neath the snow in frosty tomb. Three days o'er his brother's bier, Bjarni sat in grief and gloom." As we'll see, the ghosts of the frozen north very often relayed their fate in rhyme.

SIMPLE GOODBYES

As we have seen, sometimes there are large distances between the "agent" and the percipient. While this emphasis can certainly be a helpful literary device to impress upon the reader the miraculous nature of such seemingly instantaneous communication, the very same details are still reported in earnest. When the English poet and soldier Wilfred Owen was shot and killed in 1918, for example, he appeared to his brother, who was over three thousand miles away aboard the HMS Astrea.[29] Nevertheless, his brother reported that Owen truly came to him on the night he died, displaying a warm smile of recognition. Fascinatingly too, this encounter was said to have banished his depression.

That the apparition so simply states or emotes a goodbye before departing, what St. Clair, in her Northern Irish sample, called their "farewells,"[30] is also a common kind of experience and is often more somber for the person to whom the apparition appears than the departing themselves, who often, though certainly not always, seem rather content. From the 1960s and the somewhat overlooked collection of Aniela Jaffe, Swiss psychologist, analyst, and the editor of some of Carl Jung's work, comes a tale from an old servant named Bernadine, who declared one evening that she had seen her daughter down in the cellar, all dressed in white and saying simply, "Goodbye, Mother." News soon came that her daughter, who was then living in America, had died at that time.[31]

From Canadian journalist Patricia Pearson, we read of her friend Ellie Black who, having been roused on a quiet night, noticed a movement at the end of her bed and was shocked to see it was her father. "Why is he here?" she wondered. "And what on Earth is he wearing? Is that a top hat and tails?" Her father gazed back at her happily, tipped his hat, and bowed with a flourish before disappearing. Later the following day, word came of the man's death.[32]

There are many comparable occurrences widely found and often devoid of much content. They are, at times, rather striking in their simplicity. One may read in the Paris newspaper *Le Petit Bleu* from

January 4, 1903, the account of the apparition of a daughter in Melbourne, Australia, to her mother in Paris.[33] The daughter had spoken these words: "Mother, I am dead." This happened at half past ten in the evening. The next day, a telegram informed the mother of her death.

While the apparitions often give direct messages, commonly too, they simply appear without any fanfare or specific information. In the following memorate given by Daryl Dance in a compilation of African American folklore, the apparition comes to the door and silently ignores the percipient.[34] An elderly woman's boyfriend was deathly sick in the hospital. One evening, just about dusk, she was in her kitchen when the doorbell rang. And there was Frank. She addressed him. "Frank, I thought you was in the hospital. Where—?" He didn't reply; he just stood and stared blankly at her. "Say, Frank, don't act like that; you scare me." She then turned around to run, slamming the door behind her. Soon after, the message came that he had died right at the time of the encounter, a fact that the woman stated she would "tell on her dying day."

While so often the apparitions bid farewell, just as common, if not more so, are instances in which the figure seems barely interested in the subject. Coming to the ghostly folklore of Guatemala, we read in a Chuj Mayan memorate of Xan Malin. His wife had not seen him for days, although she was not worried as he was often away for so long.[35] One night while she slept, he seemingly came home to work on the wool, as was his usual habit. When his son went out to check on the family cornfield, Xan Malin spoke to him and said he was staying out there to watch the corn. Some time later, however, the authorities found his remains, suggesting the form had rather been some otherworldly death messenger.

Further South, the Brazilian Parintintin have dreams in which "communications from the departing 'ra'uva' of a dying relative" are experienced; those dreams in which the relative appears "close to the time of death" seem to be a clear reference to the crisis apparition or vision.[36]

Accounts of this kind, where the dying person is seen out and about at a time when they are physically on their deathbeds, are common in the collections of folklorists, wherever they collect their tales. From the shores of the Shetland Islands, Andrew T. Cluness was told by a man that he and two others saw a woman, called Betty Clarke, coming out of her house.[37] He had some days earlier finished making a straw basket for her, and told her as much when they crossed paths. However, she completely ignored him. The second time he spoke, she turned around and looked at him but didn't answer and moved on. When he was later told that Betty was not expected to live through the night and was mortally ill four miles away over the hills, this man replied that he was amazed, exclaiming, "But I've just spoken to her or tried to speak to her less than half an hour ago." Next morning, the postman brought news that she had died just a short while after he had seen her. In the Shetland Islands this kind of vision has often been called a *feyness*.

FROM POLYDORUS TO POLYNESIA

The crisis apparition seems particularly well-established among Polynesians. Polynesians widely understand dreams to be the movements of the wandering soul which, after death, can also appear in the dreams of others. Pertinently too, one of their most common uses of magic is sending messages by "telepathy." Close friends, relatives, husbands, and wives frequently report such impressions of one another.[38] Finnish anthropologist Gunnar Landtman found that it was common for Papuans of the former British New Guinea to be warned in dreams when a friend died before the news could have arrived by ordinary channels.[39] In a more specific example, Landtman wrote of a Kiwai Papuan man traveling by canoe. As he slept, he encountered the ghost of his wife, who, unknown to him, had died while he was away, something he confirmed for himself upon his arrival home.[40]

The highly influential anthropologist and ethnologist Bronislaw Malinowski noted that among the Melanesians of the Trobriand Islands, it was in fact these cases where the *baloma*, or spirit, came to announce their death that were perhaps the most common means of communication between the two worlds.[41] In a more specific example from among the Omarakana on the Trobriand Islands, Kalogusa, working on a plantation far from home, dreamed that his mother "came to him and told him that she had died."[42] When he and the others on the plantation heard the news of her death on the way home, "they were not at all astonished, and found in this the explanation of Kalogusa's dream."

On the Melanesian Solomon Islands, the soul of a dying man turns into a phosphorescent light and appears around the house of someone sleeping specifically in order to impart the message of their death.[43]

In a New Guinea tale said to explain how wasps got their color, a man was stung to death by bees while having an otherwise successful day on the hunt.[44] That night, his wife had a dream in which he came to her, told her how he died and exactly where she could find his body, just as Polydorus had in that most renowned and ancient tragedy.

We can read too of a woman named Madubang who, after eight days of seclusion, dreamed of being visited by a girl from a neighboring village She relayed this dream to another girl named Elfriede, who explained that this girl, who had come to the village accompanied by her sister, had died just a short time before.[45]

In a French Micronesian tale from the volcanic Marquesas Islands, we read that when a woman's husband did not return after the promised amount of time, she hanged herself in grief.[46] Three nights later, she appeared before her husband, who was on another island. He asked her how she could have gotten there, and she replied, "I who am here, my husband, have died."

There is an Indonesian folktale in which a woman named Dia is jealous of a happily married couple, Jenai and Menang.[47] She plotted and carried out the killing of the wife, who later came to her mother, who lived some distance away, in a dream to reveal her fate and, again, the location of her body.

From the Philippines, a woman had died while her husband was off fighting. On his way home from battle, he met his wife's spirit driving a cow and two pigs. Not knowing that she was a spirit, he asked of her intentions there, in response to which she plainly informed her husband of her death. Later, when the man arrived home and inquired about his wife, the people told him that she had died and that they had buried her under the house.[48]

From the Northwestern Philippines too, a couple of Tinguian men agreed to hunt carabao the next morning.[49] During the night, one of the men died, but the other, not knowing this, left the town and went to the appointed place, suspecting nothing. He met the spirit of the dead man, who confirmed his fate.

Among one of the Micronesian tribes of the Ifaluk atoll, a woman's son did not return after having been in the woods, but when she went looking for him along the river where he used to go, she encountered the wraith of the dead man.[50]

Polynesian folktales and memorates attest in numbers to the belief that the dead return not only generally, but specifically to reveal their deaths. In 1952, a Polynesian man dreamed of his son, who was working on another island, and because of this, he became convinced that the young man had died.[51] Two days later, word arrived confirming this.

We turn now to Turkmenistan and a Sufi vision from 1215–6 CE.[52] Pharmacist Abbas of Khwarazm had gone out alone to bathe in the Oxus River, having previously expressed the wish that God would drown him in benevolence. He entered the water and announced cryptically that "the drop of water reached the sea and became identical with the sea." He soon vanished and drowned beneath the surface. After three days, one of his disciples saw him in a dream, in which he announced that he had died.

The number of dreams in which the departed are encountered in Sufi traditions is truly vast, and often repetitive in their somewhat moralizing similarities. In another, similar story, Jamal al-Din of Kadak, having also chosen to disappear in the same manner as Abbas, above, told someone in a dream that he should now be "classified among the dead," an event after which a tomb is built.[53]

In a rural Romanian folktale told by a shepherd named Mihai, the death is suspected but not confirmed until the dream comes to him.[54] Mihai sent all his warriors to find his missing father. It was in a dream, however, that his father soon announced, "Yes, I am dead, fair son; I cannot tell thee more. My crimes were great and many, but I have loved thee well."

Among the Siberian Kumyks, indigenous to Dagestan, Chechnya, and North Ossetia, two months after a princess was reported mysteriously missing after a terrible storm, she came to her father in a dream "looking more joyful and more radiant than she had ever been in her life" and revealed her death.[55] This dream was later "strangely verified" regarding the information she gave regarding the location of a pitcher.

AFRICA, BURMA, SOUTH AMERICA, AND BEYOND

Regarding Africa, a continent where professor of comparative religion Geoffrey Parrinder noted that the phenomenon of the appearance of such apparitions at the moment of death is "very common," the dead once again make no bones about their situation.[56] An African source of author Nelson Osamu Hayashida told that one night she dreamed of a tall man dressed in purple telling her, "Don't you know that I am dead?"[57] Some days later came the news that the dreamer's father-in-law had died at about the time of the dream.

Lying one night in Senegal, a marine captain on duty awoke suddenly and saw his grandmother's form right before him.[58] She gazed at him and said, "I've come to say goodbye to you, my dear child: you will never see me again." Having been "astounded," the man found she had died far away in Rochefort, France, at that very time.

One of the Mende of Sierra Leone explained that his brother, who had died while away from home "without his people's knowledge," appeared in a dream to one of their neighbors.[59] Among the Central Cameroonian Eghap too, who believe in a separable soul, it was believed that "when a person died his ghost (*pforshei*) made itself visible to one of the townspeople on the day of death."[60]

Welsh medical researcher Dr. Penny Sartori relayed a more recent account from one of her colleagues regarding a death in Nigeria.[61] The woman, a nurse, told Sartori that around the time her father died, he appeared to her sister, who was living much further north. He was well dressed, as if for a journey, and surrounded by bright light.

The crisis apparition may technically occur either 12 hours before or after the death, and even this is somewhat arbitrary. Among the Nigerian Yoruba, we may see an example of the former.[62] Their *emi-spirit*, one of the three aspects of the individual's spirit, might sometimes visit relatives who will "learn in a dream that their kinsman or -woman is going to die soon" It is said that "even in daytime, the cold presence of a dying relative may be felt from far away, as if he were close by."

As with Amenemhat and some of the longer Polynesian tales, such crisis encounters are often woven without much fanfare into larger narratives. In Burma, there are a number of accounts to be found, including a version of an eleventh century tale based on oral tradition and the plays that the tradition later inspired. Two brothers, Byat-wi and Byat-ta, were found washed up on the coast as children and were raised by a monk.[63] Much later, one of these brothers, Byat-wi, having broken into a castle, fell in love with the daughter of the king, and although his brother, Byat-ta, warned him not to keep going back, he was eventually captured and killed. Later, Byat-ta went up the walls alone when a soldier rushed toward him; he "recognized," however, "that it was in fact the ghost of his brother," who, seemingly by his appearance and words, had made his fate known. Byat-ta was now assured of his brother's grisly fate.

Again, so far distant in time and space from such legendary tales comes a more straightforward Tlingit Alaskan account from 1933.[64] A man of the Ganaxadi tribe went to a place called Cragin in his canoe to buy some supplies but never returned. Some weeks later, his body was found on a rocky islet. His lover, however, had already learned of his murder and those who committed it from the man himself, who came to her with this information in a dream.

In a New York State Iroquois legend, He-no the thunderer transformed Gun-nop-do-yah, the thunder boy, and the human snake, Gun-no-do-yah, into thunder hunters.[65] Gun-no-do-yah was given the task by He-no of hunting and killing a monster that no mortal had been able to kill. He was given a powerful bow and arrow and instructed to follow He-no's storms. For months, he searched, but when he eventually found the monster under the last lake, he drew his arrow, ready to fire. Raising its head high, the monster opened its hissing mouth and carried Gun-no-do-yah to the bottom of the lake. He-no was sleeping at the time, and Gun-no-do-yah appeared to him in his dream and told him he had been devoured by the great snake monster of Lake Ontario.

In a far more recent example, a Hopi War Chief told of a man who saw the image of a girl with a squash-blossom hairdress standing by the wall of a canyon.[66] When he reached home, he found that his sister had died while he was away.

In Hawaii, a land where ghosts are truly ubiquitous, a legend recorded by one of the great popularizers of their folklore, William Drake Westervelt, involved the high chief of Kau.[67] One night, while awaiting the return of his traveling son, a strange dream came to him. He heard a voice calling from the land of the dead. As he listened, a spirit stood by his side. The ghost was that of his son, Kahele, who revealed that he had been put to death.

On the island of Oahu, we read of a man who laid down to rest after a long day of work. He had barely fallen asleep when he awoke to the forms of his two sons standing by his bed. They told him outright that they had been killed, and then went on to explain where their bodies could be found. When they faded away, he had "no doubt that they were dead."[68]

Living in England during World War 2, a Brazilian by birth, Sidonie, an informant of Lois Bourne, dreamed that her mother appeared to her at the front door and said, "I shall not be able to open the door to you any more my dear." Two days later, news arrived that her mother had died suddenly in Brazil at the time of the dream.

In a Yamana folktale, from as far south as the islands of Tierra Del Fuego and Cape Horn, one brother kills four of his five brothers, one by one, by asking them to fetch some cormorants from down the side of a cliff and then pushing them off of it.[70] The fifth suspected something and refused, asking his brother to go down instead. When he did so, he fell to his death. The five dead brothers then built a canoe and went to their nephew's hut. They called him out, pretending to be real people, but the nephew suspected nothing, for he "had not yet heard that the five men had died."

Grief, as it did for some of the shades of Polynesia, caused the death of a young girl further north in Colombia.[71] This woman's husband left her due to slander made against her by another. She appeared as a wraith to this man and revealed her death in this way.

Dreams and visions which announce the death of relatives are well known in Colombia, and wraiths abound there. Among the Aritama, for instance, it is said that one "always" learns of a loved one's death through a dream.[72]

Returning to Guatemala, independent scholar Judith Zur tells us that there, too, it was typical that K'iche' Mayan women of Guatemala would learn of the deaths of loved ones in their dreams.[73] Among other accounts, one woman told her that her husband had presented himself to her in a dream, announced he was dead, and let her know where his body could be found.[72] Numerous stories like this appear in relation to La Violencia, a feud that claimed many lives.

From Paraguay, and from a collection of Latin American folktales, a Guarani woman's husband went to war.[74] One night, she dreamed that the warriors came back but that her husband was not among them. Soon after, they did return, and her husband had indeed died. Whether or not he died on the very night of her dream is not made clear, but the tale is again clearly relevant to the beliefs with which we are concerned.

Similarly, pioneering Canadian anthropologist Diamond Jenness discovered that the natives of Mud Bay on Goodenough Island in Polynesia firmly believed that the souls of any men killed in battle on their side would return to their hamlets by night to inform their families of their fate,[75] while Landtman found the same on the Island of Kiwai, where a man told him that the spirits of certain warriors killed in battle came to him.[76] Far from there too, in Eastern Canada, Crawford found that during the war, many mothers had this same awareness when their sons were dying.[77] This is a common refrain the world over. In one particular Korean tale, the spirits of many departed soldiers appeared to officers in dreams to announce their deaths.[78]

SAINTS, FLIGHTS, HEALING, AND LIGHTS

With some justified reticence, the lives of the saints have been a relatively untapped area of detailed and comparative inquiry regarding these
encounters and their historical context. Some of the miracles there are
often quite elaborate and undoubtedly embellished, lending a certain
sanctity to that person's life. Others, however, are mirrors of and indistinguishable from long-established, accepted, and varied ongoing phenomena so greatly familiar to the folklorist and still commonly reported in
both domestic and clinical settings: near-death experiences, out-of-body
reports, accurate predictions of one's own death, strange healings, and
most relevant here, of course, crisis apparitions and visions in the lives
of the saints, whether conveyed through letters, literature, or art, feature
with relative and impressive prominence. It is patently clear that their
unique value was understood by hagiographers and their readers. The
likes of German theologian Karl Rahner and others, such as author Henry
Harrison, made the observation that "second sight" and "clairvoyance" do
occur in the lives of the saints, while others, such as White, examined
ESP (extra-sensory perception) phenomena among Catholic saints, con-
cluding that they were indistinguishable from modern cases.[79] These are
the same kinds of phenomena and abilities we have seen ascribed to the
shaman, the medium, and, of course, the unsuspecting layman.

While the recording of such phenomena was often calculated and
retroactive, the early vision of Sulpicius Severus, a chief authority for
contemporary Gallo-Roman history as long ago as 397 CE, is particularly interesting and illustrative in that it was documented by Severus in
his personal letters to a friend and is considered by some to have been
a very real and affecting experience. University of Utah professor and
scholar of Late Antiquity and the Early Middle Ages Isabel Moreira
notes, for example, that the account is "as close to the reporting of an
authentic experience as we come in early medieval sources."[80] While
others, such as Chadwick, were less convinced, the account is an interesting waypoint in its fundamental similarities, not only to those that
were later to be ascribed to the mystic and the saint, but to those that
had come long before.

Severus had written in one of his letters of his own crisis apparition involving his lifelong friend Martin of Tours and one of his disciples, Clarus. Severus tells us that during a light morning sleep, Martin appeared to him, clearly recognizable, in white garments and glowing with a shining face. After blessing Severus, he took his leave upward. Severus later described with awe how he was still rejoicing over the vision when two monks brought the news of Martin's death, and how he was moved both by grief and by the knowledge that God "shares the numinous depth of reality and his deepest mysteries in this way."[81] That these experiences in the lives of mystics and saints are ascribed to the favor of God in this way is something we will see repeated again and again.

Just as Severus was greatly impacted by this event, the experience of the 651 CE vision of a young boy who would later come to be known as St. Cuthbert of northern England was cited as the very impetus for him to follow the monastic path.[82] While engaged in prayer one night, Cuthbert saw the sky, which had been intensely dark, become broken by a silvery track of light upon which a troop of angels descended from heaven and again ascended, bearing with them a shimmering soul that they had gone to Earth to meet. When morning came, they learned that Aidan, the bishop of the church of Lindisfarne, an island off the northeast coast of England, had died at the very time Cuthbert saw him being carried skyward.

Before Severus, and nearly three hundred years earlier than Cuthbert, it is written that at the time that the hermit and monk Macarius of Egypt died in 391 CE, Abba Babnuda, a disciple of his, saw the soul ascending to the heavens.[83] While the source is disputed, we are interested in the idea, even though it may have been a fabrication.

As is everywhere reflected in folkloric tradition, these apparitions most often appear to someone with whom the dying person has a special connection. On the very night that Wulfstan, Bishop of Worcester, died in 1095, he appeared "in a wonderful manner" to a friend he had especially loved, Robert, Bishop of Hereford, in a town called Cricklade, commanding him to hurry to Worcester in order to bury him.[84] Similarly, at a monastery in Trier, Germany, along the banks of the Moselle River, we read of Modesta, an abbess apparently bound in "divine friendship" with thirteenth century noblewoman and abbess Gertrude of Aldenberg, who appeared to her alone at the moment of her distant death.[85]

Ignatius Loyola, the founder of the Society of the Order of Jesus, spent forty days in retreat in March and April 1538. Here, while assisting at Mass, Ignatius saw the soul of one he knew, James Hozes, pass radiantly from Earth to paradise. Rose notes that this particular vision occurred on the same spot where Benedict saw the soul of Germanus ascending similarly, suggesting a potentially romantic trapping.[86] In either case, the vision and those of its ilk retain interest here.

Similarly, at the moment St. Finbar of Cork died in 623, the early Irish saint Comgall said, "Let us pray, dearly beloved, for the soul of our Father, the Bishop Finbar. He is now borne to Heaven, by the Angels." On the following day, word was brought regarding Finbar's death.[87]

The noted theologian and chronicler Jacques de Vitry wrote of a certain hermit who spoke to a robber while imprisoned.[88] Shortly thereafter, the robber left the hermit and was pursued by people who wished to kill him. Indeed, they succeeded in this, and at the very moment he was killed, the hermit saw the angel of God "bearing his soul to heaven." Interestingly, this vision is credited with causing a determination in the hermit to "return to the world."

Just as de Vitry noted of this former and much older account of a hermit, worlds and centuries away, one Nick Yelchick, a West Virginian railway worker, had a similar experience in which, having become disoriented and fainting in a tunnel in 1927, saw his wife's face in front of him, later finding she had died at that time.[89] From that moment on, he too "was a changed man."[90]

These kinds of aftereffects had been noted early. Regarding the impacts of just such an experience upon medieval Belgian mystic Lutgarde of Aywières, American trappist monk Thomas Merton astutely noted, "We must not imagine that these visions of disembodied souls passed before the mind (perhaps even the bodily eyes) of St. Lutgarde without striking her to the depth of her soul with movements of wonder, love, and fear."[91]

Influential philosopher and theologian Thomas Aquinas (1225–1274 CE) experienced a rarely cited and similarly affecting crisis apparition of his own.[92] One night, while praying in the church of his convent in Naples, he saw a man who had recently died, Fryar Romanus. A special note had been made that Aquinas had been unaware of his death at the time of the apparition. Aquinas conversed briefly with Romanus, who left him in "great comfort and consolation," as God had "revealed some secrets" to him.

German Dominican friar Henry Suso, to whom a great number of visions were ascribed, was engaged in his studies in fourteenth century Cologne when his mother died somewhere far off.[93] At that time, she appeared to him in a vision and told him, with great joy, "See, I have departed from this world, and yet I am not dead. I shall live everlastingly in the presence of the everlasting god."

We return now of the Belgian mystic Lutgarde and another less frequently reproduced account.[94] One Jean de Lierre had gone to Rome on a mission on behalf of a number of convents but died while crossing the Alps. Beforehand, he had made a pact to visit the mystic Lutgarde if he were to die. Lutgarde, then far away, saw de Lierre standing near the door to a convent. When she engaged him in conversation, the man announced, "I am dead. I have left this world."

At the death of St. Francis, his form was said to have appeared to the Bishop of Assisi, who had gone on pilgrimage to an oratory on Monte Gargano that same night.[95] Francis told him, "Behold, I leave the world and go unto heaven." The bishop told his companions and returned to Assisi to make inquiries, where he found that the man had died at the very moment of his vision.

It is recorded that on October 16, 1246, while praying, the Belgian mystic Juliana of Liege was visited by the spirit of Bishop Robert of Liege.[96] This led her to believe he had left this world, suggesting a knowledge of such encounters and their meaning. Soon a maid came to acquaint Juliana with the news, although Juliana told her first, "You have not brought me good news, but bad; the bishop is dead."

While there hasn't been much in the way of broader observations upon these kinds of crisis accounts as they appear in the lives of the saints, there are some interesting exceptions. They seem to have been taken for granted in Ireland, for example, certainly as detailed in its magically inclined annals. In the very early Middle Ages, St. Colombanus once remarked rather nonchalantly to a colleague that in the event of his death, "and if God grant that it may be revealed" to him, he should travel to Columbanus's tomb and retrieve his letter and his staff, which should then be brought to his disciple Gallus to assure him he is not condemned by the saint.[97] This much-celebrated saint apparently saw nothing out of the ordinary if such a vision were to be "revealed" to his brothers in this way. Gregory the Great, too, the very shaper of medieval spirituality, noted that "men's souls departing out of their bodies have been seen: and also what wonderful things have been revealed unto them, at the time of their departure."[98] The renowned historian and intellectual of the early Middle Ages, Bede, even singled out the "extent and scope" of Cuthbert's prophetic visions with special reference to the fact that he could "see a soul being carried heavenwards at the very moment of death."[99]

Later monastics like the Italian Catholic bishop, philosopher, and theologian Alphonsus Liguori were clearly aware of these experiences also, and he referred specifically to accounts in which martyrs revealed their deaths to others in visions, calling them an act of God, who was "pleased to glorify" his servants in this way by "manifesting their triumph" to others.[100] Florence Capes,[101] who wrote on the life of St. Catherine De' Ricci, called such an experience "one of those revelations, so often granted to holy people when saints are called away," while Reeves[102] similarly stated that visions by which a man might learn of a saint's death at a distance "show clearly that the Lord hath conferred on him eternal honours."

We will come to many more accounts in which the saints and mystics of many religions are described in very similar terms at their deaths. Whether by way of apparition or vision, the extent to which the mystic, later the saint, is seen at the moment of death by someone nearby or at a distance, or has such a vision themselves, is widely represented in letter, in lore, and in art; they are frequently depicted as being surrounded by light, exalted in some way, rising up, or being guided to the heavens and the vision is often considered a gift imparted by God and marks the mystic as special. And while Gregory's early and influential dialogues are sometimes credited with instantiating the model of such visions, this is only part of the story. We will see many more precede them, and the very same kinds of experiences occur widely to this day, far from the inks and quills of the didactically inclined medieval monk or scribe.

Professor Emeritus of Folklore Studies at the University of Helsinki Leea Virtanen, was told by a man from rural Finland that at the moment a local had died, this man saw him in a dream. There was a strange symbol in the sky—"it means death," the man explained—before it rose up and eventually disappeared.[103]

Virtanen also tells us of a child who saw a bright cross in the sky at the moment a certain neighbor died.[104] We can note here, then, that it is said that after the death of Frankish goldsmith and bishop Eloy, his soul was seen ascending to heaven in the form of a luminous star while a gleaming cross appeared above his house.[105]

British neuropsychologist and neuropsychiatrist Peter Fenwick recorded the case of a seven-year-old child who saw her grandmother "going up in a bright light" before waking up to the news that she had died in the night.[106] In a manner which also similarly resembles a saint's death, an informant of Louisa Rhine saw her father rising up in a "beautiful light" at the foot of her bed, later learning he had died exactly at that time.[107] Had such accounts occurred in an early medieval infirmary, they too might have been a most fitting basis upon which to construct some edifying tale. With this in mind, we note here that at the time two "holy virgins," Mary and Flora, died in prison in the ninth century, they appeared to Spanish martyr Natalia of Cordoba "dressed in white robes and resplendent with glory."[108] Similarly, when Duchess Elizabeth of Hungary died in 1231 she is said to have appeared to her brother, who was in another place, "clothed in royal garments and resplendent with an ineffable light."[109]

While in-depth comparisons between more literal, legendary, and literary accounts are not the primary aim of this survey as such, there is a need to provide greater historical context than is generally offered for these visions in order for us to understand them better. In addition, it is clear that knowledge of hagiographical or folkloric motifs is manifestly not a requirement for the individual to undergo experiences that are nevertheless indistinguishable from motifs in important ways.

ROMULUS, AID, AND THE REASSURING SHADES

From the experiences of Virgil's Aeneas or Sulpicius Severus to those of playwright David Belasco and sculptor Harriet Hosmer, we have seen that the crisis apparition can be something akin to a mystical experience in its capacity to so immediately transform one's metaphysical sense of things. Not only might grief be assuaged, but beliefs concerning the soul and its very destiny may be either bolstered or engendered in the first place. Interestingly, however, it is not always the percipient alone who reaps the benefits.

In what University of Massachusetts, Amherst professor of classics Debbie Felton has called a "good example of a crisis apparition," Romulus, the legendary founder of Rome, is said to have appeared to the philosopher Proclus shortly after his death in 716 BCE; Proclus was unaware of Romulus's fate at the time.[110] Scholars have noted that hearing of the experience of Proclus consoled and assuaged the grief of the Romans, who were then despondent at the loss of their leader.[111]

Of an account in which two separate monks had visions of Welsh St. Brioc's death (which we will return to later), Irish scholar John O'Hanlon noted that it "filled all with great joy and caused them to return the Almighty's thanks for testimonies afforded, regarding the undoubted beatification of their dearly deceased patron."[112] Just as fascinating, the author went on to state that it is probable that Lan-Sieu parish church itself derived its name from the person who had this vision.

There are other crisis visions specifically credited with having inspired the construction of religious sites. In a Chinese account from some "hundreds of years ago" in the Fokien Province, the men of a certain woman's household were away at sea.[113] One night, she dreamed that she saw their ships about to be wrecked in the storm. In the dream, she swims out and takes two ships with her hands and one between her teeth. She was coming home safely when she heard her mother call, which caused her to open her mouth in reply and lose one of the ships from her grip. Some time later, the mariners returned and reported they had been in a terrible storm and had indeed lost one of their ships, while two "marvelously" outrode the storm. This vision was credited as the impetus behind this woman's apotheosis, or attainment of goddess-hood, and many temples were later built in her honor.

That such individual experiences as these most ancient crisis apparitions may impart a beneficial impact upon a wider circle than the experiencer themselves is a powerful and long-recognized reality that continues to be a source of consolation not just for the individual but for the extended family and community. Despite the commonly offered notion that such tales are casually told around the fire, more often, these particular crisis accounts are treasured, held close, and shared only with those most trusted. As Esther Kellner wrote in an issue of *Midwest Folklore* regarding this distinction, "it should not be thought [. . .] that the people of this or any rural Hoosier community took all its folk-lore seriously. Most of the stories were told purely for entertainment. A token or a warning often made a deep impression, though, and listeners would agree that it was mighty queer, and sounded like more than just a happen-so."[114]

Lending truth is one example reported by writer Luellen Hoffman, in which the percipient, having been visited by her father at a time when she hadn't been aware of his passing, felt a deep sense of comfort and closure in being able to pass this message along, noting that it "made everyone feel better."[115]

In 1997, hospice nurse Maggie Callanan was told about the case of a young man who, having been in a tragic automobile accident, was left paralyzed from the neck down.[116] This man, Steve, developed treatment-resistant pneumonia and subsequently died. Around the time of his death, his old friend Ralph was dying of cancer, and at one point just before his passing, he sat up and said excitedly, "Here comes Steve! He's come to take me swimming." Of most relevance here, Callanan noted that Steve's family and Ralph's widow took great comfort in this experience.

Max Dauthendey, a German author, painter, and poet of the impressionist period, gave an account in his autobiography, *Der Geist meines Vaters*, in which he describes, while otherwise occupied, suddenly smelling his father's tobacco while his wife smelled nothing.[117] A telegram arrived just a few hours later with the news that his father had died "at the very hour when the hallucination of tobacco occurred in Paris." According to the account, this produced a feeling of "solemnity" in the son, "rather than grief."

That these apparitions and visions might bring comfort is clear and will become increasingly apparent as more accounts unfold, but with this revelation comes the inevitable observation that this comfort often comes not from the experiences as such but from the conclusions the individual draws from them: that life persists in some way. In a 1918 case that author Andrew Mackenzie believed to be one of the best documented and most important to come to light in those years, in that the details of the experience were recorded before the news of the death arrived, a Miss Poynter, having encountered the apparition of her brother Leslie at the moment of his death, noted emphatically, "This is one of the things that makes me know there's a second life."[118]

In one experience reported to pediatrician Melvin Morse, our subject profoundly noted, regarding an apparitional encounter with her father at the time of his death, that the dream saved her life and that she now knows "for sure" that the soul continues.[119]

In an account given again to Fenwick, we read that a woman reported speaking to her husband on the telephone after the time of his death, of which she was unaware.[120] After a hospice nurse rang and relayed this news, she said that "All of this has convinced me that there has to be something more after this life."

Regarding an 1817 collective apparition at the moment of death, the informant noted that "by this circumstance and by the solemn impression it made on my mind, I was convinced of the certainty of another world."[121]

Wherever these phenomena are found, their impact is often similar. In Taichung, Western Taiwan, after a crisis apparition that coincided with a distant car crash, those present were afterwards convinced that "spirits do exist" due specifically to the veridical nature of the experience.[122]

It is written that after a nun born in Poland named Bronislawa saw a brother named Hyacinth being carried to heaven at the moment of his death, she told two with her what she had just seen, and all three went to tell others of the vision in order to console them.[123]

After the deaths of two separate persons were supernaturally revealed to Italian Carmelite nun and mystic Mary Magdalen De-Pazzi, one of which was during a spontaneous out-of-body journey, she made these occurrences known to the nuns of her monastery. While fear was presented as the motivating factor, this information caused the nuns to be "inflamed with zeal."[124]

Similarly impactful was an account from 2002 in which the informant's friend Mike visited him in a dream that felt startlingly real at a time when William had no idea that he had died; he powerfully observed, "I did notice a sudden change in my attitude after this event. Prior to Mike's death, I had been consumed by fear of death, often crying myself to sleep worrying about dying, even though I was brought up in a church environment that taught that death was not to be feared. After this incident, I lost my fear of death, but more than that, I gained a love of life, the absence of which had stifled my childhood."[125]

While numerous artworks, some renowned and others lesser known, depict such crisis-related encounters and visions in the lives of the saints, we may also find these representations in more recent works. Recorded in the 1980s, a woman from Barnegat, New Jersey, saw the "cherubic" form of her daughter gliding down the stairs at the time she had died.[126] Following the burial, this woman commissioned an artist to paint a portrait of this vision, which has since found its way into the collection of the local Historical Society.

THE LIVING GHOST

The intense, often immediate, and manifestly veridical nature of these experiences can be said to amount to something of an apparitional or visionary "apport" for the individual. Just as in those widespread tales of otherworldly journeys in which something of that world is left behind in or brought back to this one (the apport), so too does the apparent relationship between the ordinary and the non-ordinary leave its mark upon the person in these encounters. The otherwise obscure and indefinite beyond is brought crashing down to Earth in a very palpable manner, and while shocking and seemingly novel in their way, such experiences are at other times reported as having felt incredibly natural, as if this were simply the way things work.

Regarding a case more well-known in its time, English theologian Frederick George Lee wrote of the effect the apparition had upon a certain Lord Chedworth, a man who, according to his wife, had great doubts regarding the persistence of life after death.[127] Chedworth told her one morning that he had had a strange visitor in the night, his old friend Mr. B. "He is dead beyond doubt," Chedworth continued. "Listen, and then laugh as much as you please. I had not entered my bedroom many minutes when he stood before me. Like you, I could not believe but that I was looking on the living man." Chedworth was soon told by the form that "I died this night at eight o'clock."

Lee, perhaps a little ahead of his time, noted of this case that, "Whatever construction the reader may be disposed to put upon this narrative, it is not unimportant to add that the effect upon the mind of Lord Chedworth was as happy as it was permanent. All his doubts were at once removed, and forever." Whatever the truth of that particular account—or any other which has been similarly contested—we have seen and will continue to see that this powerful refrain is nonetheless a common one across an impressive variety of sources.

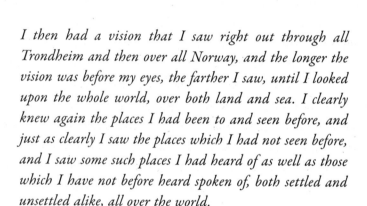

TWO

Visions, Dreams, and Men of High Esteem

I then had a vision that I saw right out through all Trondheim and then over all Norway, and the longer the vision was before my eyes, the farther I saw, until I looked upon the whole world, over both land and sea. I clearly knew again the places I had been to and seen before, and just as clearly I saw the places which I had not seen before, and I saw some such places I had heard of as well as those which I have not before heard spoken of, both settled and unsettled alike, all over the world.

KING OLAF II OF NORWAY (1015–1028)

While in the accounts so far, the mystery has primarily come to the individual in the form of an external apparition, in the visions presented in this chapter the individual seems to attain information by some mysterious mental means. Whether by way of an apparent viewing of the distant event from a vantage point in space, out-of-body travel, or some other occurrence, these visions involve the attainment of accurate knowledge regarding the murder or death of someone at a distance. They seem to have, as noted by Kenner and Miller, "a box seat at the theater of death."[1]

While, in places, the importance of the dream as an overt cultural entity has dimmed over time, its central and firmly embedded importance was historically far more considerable. It would be a challenge to overstate the extent to which the dream has been valued as a direct channel of communication with the realm of the dead and of revelation in general, in almost all places and times. This is especially true of the veridical dream. Those kinds which seemingly reveal information pertaining to actual worldly events have been and continue to be valued, for example among the indigenous tribes of the Americas or in many Islamic societies. The observation of Professor of Anthropology Deward E. Walker Jr. regarding the Native American Menomini tribe that dream revelation was indeed the central experience of their religion could be extended to many regions.[2]

It is important to note that distinctions between *kinds* of dreams were often very carefully made. Most ancient and indigenous cultures delineated with care between those visionary experiences that represented a literal viewing of or attainment of knowledge regarding events in the external world or otherwise legitimately "supernatural" dreams, as opposed to the smorgasbord of content that constitutes the more common or everyday dream. Those reporting comparable visions and dreams today commonly make the same distinctions, and while historically the dream has been regularly disregarded as a reliable form of testimony, particularly by the scientist or similarly inclined historian, here we offer them freely, and in this way we significantly broaden the historical catalogue of crisis-related visions. Furthermore, the dismissal of visions of this kind as lacking historical interest seems unwarranted. Whatever our opinions of their ultimate origins, their objective veridicality has, in certain cases, been established beyond a reasonable doubt and thus constitutes at least a considerable curiosity—and at most a genuine mystery.

That visions and dreams have occurred which exactly describe the scenes of murders, crises, and events in general is a matter of both legendary, romantic, literary, and public record. "Perhaps nothing," noted Lang, "not even a ghost, is so staggering to the powers of belief as a well-authenticated dream which strikes the bull's eye of facts not known to the dreamer nor capable of being guessed by him."[3] The number of visions and dreams that strike Lang's bullseye are uncountable, ongoing, and constitute a somewhat hidden major social phenomenon. While later we will explore a variety of dream types, this chapter will take a predominantly cross-cultural approach, presenting dreams and visions coincident with a death from as wide a variety of sources as could be attained.

Generally speaking, it has been widely held that some dreams tell true. There are not many ideas older than this, and they are attested widely. From the shamans at the furthest ends of the Earth to the sinners and saints of the long Middle Ages and further to events recorded more recently in intensive care units, these visions of death are perennial, and considering the extent to which they are tied to and related to violent or unnatural death, we begin fittingly with what has been referred to as the "first murder."

VISIONS OF FRATRICIDE

Among the pseudepigrapha of the Old Testament, those early non-canonical Christian texts, there is described in The Life of Adam and Eve a prototypical vision in which Eve witnessed the infamous murder of her son Abel by his brother.[4] "This night," she noted she had seen "the blood of my son Abel being poured into the mouth of Cain, his brother, who drank it without pity." Having been told of this vision by Eve, Adam states, "Arise and let us go to see our children and learn what hath happened to them." Together, they went and discovered the body of their son.

This relatively simple narrative, widely agreed to have been composed around the first century CE, consists of the fundamental and often straightforward characteristics of the uncountable others that would follow and spiritually constitute the basis for some common folkloric motifs, including most apparently that of a "murder made known in a dream."[5]

Nineteenth century American congressman Robert Dale Owen, in his classic study of related phenomena, recorded something which he noted "must be considered remarkable, from its unquestionable authenticity, and its perfect coincidence in time and circumstances with a most horrible murder."[6] On the evening of February 8, 1840, two brothers murdered a Cornish man. At around ten o'clock, the dead man's brother awoke from a dream in which he saw two men kill his brother. The man was able to describe very specific details such as how his brother had fallen from the horse after one man caught it by the bridle. The death, according to the trial that was to follow, was exactly as shown in the dream in every detail.

Whether drawn from memorate or myth, these visions may be found wherever they are sought. From an 1893 Kurdish tale (of much older origin), we read similarly of a man with two children who married again after the death of his wife.[7] After two years, this second wife had her own daughter by him and started hating the children of the first. The man's daughter once went to tend the cattle, and when she came home, she asked where her brother was, to which the woman replied, "Thy brother has gone to his uncle's house." The girl then went to sleep, and in her dream she saw that her brother had been killed and his body thrown into a pit. She arose and told her father, who advised her to heed the dream and see if it was true. They went together and found the body thrown into a pit and covered with a stone, just as she had seen it in her dream.

AFRICAN DREAMS OF DEATH

The accounts are often striking in their unembellished simplicity and in their basic similarities across continents. In a tale from the former Zaire, a man from a village, when hunting in the forest for meat, met another who had his same name, Mbunga.[8] That night, Mbunga of the village dreamed that his mother was dead and that Mbunga of the forest had later healed her. Upon returning home, he found that his mother had, in fact, died in his absence.

From what is now the Democratic Republic of the Congo, we read of a hunter named Nenpetro out stalking an ox. He shot it, but before he could reload, the angry ox charged and killed him on the spot.[9] Back in town, "they knew nothing of this," but one of his three wives,

Ndoza'ntu, dreamed that he had been killed by an ox and that he had made a kill just before his death. At nightfall, they reached the body, confirming the dream in both details.

The crisis vision seems to be a firmly established phenomenon in central Africa. The Lambas of former Rhodesia consider nearly every dream to be portentous, including things occurring at the very moment of the dream. Other than crisis visions, this could include signs of visitors coming or signs of coming food/game.[10] In one someone who had a "journey dream" might afterwards hear that "so-and-so has died!" and then say, "I saw it where I went. I did not dream well."[11]

NORTH AMERICAN NATIVES

Three years after the tales above were reported, ethnographer Thelma Adamson recorded another from the Salish Indians regarding a murder committed by a man named Tapeworm.[12] When the murdered man failed to return home, five of his brothers, in turn, went out to look for him and also never came home. The seventh and youngest brother dreamed that someone had murdered them. The murderer was described to him in this dream so exactly, it was clear that Tapeworm was the culprit.

An old Ojibway legend gave a certain cliff in Michigan its name, "Lover's Leap."[13] An Ojibway girl waited on this cliff for her lover to return from war. Her people were returning, and she looked for him but could not see his face among them. Just at that moment, her lover was tied to a tree, dead, and with an arrow in his heart. As she looked in vain, a "vision of his fate revealed itself," and soon his ghost came to her, too. She killed herself by plunging into the water.

According to American anthropologist and ethnographer Frances Densmore, a Chippewa Indian man named Niskigwun, specifically renowned for being able to know things that took place in his home while he was away, had, on one occasion, been absent for three weeks, and on the third night dreamt that a certain one of his children had died.[14] Although he had left the child and his family in perfect health, he found this to be true upon his arrival home.

A number of creation myths implement such veridical visions as well. From among the Pomo Indians of California, for example, it states that when the people were behaving badly, they were destroyed by snow and ice.[15] One named Marumda dreamed that all the people on Earth were dead. "Wah!" he said, "I'll go and see if they are all exterminated," and he went south to discover they had all died, just as his dream had suggested.

From among the Coos Indians of Oregon, we learn of a young man who dreamed about the fate of the many husbands of a woman at Takimiya who was in the shape of an eagle.[16] Every man who came to Takimiya became her husband. After the wedding ceremony, she would say to her husband, "Let us go to a nice place where there is lots of fun." She would then make him sit on her back, and she would fly off with him to a place where there was a lake. After her arrival there, she would turn right over and throw the man into the lake, where he met a miserable death. She did this for a long time, until the young man discovered in a dream that she had been killing her husbands.

TALES ACROSS CONTINENTS

A similar story involved a bloodthirsty tiger as the apparent murderer. This one is a tale from the Baiga, a lesser-known ethnic group of Central India.[17] The tiger had been eating people for five years, and none of the Baiga could do anything about it. The informant says that he "saw in a dream that this was happening" before going there himself and settling the matter for himself, confirming the contents of his dream.

From the *Manyoshu*, or *Collection of Ten Thousand Leaves*, an anthology of ancient Japanese poetry compiled sometime after 759 CE, we read of a maiden who kills herself in grief.[18] A man named Chinu, who was vying for her heart at that time, "dreamed of it that night" and soon attempted to follow her to the underworld.

Just as the crisis apparition and the crisis vision are often woven without fanfare into grander and more elaborate legends, romances, or moralizing tales, we find a similar story continents away. In the last book of *Le Morte d'Arthur*, a fifteenth century Middle English prose reworking by Sir Thomas Malory. In it, Lancelot, legendary knight of the round table, is "warned in a vision that Guinevere was no more."[19] He quickly departed for where she was at Almesbury, "and found her really dead."

The beloved eleventh century yogi-hero Milarepa once dozed off and had a vision of his old home, which he had left behind on his travels.[20] He noticed the house was cracked "like the ears of a donkey," the rain had leaked through and damaged sacred books, his field was overrun with weeds, and tragically, his mother and other relatives had died in his absence. Having pleaded with his lama to send him home, and after a prolonged sequence of gaining the powers required to do so, he was eventually allowed to return and found that his mother and relatives had died, just as he had seen in his vision.

The following century brings us an Islamic vision. That Islam has historically placed an incredible value on the potential revelatory capacity of particular kinds of dreams, seemingly more so than many of their most remembered contemporaries, should not be entirely surprising. The story of its founding prophet is filled with dreams related to the great events of his life, without even mention of their place in the founding of the religion itself. It has been said that he would make morning conversation with his companions as to the contents of their dreams, from which he might draw portents or insights. Indeed, those fundamental ideas regarding dreams found in the Qur'an are still an ongoing influence in the Muslim world.[21] As recently as 1990, for example, Saddam Hussein prepared public opinion for a withdrawal from Kuwait on the authority of a dream.[22]

During a ninth century earthquake in Syria which destroyed a church in the ancient city of Edessa, Mu'awiya I, the founder and first caliph of the Umayyad Caliphate, is said to have had a vision which revealed to him that Ali, son-in-law of the Prophet, had died in the tragedy.[23]

The grandfather of thirteenth century Shafi'i Islamic scholar Ibn Khallikan dreamed of the death of Ibn Hubaira, the vizier of the caliph al-Mustanjid, in 1165.[24] The night the vizier died, as Khallikan tells it, he was "in the palace of the vizir and that he was there seated. A man came in with a javelin in his hand and struck him with it [. . .] so that the blood gushed out like a fountain and struck the opposite wall." When Khallikan woke up and was relating the dream to his friends, he was "scarcely finished" doing so when a man arrived and exclaimed that the vizier had died that very evening.

A century after the death of Khallikan came the much geographically and culturally removed passing of the third Earl of Salisbury in England, William Longespee, who was killed in cold blood by a group of Saracens.[25] His mother, the Abbess of Lacock, is said to have had a vision of an armed knight being received into the opening heavens. Upon questioning those who seemed to be attending him, she was told plainly that this was her son. In a manner which echoes the apparitional accounts and a theme which will recur as we continue, the vision seems to have had a great impact upon the Abbess. When the messengers came, fearful of imparting the news of her son's death, they were astonished at her "maternal piety," as she expressed words not of sorrow and sadness, but rather of spiritual joy.

According to one of three Irish annals extracted from a vellum manuscript, Gilla-na-naemh Mac Egan, who was a legal expert, polymath, and one of the three sons of the ancient Irish King Albdan of Lochlann, had a portentous dream.[26] After killing and plundering in Spain and elsewhere, he told the brother who was in his company that the death of their third brother, who had not accompanied them, had been revealed to him in a dream.

In another, lesser-known account, Italian Dominican Confessor Constantius of Fabriano, on an evening in 1459 CE, saw a vision of the soul of one Antoninus of Florence being "borne marvellously beautiful" to heaven.[27]

While somewhat tangential and debated in certain particulars, in this spirit we must return to antiquity and include one of the best-known death scenes in the *Iliad*: the slaying of the Thracian King Rhesus. We have noted that dreams which coincide with death were recorded with relative sparsity in antiquity. However, the following occurs almost simultaneously with the external incident. In a dream that occurred at the very moment before his death, Rhesus is said to have dreamed of his killer, the son of Tydeus, standing over his head.

He then awoke to this very same unfolding scene before being famously "robbed of his honey-sweet life."[28]

Something similar was recorded of the Roman Emperor, Julian the Apostate. According to Eutyches of Constantinope, Julian, sleeping in a tent and planning to march on Babylon, dreamed that a man in a light cloak entered his tent and stabbed him with a spear.[29] When he awoke, all his soldiers entered the tent and saw that he had been stabbed, and he died on the spot.

If accounts like those of the pharaoh Amenemhat or others found throughout the pseudepigrapha have been less mentioned by parapsychologists, so too have many others, literary or otherwise. A badly tattered papyrus from the fifth century contains the remains of Aeschysus's ancient tragedy the *Glaukos of Potniai*.[30] Glaukos, according to legend, is said to have died after having been devoured by his own team of horses during the funeral games held for Pelias, king of Iolcus in Greek mythology. In one scene of the play, a woman who knows Glaukos seems to be relating a dream that involved horses, the nave of a chariot wheel, biting, and dragging. A messenger soon comes and tells her about the death of Glaukos, saying that he had died in this very manner.

According to Roman monk and chronicler Theophanes the Confessor, the Byzantine Emperor Romanus I Lekapenos had a dream in which he saw his son's throat being cut.[31] In the same dream, he saw Anastasios, the metropolitan of Herakleia, thrown into a fire. This turned out to have been on the very day they both died, around 946 CE.

While there is truth to classicist E. R. Dodds's assertion that the evidence for telepathy and clairvoyance in classical antiquity is "curiously scanty," there is nevertheless far more "evidence" for both than has been suggested, and literary sources have been generally ignored.[32] More importantly, here we are not at all restricted to solely evidentiary or corroborated accounts; such an approach, while having its place, fails to attend to the ideas and beliefs of what a culture might consider important or deem possible.

Dido, the legendary queen whom the Romans and Carthaginians

claim founded Carthage, had a similarly revealing dream, according to Greek historian Appian.[33] Her husband had been killed "clandestinely" by Pygmalion, then ruler of Tyre, and according to the account, this was "revealed to her in a dream."

From 341 CE, it is written that St. Anthony the Hermit was asked by a sick Paul of Thebes to fetch his cloak.[34] While he was away, Paul died; as Anthony was returning with the cloak, he saw a vision of Paul ascending to heaven. When he arrived back at the cave, he found Paul's body, dead.

Over a century later, in 451 CE, the abbot of the white monastery in Egypt, Shenoudah of Atripe, likewise had a vision in which he learned of the death of a certain monk named Thomas and went to bury him.[35]

A brother of Benedictine hermit Bartholomew of Farne dreamed one night in 1193 that Bartholomew was dead.[36] He immediately awoke the convent, and they sailed the twenty-four miles or so it was to his abode, and "sure enough," Paterson writes, "the holy hermit was lying in his stone coffin, having just died at the time indicated by the dreamer."

We come now to the better-known, and loathed monarch Herod the Great and his vision of his brother's death in 4 BCE.[37] In a rather brief reference to what was nonetheless an impactful vision, Herod the Great, former King of Palestine (37–4 BCE), had multiple dreams of his brother's defeat and death at the hands of the forces of Antigonus, a successor to Alexander the Great. His brother, having neglected Herod's prior warnings, marched towards Jericho but was killed in battle. When Herod was at Daphne (in modern Syria), he had some foreboding dreams to this very effect, and as he leaped out of his bed in a disturbed manner, there, at that exact moment, came messengers bringing him news that his brother had died.

One similar experience, although separated by many thousands of years, comes from 1662 regarding former Governor-General of Batavia John Maatzuiker and his visions at sea.[38] Dutch Calvinist minister and naturalist Francois Valentijn related that Maatzuiker had dreamed that he saw Arnold de Vlaming van Oudshoorn, member of the Council of India, who had sailed from Batavia for his native country of Holland on December 23, 1661, in mortal danger and heard him call for help. Maatzuiker awoke disturbed. When he returned to sleep, he had a similar dream, but this time he seemed to see de Vlaming van Oudshoorn perish. Once more, Maatzuiker noted the day, the month, and the year with the whole history, sealed it, and gave notice that the sealed letter was to be taken good care of until word of this fleet arrived from the Cape of Good Hope. Accounts were afterward brought that on the very same day of Maatzuiker's dreams, Arnold de Vlaming, along with some others, had sunk and he had died.

Recorded among the Mocovi Indians, some of the indigenous peoples of the Gran Chaco region, we look to the experience of a shaman named Salcharo.[39] He had sent acquaintances out along a trail to gather roots for his medicines. That same night, he had a vision that those people had been killed by a jaguar. The death is announced by Salcharo to his people "as soon as it dawned." He went out and found them dead, just as his dream had told it.

Similar in this way was a case from 1924 Tibet.[40] A young man on the mystic path is sent into the forest for three days and nights but never returns. On the fifth day, his master suggested a party look for him. The man's corpse was found tied to a tree. One disciple then questions openly whether or not his master had a dream that revealed this death to him. While this was not confirmed by the man, the possibility is clearly considered a very real one.

Naturalist Joseph Sinel noted that those who lived among the natives of both Central and South America "frequently" reported amazing instances of telepathy.[41] While Central and South America are greatly underrepresented in "paranthropological" work related to visions of death, he did give some other related examples, including an account from some English explorers further north on Baffin Island, now Baffinland, in the Canadian territory of Nunavut.[42] They were told by an old Eskimo there that a friend of theirs had just that very moment been murdered in a town in Central America, two thousand miles distant, giving specifics as if he had been present himself. A year later, when visiting the scene, they found that the old Eskimo's account had been "correct in the minutest detail."

Something alike is said of Roman Catholic mystic Teresa Higginson. In her letters, compiled by Anne Cecil Kerr, Higginson claimed she learned of the death of an African chief named Jaampuda during an apparent out-of-body visit to the tribe from her home in England.[43] Higginson also wrote in a letter to a Miss Ryland on the day her father died in 1877 that she had a vision of the man dying in the street at St. Helen's.[44] A priest soon brought her a telegram confirming the news.

These beliefs were sometimes so prevalent that they could be used to the advantage of the storyteller. Returning to South America, specifically Venezuela, we read in one such Wakuenai narrative, said to explain the origin of evil omens, of a man named Inapirrkuli who tells a woman he is in love with that he dreamed of the deaths of her two brothers and that they should leave the forest where they had been and see how they were at home.[45] While in this particular narrative, the man himself had actually killed both other men and pretended he had slept through the night to cover up his crimes, it nevertheless shows clearly again, as the author also explains, the belief amongst the Wakuenai that deaths may be discovered while dreaming.

In a very recent Brazilian account regarding a wife's vision of her husband Joaquim Maradezuro's death, we read that, having left his wife at home to go fishing, Joaquim didn't return as usual.[46] That night, his wife dreamed that he was covered in blood, which poured from his body across the earth. The next day, it was discovered that he had indeed been killed by farmers, his body having fallen and bled on the earth as in the dream.

Pionerring Danish anthropologist and explorer Knudd Rasmussen (1927: 12-17) retold the story of an Inuit man who, on a journey from Igdlulik to Ponds Inlet, had a dream in which he saw a friend of his being eaten by his own kin. Later, he and his wife came to a strange spot where they heard a voice state, "I am the one who can no longer live among humankind, for I have eaten my own kin."[47] They eventually came to a snow shelter, where they found the voice to be coming from, and indeed, a woman inside confessed to having eaten her own husband and children.

While there are uncountable analogues to be found closer to home, for example in the publications of the Society for Psychical Research, those have been widely reproduced. An earlier *Report on Spiritualism* in which such visions were also recorded, however, is less cited; the following is an example similar to the one above in which a wife discovers her husband's death. It is the story of the wife of a man who served in the army and went out to India who, one night in the drawing room, screamed and fainted. After recovering, she said she saw her husband shot. The time was noted, and intelligence soon arrived that he had been shot at the precise moment when she saw the vision.[48]

We come now to a version of a tale widespread in Venezuela, from the Karina people of the lower Orinoco, in which a man offended the water spirits by killing too many of them.[49] As punishment, a wave washed over him, drowning him. In that very instant, a dream came to his wife and children, saying that their beloved father and husband had been turned into a water spirit. They immediately went to the place he was fishing and had their fears confirmed. They saw his spirit, but it quickly disappeared into the waves.

Comparably, in Malaysia, a woman dropped her child into a river while bathing. She was unable to swim, however, so she couldn't follow.[50] That night, the child confirms its fate in a dream, telling her he has been turned into a crocodile.

While without the rather poetical interpretation of having been turned into a water spirit or a crocodile, both very much symbolic of death in those cultures, the editor of the Welsh *Blackwood Magazine* reported in 1911 of a young man who worked in a china factory at Swansea who dreamed that he saw a man drowning in one of their pools.[51] He dreamed the same thing a second and a third time, and then, unable to resist making an effort to rise and satisfy his curiosity, he went to the spot and found the man drowned.

Whatever the explanation, what becomes clear is that the notion that a dream may reveal a murder is as much part of the public record as it is of the more legendary tales, as much to be found in the depths of the Amazon as it is in a village in Wales. Recorded in the *Cincinnati Times* on December 6, 1884, a young woman dreamed of her brother, who lived in California, rising from bed, fishing out a revolver and a knife from under his pillow, and attaching them to his belt.[52] She saw him sever the hand of a stranger who was trying to kill him. The man then ran outside, drove the knife into himself, and died. Having awoken and being greatly impressed with the vivid nature of the dream, she told her husband. Not long after, they received a letter from their brother relating an adventure that corresponded in every detail with the scene witnessed by the woman.

In a vision that, in its essential details, echoes those still being recorded, we read that on the day a Roman lord, John Patrizzi, died, a monk was apparently rapt in ecstasy and transported to the Basilica of St. Cecilia, where he learned that the lord had "just died."[53] The vision apparently made him more devout.

A similar account that occurred as much later as the nineties involved a man named Mark.[54] He was riding back to his house with a friend and was convinced he could feel his father's presence, who was close to dying at the time. With the urge to check on him, Mark states that he somehow "sent" his "spirit" to that location and had a rather extraordinary experience in which he witnessed his father's death and helped him cross over to the other side. The next morning brought news of the passing.

VISIONS OF GAME AND OTHER ANIMALS

By no means are only the deaths of people revealed in these visions. Among the relevant groups, visions (spontaneous or induced) regarding game often involved ritualistically anticipating a good hunt or related prophetic omens, while others, from cultures at a great distance, involved more pointed messages about things *presently* happening or having just occurred pertaining to the hunt. This could be a dream telling of an animal's death or the information that the animal has been trapped. Some short examples of both will speak to the broader beliefs in veridical dreams among these groups. Given to us by German-American anthropologist Franz Boas is a Kwakiutl Indian tale from the Pacific Northwest Coast of a father telling his children he had dreamed of a dead animal in a particular spot. He sent his children and four dogs, and they confirmed the death of the animal exactly where their father had seen it.[55]

Boas also mentions a man named Wren who built a weir, a kind of fish trap, before returning home.[56] When he slept, he had a dream in which he noticed that both of the fish baskets he had made were broken and that there was a salmon trapped in the weir. In the morning, he set out and saw that the dream had told true.

An Ndembu African from the Congo named Mucbona dreamed that his dead mother's brother came to him and told him that he had caught game in his traps.[57] Mucbona went and found the trapped animals, noting that "this accords with my dream."

Landtman noted that among the Kiwai Island Papua New Guineans, for example, a man might be warned in a dream when a pig was caught in a trap,[58] while similarly, among certain indigenous hunters as distant from there as Idaho, dreams of where game could be found "always" turned out to be accurate.[59]

A Walapai Indian similarly told Kroeber: "I acquired my ability to hunt through a dream. In this the spirit of a man pointed out to me all the springs and feeding places of the animals, and also the methods of hunting."[60]

While sometimes not revealing a death as such, the capacities are implied in many of the tales. On the Torres Strait, the father of a man named Bukia came to him in a dream and told him to go to a certain place where he would see many pigs.[61] Bukia did so, shot one of them, and brought it home to his mother.

A tale from "long ago" told among the Bondo tribe of southwestern India involved an old chief and his wife who lived alone on a mountainside.[62] One day a tiger killed a deer near their house, and the chief saw it happen in a dream. Afterwards, he went and found the carcass and he and his wife cut it up.

Among the Bulu, one of a number of related peoples inhabiting the south-central area of Cameroon, as well as mainland Equatorial Guinea and northern Gabon, one named Turtle told his father, a hunter named Leopard, "Ah, father mine, have you been out to examine your pits today?" Leopard replied, "No. Why do you ask me thus?" Turtle said,

"Because I dreamed a dream that an animal had fallen into your pit." They went together to the pit and found the dream to be true.[63]

Similarly, there was a Chukchi fox hunter who explained that he always knew when a fox was in one of his traps, as this was always indicated to him in a dream of being attacked by a beautiful red-haired woman.[64]

One area of interest to which we can give only little notice is that, in the lives of the saints, there were also many veridical visions of game, as in animals you hunt, not games to play recorded, though the messengers are fittingly particular. For example, in a community where concern was building as to how much food would be available as the important feast of St. Benedict was growing near, a monk "had a dream-vision of an area of the Loire [France] which he recognized."[65] Several people went to the spot and caught an abundance of fish, the event being later ascribed to Benedict by the Benedictine writer Adrevals of Fleury.

While saintly literature is more concerned with the more common future-related visions, these others, of course, hold greater interest here and could be much expanded upon. At times, both aspects of events happening contemporaneously as well as those which will happen in the future are present in a single vision. An example of this can be found amongst the remote Yaghan of Tierra del Fuego and Cape Horn, where Gusinde, in his much referenced historically significant work, recounted the story of a certain of their shamans, one of the most skilled ever.[66] During the night, having set the intention to be "active in his dreams," this shaman incidentally discovered the deaths of two whales while he was attempting to affect the weather. He saw two pregnant whales approaching, and saw how they and their calves were killed by a type of killer whale. He told his people they would soon wash ashore, and on that same evening, the tide washed up two large whales on the coast. When they cut them open, they discovered the calves were dead inside, just as the dream had predicted. According to Gusinde, their astonishment "persisted for quite some time."

Curiously similar, although on the opposite end of the globe, a shaman woman of the British Columbia-based Haida people dreamed she saw a fine whale come ashore opposite her village.[67] In the morning, she called her neighbors together and told them of her dream. They all went to the beach and found the whale.

Instances of clairvoyance related to the deaths of animals are found in indigenous, romantic, legendary, fairytale, and folkloric sources alike. In a Russian folktale, a Russian man and a Tatar were traveling through the southern steppes and couldn't agree on who would watch over their horses.[68] After they had slept, the Tatar awoke, and the Russian told the Tatar that he had dreamed that the Tatar's horse had wandered into the swamp nearby and died. While this was a trick on that man's part (he himself had driven the horse to its death), the fact that the Tatar "anxiously leaped to his feet and rushed there" speaks to how seriously this dream possibility was taken.

From China comes the story of a king, Shih-Huang, who lived during the Chinese Ch'in dynasty, who dreamed that his horse was dragged into the sea by a giant fish.[69] Shih-Huang awoke in terror and put out a bounty for anyone who could go and kill this fish. Some of them saw it but couldn't kill it, so then the King went, found the fish, and killed it himself.

In a Japanese account from the Meitoku era (1390–1394 CE), a priest had a fairly elaborate dream in which a voice from a shrine commanded soldiers to kill a great serpent.[70] After waking up, the man went to the field and the shrine from his dream and saw that it had been burned to ashes. The priest inquired among the local villagers, who told him that they had seen a great serpent lying dead and headless on the ground. The priest later learned that the event coincided with the time of his dream.

Former professor of Spanish at UCLA Stanley Linn Robe gave an example from New Mexico in which a man and his father castrated calves one spring.[71] That night, the father was awakened by his son, who told him he had dreamed that the calves had been killed. While skeptical, the father was astonished to find the four dead calves on the very spot indicated the next morning. Regarding an instance of a similar kind from rural Finland, we read of an informant who, in his dream, took a knife in his hands and began to cut the throat of his rooster.[72] After he awoke, his sister came in and told him that a stoat or polecat must have been in and killed the rooster, which was covered in blood. Like in the tale from the Yaghan, this apparently made a great impression on the family.

While so often found there, such discoveries are of course not relegated to the experiences of the specialist or the pages of folklore, nor are they culturally unique—quite the opposite, in fact. These are stand-alone phenomena which commonly manifest without such discrimination.

ETHNOLOGY, TELEPATHY, AND PARANTHROPOLOGY

While spontaneous apparitions, visions, and dreams in which the individual seems, as Mark in a previous account had described it, to "send their spirit" to some distant location and retrieve information or dream of the scene itself are surprisingly common today, they are nevertheless frequently considered novel in many cultural contexts. However, as we have already seen, such experiences and capacities are entirely known, accepted, and actively elicited in many indigenous and traditional cultures. Many sources report that the shaman in a trance state could see at a distance where game was to be found, the approach of visitors, or if his tribesmen were in trouble. Regarding the documentation of these facts and experiences as they pertain to our study here, there are many more than have been compiled to this point, and they are particularly interesting in both the extent to which they were collected independently and the number recorded by scholars who expressed awe or disbelief when coming upon them.

Such cross-cultural, paranthropological reports of ESP have been referred to generally by scholars in different fields, though they are very rarely collated. Many, including German ethnologist and psychologist Holger Kalweit and author Vincent Gaddis, considered telepathy and clairvoyance as part of the full range of shamanic knowledge; the latter made the general connection that "just as today's psychic sensitives exhibit ESP, clairvoyance, and psychokinetic abilities, so did the shamans of our native tribes."[73] Influential social anthropologist and folklorist James Frazer held that, in fact, the capacity to exert influence at a distance is the very "essence of magic" and that "faith in telepathy is one of its [magic's] first principles."[74] Author Max Freedom Long, speaking of the Polynesians, wrote that telepathy was "common," and that relatives frequently received such impressions from each other at a distance.[75]

While even the Society for Psychical Research and the majority of their contemporaries were somewhat tepid on the idea of dreams as impressive evidence for telepathy, they nevertheless concluded rather firmly that the coincidence theory was not applicable here either and that it clearly becomes "unreasonable to argue that the coincidences are sufficiently accounted for by the law of chances."[76] The authors also wrote that out of the 149 coincident dreams that are included in the first volume, no less than 79 have represented or suggested death. "This, it will be seen," the authors went on, "is entirely in accordance with a theory of causal connection between event and dream, where the abnormal state of the person dreamt of is regarded as part of the cause; but it is not at all in accordance with what we should expect accident to bring about."

LOCATING THE LOST

While dreams and spontaneous visions are, at least in the West, the primary means of revelation of this kind, it was very much the case in tribal communities that the shaman, sometimes under the influence of a psychoactive substance, could actively make use of such supernatural vision toward different ends: to locate game, to find lost items, and to discover invasion or illness, for example. Tribes relied on the shaman's clairvoyance to solve numerous problems. By myriad means, the shaman claims the ability to discover events occurring in real time from a distance.

The examples are numerous and relate to more than just the discovery of deaths, although their existence speak directly to those accounts in that the capacities are entirely comparable and beliefs in each related. Pioneering Canadian anthropologist Diamond Jenness, living among the Copper Inuit, once lost a tin full of matches and a shaman "discovered in a dream" who had stolen them.[77] On Ambae Island, 1,800 kilometers east of Australia, in case of theft or of any hidden crime, some wizard who understands how to do it drinks kava and so throws himself into a magic sleep. When he wakes, he declares that he has seen the culprit and gives his name.[78] A Tillamook Indian man fasted atop a certain mountain specifically to dream of his missing brothers' location.[79] These stories are common—and found continents apart.

We may again draw an interesting shamanic parallel among the mystics of the church: at times, certain people came to St. Theodore Phanariot, or "the revealer," to locate lost items, including a man who wished to know the location of his escaped servants.[80] In a related Jewish example of interest, before going to sleep one night, a certain rabbi specifically wished to learn the location of a missing girl, and in his dream he "learned the truth."[81]

These are ancient ideas. The procurement of "professional clairvoyants" to discover things lost is referred to in a fragment of an ancient short play by Pomponius.[82]

We may draw from a collection of Maryland folklore in which a similar event occurred, though in an entirely different cultural milieu and spontaneously rather than sought.[83] A man lost his son to a vicious storm one winter. He dreamed some weeks later that his son's dead body had drifted into a creek south of town. The next day, the bloated corpse was found exactly where he'd dreamed it had been.

Dr. Laubscher, who studied divining among the natives of the unrecognized Republic of Transkei, became convinced that, apart from some clear cases of fraud, genuine clairvoyants were to be found among the natives he worked with.[84] He gave as an example a diviner who located stolen cattle sixty miles away and named the thief. Laubscher noted, in fact, that "the native territories abound" with these stories regarding the discovery of lost items. As Shirokogorov and Berndt and Berndt respectively clarified and implied, however, it was especially in "urgent cases" that such capacities were invoked, just as today it is a crisis that seems to prompt the majority of spontaneous cases.[85]

Casagrande, in his work among the North American Ojibwa and Comanche tribes, relays an instance in which one of the tribesmen intentionally discovered that two missing boys had been drowned and located their bodies' exact position in a nearby lake using some form of clairvoyance or soul travel.[86]

Relatedly a Nova Scotian man was fishing with his brother. Another brother, Peter, was fishing off Halifax. One stormy day, the brother who was with him jumped up from his sleep and said, "My God, Peter is drowned." They found out afterwards that he was drowned at that very hour. The brother had seen it happen.[87] Perhaps in another time or place, these men too would have been shamanic candidates.

Such dream discoveries of something or someone lost are found far and wide. The Sufi Sultan Veled once dreamed of the recently killed Shemsu-'d-Din, wherein he was told where to find the body, which he and some others soon recovered from the bottom of a well.[88]

For a far more ancient analogue, we can look to the Epidaurian Temple Record. The text speaks of a boy named Aristocritus who failed a landing after a cliff jump and fell into the sea and disappeared. His father, in a dream, is led by the godly Asclepius, who shows him where his son is. Upon waking, he returns home, identifies the spot, cuts a passage through the rocks, and finds his son. We may conclude, as did Dodds, that the boy's death was revealed in this way.[89]

In an Icelandic tale from 1780, a "wizard" was employed to find the location of the bodies of brothers who had perished, and according to the tale, he was successful.[90] Lang noted that "the Maori oracles are precisely like those of Delphi."[91] He lends truth to this by quoting a relevant example from the work *Old New Zealand*: after a party chief left his tribe for a distant part of the country, his condition was inquired about by means of an oracle.[92] "He will return, but has not yet returned," was the cryptic response. Six months later, the chief's friends brought him back, a corpse.

Also far from Delphi and its famed oracles, in 1911, an incident from the Orkney Islands occurred in which, after a boating accident, a fisherman experienced a remarkable dream in which he discovered that the body of one of the unfortunate men was lying in a creek well known to him.[93] This dream so impressed the man that, on getting up for the day, he went directly off to the little inlet specified. Upon his arrival, he found the body lying there exactly as described in his vision.

Something similar was reported in the *New York American* on October 18, 1915, in which a mother had dreamed accurately, as was later shown, regarding the details of her son's body being lowered into a pauper's grave, which led to the discovery of the body. This was "one of the strangest incidents in local police history."[94] The folklorist has sometimes observed that these visions are now less dramatic than they had been in older accounts; this is a simplification, however, as many of the old accounts, mostly those that have been ignored in this context, are equally straightforward and lack embellishing details.

Returning to Polynesia, the native history of the Gambier Islands of French Polynesia and the islands of Tahiti and Mo'orea tells us that a chief named Taratahi was forced to leave Mangareva and sail to an island named Mata-ki-te-rangi.[95] His grandson, Te Agiagi, had a vision that his grandfather had been killed by his people, the Meriri. He and some others sailed to Mata-ki-te-rangi in a double canoe with the express intent of verifying this vision. Soon after arriving, Te Agiagi went ashore and found the corpse of his grandfather where the vision had revealed it to be.

Comparable accounts may be pulled from almost any century and feature heavily in the lives of the saints. In just one example from 695 CE, after the murder of two priests who were subsequently thrown into a river, one of the martyrs appeared in a vision by night to one of their companions, telling him that their bodies would be, and indeed later were, found at "the place where the heavenly light should be seen." The bodies were later found in accordance with the information.[96]

Far from the tundra of the Tungus or the rainforests of the Cashinahua where the shaman might find something lost, psychoanalyst Elizabeth Lloyd Mayer tells us that in 1991, when her daughter's hand-carved harp was stolen, her familiar world of science and rational thinking was "turned on its head."[97] Having failed to turn up any leads, a friend suggested she call a dowser, a man who specialized in finding lost objects. Dr. Mayer agreed, initially to humor her friend. Within two days and without leaving his Arkansas home, the dowser located the exact California street coordinates where the harp was found. Elizabeth noted that this "changed everything," and was the catalyst for her fourteen-year journey collecting similar accounts.

These things have been long remembered. The lover in *Child Waters*, an old Anglo-Scottish ballad, dreams that his best steed is stolen.[98] The man, Willie, is concerned with verifying his dream, which turned out to be true:

> *I dreamed a dream san the straine,*
> *Gued read a' dreams to gued!*
> *I dreamed my stable-dor was opned*
> *An stoun was my best steed.*
> *Ye gae, my sister, An see if the dream be gued.*

SHOCK AND AWE ON THE WIRELESS

As noted, many explorers, anthropologists and ethnologists, in coming to terms with these unusual events, simply discounted them; others, however, could only marvel. South African explorer Laurens van der Post considered his skeptical mind "humbled" after certain interactions with the bushmen tribes there.[99] In one of his recorded instances, he and a group, having made a kill, were about a hundred and fifty miles from where the rest of the tribe had camped when one of them remarked, "I wonder what they'll say at the sipwells when they know we've killed an eland." When van der Post asked how they could know this, the man replied, while tapping his chest, that they "know by wire." When they returned to the camp, it was confirmed that they knew.

When Swedish explorer Sven Hedin was charting large parts of the interior of Asia, a guide whom he had hired died some months into the trip in Tibet and they had to turn around.[100] The journey back was challenging, though eventually they "saw the glow of fire in the darkness" as they sighted some of their men scouting for them. The first one who rode up was the guide's brother, who came up to Hedin and stated, "My brother Aldat is dead." Hedin, inquiring in what he calls "amazement" as to how he could know this, heard the reply, "I know it. In a dream, I saw him die." According to Hedin, he saw this occur on the very day of Aldat's death.

South African journalist and writer Lawrence George Green, while among the Kalahari bushmen, noted that the desert is believed to encourage psychic awareness.[101] One afternoon, a bushman told him that he knew that his fellow hunters had killed two springbok near the Nossob River, and this was explained as something he knew by "Kalahari Radio." Green later had it clarified that this apparently referenced "thought reading." They would use the smoke signal not to convey a particular message but to alert them that something significant had occurred. They would then "look at the smoke, and the message came to them." Green, like parapsychological researchers before and after him, expressed doubt that coincidence could explain as many instances as there were.

Green relayed other instances too, including one in which a friend of his had set off hunting with some of the natives, one of whom suddenly announced, "Bwana Jack has shot a cow kudu."[102] Green's friend asked him how he knew, and he gave the "usual" reply: "I just know." Soon after, confirmation came that a kudu had been killed at that precise moment, with the possibility of the shot being heard by ear ruled out.

This capacity to "just know" is a common refrain in cultural contexts far removed from the African bush. "Sometimes," an American informant told McClenon, "I can tell when things are wrong back home without coming in direct contact with them."[103] This included an instance involving the death of his grandfather. These more general intimations are found widely. Shirokogorov noted that among the Tungus when people die, certain clan members "may know it and relate what has happened and the circumstances of the death."[104] The author gives a specific case in which a boy "saw" his father killed and told accurately that the murderer would return in three days with the antlers of a red deer which his father had killed. The body was soon found where he had seen it.

While some, such as British ethnologist Dudley Kidd, have speculated and others have indeed shown clearly that certain types of information are transmitted among natives through drums, smoke, and other signals and later mistaken for more mysterious circumstances, this can only explain a portion of these accounts and ignores entirely those in which the natives are emphatic and clear that the information comes through vision, dream, or intuition.[105] We have already seen this in the previous account, or when the Kalahari Bushmen told George Green that it was a combination of smoke signals and "thought reading." Gaddis has in fact noted that even where smoke signals are used, these are often for garnering general attention, while more specific information might then be discovered by the relevant visionary or other means.[106]

Although Long failed to make it clear that the term also references other more conventional means of communication, he notes the common use of telepathy in Tahiti; the so-called the "cocoanut radio."[107] The language used is often strikingly similar. Others, such as author Graham Bound, similarly relayed that "instinctive feelings" were another part of the cocoanut radio.[108] The so-called *gurungu* of the Aboriginal Muruwari is comparable.[109] *Gura* means string, while the literal meaning of gurungu is "magic string." This form of communication was "used and discussed frequently" during an Aboriginal man's time at a certain mission. "I still believe in it," the man, named Barker, told Janet Matthews. "Men and women talked about getting news from others who were far away—it might be of an impending visitor or a death." Like Green, Matthews expressed awe regarding specific instances, noting that it had happened so often that it had been "difficult to believe that it was coincidence."[110]

According to English archeologist and anthropologist Katherine Routledge, the natives of Easter Island are strongly attuned to their dreams.[111] In one example, they relayed messages such as those regarding someone returning from a journey with "all the assurances of a wireless message."

Creighton, comparing one of her Nova Scotian accounts to those of the Micmac Indians, wrote of a recording she made in which Peter Michaels told her of a certain sound like a moose call, which "means there is trouble at home."[112] It happened when this man's father died, and he called it the Indian's "telegram."

Author Jean Godsell, wife of Philip Godsell, a Hudson's Bay Company inspector-turned-fur trader, was greatly impressed by the so-called "moccasin telegraph" in the Canadian Northlands. It was a source of "never-ending wonder" for her. In one instance, having been awaiting the return of some Indians, one named John told her they were coming that day and also later explained that one of them had died out in the bush. When Godsell asked the man how he knew all this, he replied, "Last night I had a dream. . . . Saw everything."[113]

Godsell relayed another case in which a medicine man took his tobacco home and went into a trance specifically to discover the whereabouts of a ship. He returned later and said he sent his spirit over the water, ascertained the ship's location, and said that one man, "wearing clothes like a woman," had died and been buried at sea. This was found to be exactly true. The dream or trance was "fulfilled in detail."

Something remarkably similar occurred on the Melanesian Ambae Island. A group had left the island on a ship, and their friends were anxious to know how they were doing.[114] They recruited Molitaville, who used kava to leave his body "in the form of a bird" and follow the ship. He soon returned with news that one of the men had died, which was proved to be true upon their return.

Award-winning American folklorist Barre Toelkan gave numerous relevant examples from among the Navajo. One from 1956 had the author driving from Salt Lake City to a Navajo reserve in Blanding. When they arrived, Toelken found an old Navajo woman preparing food.[115] When Toelken spoke to her regarding his arrival, she said, "Of course, that's why I cooked up all this food!" Toelken expressed great disbelief, noting this woman had no way to know they were coming—no electricity, phone, or even windows. The author had "no doubt" these things happened while noting the difficulty in explaining them.[116] While singular incidents may not impress, Toelkan notes that these anecdotes are common and that while outsiders reacted with surprise, for them it was rather taken for granted.

The previously mentioned and skeptical Dudley Kidd noted of certain South Africans that it is "well known that the natives—occasionally but not often—learn news with amazing rapidity, sending information concerning the main outline of certain events over large tracts of country even faster than it is conveyed by telegraph."[117] Kidd referred to this as "native telegraphy" and gave an example in which the son of the enemy's chief came into court with a shaved head, a sign of mourning among the native men, which the magistrate recognized and inquired about. The young man stated that his father had been killed in the war and even mentioned where the body was lying. The magistrate didn't understand how he could know this, as even he hadn't heard the news yet, but soon after, a telegram came that confirmed both details.

Remaining in Africa, the old men of the Pudu section of the Sapa in Liberia, where warnings of death are "firmly believed in," told Presbyterian minister and missionary George Schwab that once, when the Tic were about to attack their country, an old woman "heard of it" through a dream.[118]

This is a fairly common kind of observation made among indigenous tribes. Once more among the Maoris, we hear of something similar. In *Old New Zealand*, author Pakeha Maori wrote of a priest of the Ngapuhi tribe who had been consulted regarding the location of a young girl who had sailed away with a man.[119] When this man made contact with an otherworldly "relative," he and those in attendance made their request that he "drive back the ship which had stolen his cousin." The response was, "The ship's nose I will batter out on the great sea." The ship returned ten days later, forced back by a storm, with the author noting, if with the condescension typical of the time, that "Now after such a coincidence as this, I can hardly blame the ignorant natives for believing in the oracle."

Britten made the observation that *Tohungas*, those being certain skilled practitioners among the Maori, are "unmistakably 'mediums,' in the modern sense of the term."[120] Redesdale made the same comparison in his *Tales of Old Japan*: "The class of diviners called *Ichiko* profess to give tidings of the dead, or of those who have gone to distant countries," further noting that "the Ichiko exactly corresponds to the spirit medium of the West."[121]

We might draw a fascinating historical parallel here. Just as the shaman has discovered distant events in trance, so too again have the monk and the saint. In the fourth century, Bishop Paphnutius of Thebes, as depicted in a beautifully elaborate painting in a fast-induced trance worthy of the shaman himself, sees the soul of a man he had recently left in the desert being transported to heaven at the very moment he died.[122]

These parallels at times mark the saint and the shaman as strikingly related bedfellows; St. Thomas the Armenian, for example, often fed on "pulse and some fruit only, sometimes from one week to the next and again on the first day of the week, and sometimes every two or three days, so that he was granted the gift of secret vision," just as would the shaman.[123]

It should be noted that in a great number of these accounts, the individual in question is observed to have been in a trance, praying, sleeping, or otherwise distracted, the idea being that one is therefore more receptive to such supernatural influences. This is greatly emphasized in, though not limited to, stories about the lives of the saints and seems to have been specifically implemented by hagiographers. Bilocation—appearing somewhere far distant from one's body, for example—occurs primarily during these states.[124]

We find the same dynamic in an old Japanese tale in which the fact that a man, Taicho, had dozed off gave a certain god the chance to speak with him. He had been waiting for the man to go to sleep before initiating communication.[125]

Rodulfus Glaber, an eleventh century Benedictine monk, wrote of a man who had a vision while praying in church.[126] He saw a company of solemn men wearing white robes led by a bishop with a cross in his hands. He explained to the man that there were monks who had been killed in battles with the Saracens and that they were on their way to the land of the blessed, that is, paradise.

Hagiographers often drew upon oral tradition, ballads, and other material related to the saint. This was as true for Welsh Saint David as it was for many others. We know in fact that not all of these tales are true; what is interesting is that even in those that are not, such as the following, they seem as if they could have been gleaned from the kinds of folkloric or other related sources we have seen. Thus it is written that while kneeling to receive the Eucharist, Edward the Confessor is said to have had a vision that revealed to him the drowning of the King of Denmark in the eleventh century, a scene represented in artwork.[127] Despite accounts that messengers were sent to Denmark at that time and confirmed the king's death, in reality the king died after Edward.

It is of course of great interest as to why something should be fabricated and to what extent the contents of that fabrication might nevertheless speak to the expectations of the reader and the author's understanding of these things. The hagiographer comes to mind. In this regard, such tales have their importance, just as do the literary examples.

Returning to Australia now, Anglican clergyman and anthropologist Adolphus Peter Elkin also expressed awe regarding occurrences among the Aboriginals there, noting their "remarkable" power to "know what is happening at a distance, even hundreds of miles away," later observing that they would sometimes be so sure of these intimations that they would return home at once. The author later notes often these intimations had turned out to be correct.[128]

American anthropologist William Montgomery McGovern wrote that, while under the influence of the specially prepared and psychoactive "kaapi" (*Banisteriopsis caapi*) root, certain Peruvian Indians "fell into a particularly deep state of trance, in which they were possessed of what appeared to be telepathic powers."[129] On one occasion, the local medicine man told him that the chief of a tribe on the Pira Parana River, miles away in Colombia, had suddenly died. McGovern entered this in his diary and weeks later found it to be "true in every detail," leading him to urge further investigation of such phenomena.

In his ethnographically and linguistically oriented field notes among the Peruvian Cashinahua, Kenneth Kensinger recounted something very similar.[130] He wrote in a footnote that many of the Cashinahuans who have never been to or seen pictures of Pucallpa, a large town at the Ucayali River terminus of the Central Highway, "have described their visits there under the influence of ayahuasca with sufficient detail for me to recognize specific sites and shops." In one "particularly memorable" ayahuasca session, six of the nine men informed him that his grandfather had just died. Two days later, the anthropologist reports in his notes that he was informed of his grandfather's death via field radio.

While ingesting ayahuasca, one Colonel Morales similarly reported seeing a vision of his dead father, even though the news that he had in fact died couldn't be confirmed by courier until a month later.[131]

It seems appropriate to note here just how incredibly fitting that the name initially given to ayahuasca was "telepathine," based on the conviction that it facilitated telepathic communication.[132] The observations of the influential psychiatrist Stanislav Grof regarding experiences related to the ingestion of LSD seem relevant too; he wrote that encounters with the deceased were "frequent" and often involved "telepathic exchange."[133]

Apart from the likes of the Cashinahua or the Zulu, the same capacities are, again, ascribed widely to mystics. The Dutch mystic Lydwina of Schiedam, while in conversation with someone, gave them an exact and detailed description of their house as though she had passed her life there.[134]

In 1218, the Cistercian monk Caesarius of Heisterbach, in his *Dialogue on Miracles*, a collection of edifying tales rooted in popular beliefs and attitudes, noted that at the very moment of the death of Gerbrandt, abbot of Klaar-Kamp in Friesland, a nun of Syon, a house of the order belonging to Klaar-Kamp, went into a trance and saw his spirit being carried to heaven by angels.[135] Like Lydwina of Schiedam and the shaman before, she also later described the details of the house in which he was buried.

Nearly a century earlier, at the moment of its occurrence in 1123, the death of the Italian abbot and bishop Peter of Pappacarbone was revealed to one of his monks, who had a vision of three previously dead abbots coming to take him away with them.[136]

From Africa again, the skeptical author David Leslie was waiting in "Zulu country" to meet Kaffir elephant hunters.[137] But they did not arrive as they should have. It was suggested that he see a doctor in order to learn of their location. He went, and the doctor fell over into a trance after having ingested some "medicine." Ten minutes later, the doctor awoke, described a man faithfully, and said of him, "This man has died of the fever and your gun is lost." He then went on to also note the deaths of four elephants and another hunter. The men and the details of their success or failure had been "minutely and correctly described," and he was soon told where the bodies were and when the remaining men would return home. The author noted that to his "utter amazement," it "turned out correct in every particular."

As had so many later folklorists, the author noted, "I could give many more instances of this 'power,' 'diablerie,' or whatever it may be called . . . and I must acknowledge that I have no theory to urge or explanation to offer regarding it, for I have in vain puzzled my own brains, and those of some of the shrewdest men in the colony for some sort of elucidation of the mystery."[138]

American journalist, ethnographer, and historian Stephen Powers recorded many instances of what he too called clairvoyance among the native tribes of California, though he did not take them seriously himself, rather suggesting that they were simply pretending to speak with spirits.[139] He nevertheless related a shaman's vision of a distant murder at the moment of its occurrence among the Californian Tsunungwe. The author tells us that a reservation agent and two others had been murdered, and that one day a Kelta shaman cried out that he saw the killer with his "spiritual eyes," describing "minutely" the place where he was hiding. According to Powers, subsequent events revealed that the shaman was substantially correct.

From South Africa, we hear of an incident between missionaries themselves rather than with the natives. A man named Sutherland had just been buried that night in a grave into which loose sand continually poured. The next morning, seventy miles distant, another missionary, Dr. Elmslie, awoke and exclaimed, "Sutherland is dead, and buried in a grave with the sand slipping in on both sides." This being accurate, author and Scots missionary James Horne Morrison could only put the incident down to a "mysterious sympathy" among the little band of pioneers.[140]

Regarding another clairvoyant visualization of the grave itself, it is recorded that a pilgrim in Jerusalem in 866 CE learned of the death of Fremund the Hermit, in which he saw Fremund's grave.[141] While this man, Edelbertus, initially refused to believe the vision, he eventually traveled and found the grave himself, exactly where the vision showed it to be.

Among the Tangu people of Papua New Guinea, there is a myth of a woman who left her daughter alone at home, during which time a stranger came, killed the child, and buried the body.[142] The location of the body was revealed to the absent woman in a dream. The fact that the death itself was learned of in this manner also seems clear.

Returning for a moment to the ballad dreams, the extent to which the veridical visions of these kinds are represented there deserves our interest. Here we note *The Lass of Lochroyan*, in which its Lord Gregory has the following dream:

> *I hae dream'd a dream, mother,*
> *I wish it may prove true!*
> *That the bonny Lass of Lochroyan*
> *Was at the yate e'en now.*
> *I hae dream'd a dream, mother,*
> *The thought o't gars me greet!*
> *That fair Annie o' Lochroyan*
> *Lay cauld dead at my feet.*

Having left to see if his dream was true, he eventually found her dead:

> *Lord Gregory tore his yellow hair,*
> *And made a heavy moan;*
> *Fair Annie's corpse lay at his feet,*
> *Her bonny young son was gone.*[143]

VISION AND BELIEF

Sinel noted outright in his early twentieth century study that he thought these experiences may have instilled the conception of an afterlife in the first place.[144] While such kinds of beliefs are certainly predicated upon a variety of different experiences, it is clear from the accounts that these visions have played an important role and have often been overlooked in favor of those account types, such as the near-death experience, which has garnered far more attention in recent decades.

Ronald Rose, in his singular study on Australian Aboriginal tribes and their relationship with psychic experiences, wrote specifically regarding the crisis apparition, telling us that "the conviction associated with a so-called crisis case, a type of incident that appears to be far more common among them than with white people, is often so profound that it moves them to action."[145]

Rose gives several interesting accounts, including one in which his informant's acquaintance suddenly exclaimed that his father had died.[146] "Don't mind telling you, I felt spooky," the man went on. "Here was this fellow, a hundred miles from his home, and apparently knowing what was going on there. And that's not all. A couple of weeks later I found out that he'd been right. His father had died—bitten by a snake that day. Work that one out!"

Rose had also suggested that the similarity between the crisis experiences of Aboriginal tribes and those so voluminously recorded of the "white man" is to be expected if the experiences are genuine, and that this was indeed collateral evidence for them.[147]

Bronislaw Malinowski wrote that one of the key experiences in North-Western Melanesia that distinguished the true dream from the false dream were those in which a recently dead person appears to announce their death.[148]

Returning to Shirokogorov, he had written that the Tungus cite their capacity to induce "vision on distance" amongst their evidence for the existence of the soul itself.[149]

Botanist and pioneering parapsychologist J. B. Rhine was similarly moved, if even indirectly.[150] Rhine tells us that, as a graduate student, one of his most respected science professors told him of an incident in which his wife dreamed that her brother had killed himself. "I was only a boy then," noted Rhine, "but it made an impression on me." Rhine was entirely sure of the veracity of the account, that the man was "sane and balanced," and noted that this was a story that "seemed to point so definitely to possible revolutionary facts in the interpretation of the working of the mind." While Rhine's looking back on the account seems to suggest there was an ultimate "disbelief" among he and his students, which was why they didn't follow up on the subject, this seems clearly to be a reference in the subconscious sense. Even if the singular event doesn't instill a new belief, it is clear it may still greatly affect.

Visions and dreams of a general crisis, rather than death, may similarly be the catalyst for change in the life of an individual. When Hans Berger, inventor of electroencephalography, was serving a year in the German military in 1892, he was thrown from a horse.[151] While not particularly unusual in and of itself, that day, as the neurologist David Millett recounts in the journal *Perspectives in Biology and Medicine*, Berger got a telegram from his father just checking on his well-being. Berger's father had never sent him a telegram before, but his older sister just had a feeling something was wrong with him. While not as eventful as many of the crisis accounts presented, for Berger this uncanny encounter would nevertheless determine a lifetime of research.

◆

We have already seen and will continue to see that Rose's conviction, along with that of others such as Virtanen, Jaffe, and McLenon, holds true in all times regarding the potential impact of these visions. Like the apparitional accounts, such impressions really do move people to action and can affect and alter the individual's beliefs in a variety of ways, regardless of era or location. Just as those anthropologists and ethnologists had been brought to awe in the face of these strange occurrences and suggested a role in the engendering of belief, this is also demonstrably true wherever these experiences are found. We have seen also that in all times, whether by means of spontaneous or sought-after visionary experiences, it has been attested that distant events, including deaths, have been discovered at the moment of their occurrence. This is a widespread reality. These people are frequently identified as shamans, seers, or saints, but as we have seen in our own time, the Finnish truck driver, the Texan salaryman, or the hobbyist psychonaut might also exercise such capacities even if a culture allowing for their assimilation is lacking. We have also seen that, as with apparitional encounters, these visionary experiences might similarly impact the individual's personal philosophies and belief systems at an impressively fundamental level. That the individual expressing these capacities as opposed to those who don't is often marked as special is clear. We will now explore these very distinctions in greater detail.

THREE

Those Who See, Those Who Don't

The circumstance that an actual spirit is present when none but the sensitive can see anything, as proved by the news of a death at a distance being sometimes psychically communicated, tends to set the seal of authenticity upon occasional real spirit presence at the séances of trance and clairvoyant mediums, a fact which some uninformed authorities deny altogether.

WILLIAM HENRY HARRISON

We have seen the tribesman inform the surprised explorer or the anthropologist of distant events. We have heard from both the Maori and the medieval monk about how they have witnessed apparitions which others did not see. The man or woman known for seeing visions or ghosts that others do not, even when in the same company, is a common folkloric trope. These facts speak to an old and widespread division between the specialist and the layman, although this is *somewhat* redundant in certain cases, in that, through such experiences, it is often the case that the latter graduates to the status of the former. As becomes apparent, whether by vision or dream, by mirror or by magic, by incubation or trance, there have always been those who see and those who don't. This distinction is made, perhaps most famously, in Numbers 12:6, where the Lord states that he might make himself known in a vision or dream, but only if there is a "prophet among" those ranks.[1] Of similar repute was Saul in his famous encounter with the Witch of Endor; Samuel's ghost was visible to the witch but not to Saul.[2] Much earlier, however, upon a most ancient near-Eastern clay tablet, it is stated that ghostly cries are heard only by "one who can hear."[3]

While such examples are renowned and often recounted, the notion is far more widespread, and where it hasn't been so well documented, it is often plainly implicit in the existence of the shaman or psychopomp and his particular skills and role in relation to the broader community.

In a Hawaiian tale, a man named Wahine-oma'o could not see a spirit; he lacked so-called spiritual sight, but another could.[4] Far north in Lapland, rather than there being a special class of seers, nobody sees or hears spirits except the man with whom they have very particular business.[5] In Jamaica the habits of ghosts or *duppies* are established according to those who have the "powers of seeing them,"[6] while among many West Africans a man's soul is only visible to a *wong-man* or spirit doctor.[7] The African examples alone might fill pages; among Nigerians, it is said that those who are able to see spirits have the "four eyes," and only they possess this gift.[8]

Among the indigenous Euahyahli of southeast Australia, a *wirreenun*, their medicine man or sorcerer, has the power to conjure up a vision of his particular *yunbeai*, a helping spirit, which he can make visible to those whom he alone chooses.[9] Likewise, the Gros Ventre Indians of North Central Montana say it is only the man who controls a ghost (the medicine man) who can see his spirit; it is invisible to other people.[10] The Argentinian Toba also ascribe to these ideas, as among them it is only the medicine man with his "special clear-sightedness" who can see and communicate with spirits.[11] From an old tale told in Palestine, when a father who had taught his son the ways of medicine was on his deathbed, he told his son that even after he died, he would be beside him, aiding in his work, but that only the son would be able to see his father.[12]

The distinction between those who see and those who don't was commonly expressed by prominent medieval authors as well. Caesarius, for example, referred to this quality or lack thereof many times. One of those references is in the story of a recluse who had been accosted by a demon in the form of an angel, and showed he did not have the "gift of the discernment of spirits."[13]

Gregory, in his dialogues, opens chapter seven with an observation aimed at a brother of his who complained that he could not see the soul of a person when it departed from their body, to which Gregory replied, "But that was your fault, who desired with corporal eyes to behold an invisible thing, for many of us, that by sincere faith and plentiful prayer, have had the eye of our soul purified, have often seen souls going out of their bodies."[14]

Howells long ago noted that in Wales the ghost is "rarely visible to more than one person although there are several in company."[15]

While these examples speak to something perennial, it was perhaps in Scotland, with its seers, that this belief gained a particularly strong footing. In the year 1799, a traveler writing of the peasants of Kirkcudbrightshire related: "It is common among them to fancy that they see the wraiths of persons dying, which will be visible to one and not to others present with him."[16]

In their essential elements, these sometimes hallowed visions, so often meant to separate the mystic from the ordinary woman or man, tend rather to unite them in some way or mark the former as the latter in the first place. Among the Amazonian Kamayura, for a more concrete example, at the burial of a shaman, the young man who sees the shaman's helper spirit himself becomes highly regarded and attains that spirit for himself, as opposed to those who do not see the ghostly form.[17]

One night on the Orkney Islands, a woman who was looking after someone ill had left for home.[18] A short time after laying down, while the lamp was still burning brightly in the room, she was surprised to see the clear form of the woman whose sickbed she had just left. The vision vanished as fast as it had come. Her husband wondered why she looked pale, and she balked, puzzled as to how he hadn't noticed the figure. When the next morning arrived, bringing with it the news that her friend had passed away the previous night at or near the approximate time at which she had seen the apparition, she had no doubt about the actuality of what she had seen.

English author Frank Podmore related a case from Cambridge in 1890 involving one Berta Hurly, who, in the spring and summer of 1886, often visited a poor woman from her parish, Mrs. Evans.[19] She was very sick, although there was no sign of immediate danger. Having not called on her for a few days, Berta, after dinner with her family, saw the figure of a woman dressed like Mrs. Evans pass across the room from one door to the other, where she disappeared. Berta exclaimed, "Who is that?" Her mother said, "What do you mean?" to which Berta replied, "That woman who has just come in and walked over to the other door." Her family laughed at her; however, she felt sure it was Mrs. Evans, and the next morning they heard she was dead.

In a case given by Mason Neale in the nineteenth century, we read of a surgeon who was attending to his brother-in-law's ill child.[20] This little girl of about five was playing in a dressing room when she suddenly cried out, "Oh, aunt, I come and see the baby, the poor baby. There he is—there!" As the child pointed to a corner of the room. Mrs. B. saw nothing, but she was insistent. Very soon, word came that the infant had died at that very moment.

Just as the soothsayer, the shaman, the witch, the seer, the scryer, or the medium have historically seen what others have not, so too have people continued to have these experiences right up through present day—indeed, they might have been candidates for the above monikers had their experiences occurred in a different time or place. They are designated as a diviner.

DAYLIGHT GHOSTS, WITNESSED AND TOLD

While we have seen the medicine man, the mystic, and the hero express his or her telepathy or clairvoyance, these visions and apparitions have historically occurred to ordinary people while fully awake and in the full possession of their senses. The authors of the *Phantasms of the Living* referred to these accounts, in fact, as the "most important class of all."[21] It was very much in vogue for at least the two hundred years or so before the publication of their seminal work on visions which occur at the time of a death: that of *course* people dreamed of apparitions and ghosts, and that such things rarely, if ever, happen in daylight. This is a common objection to the informatory vision or ghost in general, but it is also somewhat surprising that it has gained such ground, considering the impressive number of even the very oldest ghost stories which had neither taken place during the night nor during sleep. About half of the ghost stories from antiquity in Ogden's work, for example, took place as waking experiences, despite the prevalent notion that dreams were overwhelmingly the means by which one might consort with the dead.[22] Furthermore, while most early Greek dreams were dreamed indoors, the majority of those that were supernaturally caused actually occurred outdoors.[23] Similarly, while many ancient Egyptian encounters with supernatural entities came at night, others were specifically noted as having occurred during daylight hours—such as the man Ipuy, who stated, regarding a divine encounter with the goddess Hathor, that it was during the day when he saw her beauty.[24] As Hornung noted, in fact, for Egyptians, there were dreams both "by night and day," implying that the concept of a dream also included waking visions.[25]

The most ancient of Mesopotamian ghosts too had no qualms about appearing to the unsuspecting man or woman during waking hours and were "perfectly visible in a daylight hour sighting."[26]

The common idea then, however misaligned with the truth, that an overwhelming majority of ghosts appeared only by night and often to those not seemingly in their right mind, was certainly bolstered by some influential figures. The likes of Franciscan Friar Noel Taillepied wrote that ghosts most commonly appeared around midnight.[27] Others, such as author John Wade, repeated these sentiments, agreeing with Taillepied but even further explaining that it was only the "audacious spirits" who appeared by daylight, later falsely suggesting that there are only a few such instances.[28] Of even greater influence was surely the fact that the majority of early Christian visions of martyrs occurred during sleeping hours.[29]

The trope is apparent in some of the most influential literature, too. The revenants of ballad poetry as in *The Wife of Usher's Well,* often felt the need to be "off before daylight."[30] In Shakespeare's *The Winter's Tale*, it was daylight that drove the revenants back under the earth while in *A Midsummer Night's Dream*, Puck reminds Oberon that at the approach of the coming sunrise, ghosts who previously wandered here and there will troop home to the churchyards.[31] It should not be said that there is no truth to the idea, as the overall number of accounts by day and by night seems to be similar. It is simply interesting that one idea became more popularly accepted as truth.

WAKING VISIONS

Apollonius of Tyana, the Greek philosopher, mystic, and magician, was said to be able to speak with birds, divine the future, and was often sought out as a healer. We shouldn't be surprised, then, to read in Philostratus's *Life of Apollonius* that the veritable visionary himself is recorded as having mysteriously witnessed the death of the emperor Domitian at the moment of its occurrence. While delivering an address around midday, he is said to have dropped his voice, lapsed into something of a trance, and cried, "Take heart, gentlemen, for the tyrant has been slain this day." It should also be noted of this vision that its later accuracy is said to have caused the emperor Nerva to invite Apollonius to assist in ruling the empire.[32]

While this account has sometimes been passed over as an instance of ESP in antiquity,[33] it too benefits from being placed within the kind of context we are developing here. Furthermore, this particular narrative ascribed to one mystic the learning of a distant death at daylight, the vision witnessed by others, happens to strongly resemble a 1762 vision attributed to another revered mystic of his own time, Emanuelle Swedenborg. The incident, concerning the death of another emperor, Peter III of Russia, was relayed by his friend.[34] Of Swedenborg, his friend noted that "In the midst of our conversation, his countenance changed. It was evident his soul was no longer present, and that something was passing in him." As soon as he had come back to himself, he was asked what had happened. Swedenborg said, "This very hour the

Emperor Peter has died in prison." Peter's death was announced on that same day.

Yet another of the neglected visions from much earlier relates to the Decian persecution of Christians, which occurred in 250 CE. As recorded in the life of Gregory Thaumaturgus, it is said of the martyrdom of a young member of a noble family named Troadius that Gregory "in his wilderness" described to his companion the details of the trial, the torture, and the death of Troadius as it happened, step by step.[35]

Virtanen gave a similar account, this time again from rural Finland, where a truck driver also verbalized the details regarding a tragedy he was perceiving, apparently in real time.[36] One day, having just laid down, he said something awful had happened—that a woman had been killed on a certain bridge. Just moments later, this was confirmed.

The distinction between those who see and those who don't seems particularly stark in the apparitional cases. Thus one of Spain's most celebrated magicians, Doctor Eugenio Torralva, was called to the house of Donna Rosales in 1510, who had complained of seeing a ghost in the form of a murdered man, though it was noted that her physician could not see it.[37] Similarly, when Torralva arrived, Morales, the man who had set up the meeting, could not see what Torralva saw, which was the apparition of the dead man along with a woman who told him she was looking for treasure—Torralva apparently being "better acquainted with the spiritual world." They dug up all the cellars of the house and found the corpse of the man whose vision they had seen.

This distinction was clear again in an account involving a Maori.[38] Two men, Frank Philps and Jack Mulholland, were cutting timber at the mouth of the Awaroa Creek with the assistance of a Maori who came from a village on the other side of the river, about six miles away. As Frank and the Maori man were cross-cutting a tree, the native stopped suddenly and said, "What are you come for?" Frank replied, "What do you mean?" He said, "I am not speaking to you; I am speaking to my brother." Frank said, "Where is he?" The native replied, "Behind you." Frank looked around and saw nobody. The native man no longer saw anyone but laid down the saw and said, "I shall go across the river; my brother is dead." Frank laughed and said that he had just recently left him in good health and there had been no contact since. When the man returned home, he discovered this to be true.

When Ikuko Osumi, a Japanese healer, was young, she had a vision in the back of a cart and told the driver there was a dead man lying in the back of it.[39] The man could not see anything; however, when Osumi described his very particular clothing, the man thought she was seeing his brother. He soon returned home and found that his brother had fallen from his boat and drowned.

More well-known and again in broad daylight was a vision recorded in 594 CE by Gregory the Great of the death of a man named Speciocus.[40] While Gregory was sitting for dinner among the other monks of his order, he somehow became aware of his friend's spirit departing from his body, which he immediately told those around him. He took off for Capua and found his brother just buried, coming to know that he died at the very time of which he witnessed the vision.

Thanks to his biographer Widric, we have the record of a "strange story" related to the death of Gerard of Toul, a French bishop from 963 to 994.[41] A man he knew woke at dawn and walked the streets, declaring with "lamentations and outcries" that Gerard was "about to be removed from this world" and that he knew this from a vision. Accordingly, the bishop died on the same day.

As an aside, while among our contemporaries, in the majority, such visions often occur but once in a lifetime; among the mystics, shamans, and saints, it was sometimes part of their claim to such titles that they were the subject of multiple visions. Another Irish account is of such a person, as reported by hagiographer Adamnan. He wrote that as St. Colomba was living on Iona Island, he suddenly, and to the surprise of all those present, moaned heavily while reading.[43] One of his brothers asked about the cause of his grief. Columba, in "very great affliction," told him that "two men of royal blood in Scotia have perished of wounds mutually inflicted near the monastery called Cellrois, in the province of the Maugdorna, and on the eighth day from the end of this week, one shall give the shout on the other side of the Sound, who has come from Hibernia, and will tell you all as it happened." Soon came news that Colman the Hound, son of Ailen, and Eonana, son of Aid, had indeed died of their wounds at exactly that time.

At another time, a stranger from Hibernia came to him and stayed with him for some months on his island.[44] Colomba one day said to this man, "One of the clerics of thy province, whose name I do not yet know, is being carried to heaven by the angels at this moment!"

Recorded by Athanasius of Alexandria is an ancient vision of St. Anthony, to whom, again, a number of related visions had been ascribed.[44] When two of his brothers were coming to him across the desert, one died while the other was close. Anthony, sitting upon a mountain, called two monks who were in his company and told them to take a pitcher of water toward that road, for one of those two men had died and the other was in peril, noting this had been revealed to him as he was praying. The monks went and found the situation to be just as they had been told. This was ascribed again to the will of the Lord.

Italian Carmelite nun and mystic, Mary Magdalene De'Pazzi, was also subject to more than one vision. We read in her life that in 1591, on a Friday evening, while about to eat with her sisters, she suddenly arose from the table and, swiftly going to the superioress, told her insistently, "Mother, that soul passes away!" Without explaining further, she ran to the room where Sister Mattea Focardi was confined because of a sore on her right leg, which was apparently "far from threatening death." When she arrived, the woman was in her last agony and died moments later.[45]

Again referring to De'Pazzi, we read that at one time, being "alienated from her senses," she saw the spirit of one Francesco Santucci, of a distinguished Florentine family, passing away.[46] She went to his daughter and, taking her by the hand, said to her, "Sister, weep not; thy father, by the merits of Christ and the intercession of St. Francis, for whom he entertained so much devotion, has passed at this moment to a place of salvation." The steward was immediately dispatched, and in a very short time he returned with confirmation.

Many waking visions that have made their way firmly into popular legend pertain to important people and events. As recorded by the English monk Bede, one such 685 CE vision concerned the King Ecgfrith, who was once the King of Deira, a former northern Anglo-Saxon kingdom in

Britain.[47] Here again we meet with Cuthbert. Bede tells us that the King's queen, Eormenburg, was touring the church at Carlisle with Cuthbert when Cuthbert stopped, paused, and said to her and the others present, "I have just had a vision of your husband's death. Return to your palace and escape with your children." Almost immediately, a messenger arrived from the field at Nechtansmere with the news that Ecgfrith had been killed at the very same hour as the vision.

Cuthbert also had numerous related of this kind. In one of those, his limbs were said to have gone limp, as so commonly did those of the shaman, as he clearly beheld something in a trance. When asked, he eventually revealed to the questioner that someone from their monastery had died. It was later found that a certain man had fallen from a tree and been killed at the very moment Cuthbert had had his vision.[48]

VISIONS OF BATTLES AND DISASTERS

While the number of prophetic or generally psychical occurrences surrounding historical or large-scale events such as battles or tragedies is often overstated, those which do occur are almost invariably remembered well, perhaps the more for it. We have already seen references to visionary indigenous knowledge of incoming ships or tribes. Such visions constitute an intriguing sub-category in our survey of related experiences.

One of the earliest examples relates to the Battle of Pharsalus in Central Greece, the decisive battle of Caesar's Civil War in 48 BCE.[49] In an event given by Plutarch, a priest called Cornelius, residing far off in Italy, was suddenly seized by a "prophetic inspiration" and saw the battle taking place far off, before announcing the victory of Caesar. Roman author Aulus Gellius wrote, "At the time the prophecy of the priest Cornelius seemed unimportant and without meaning. Afterwards, however, it caused great surprise, since not only the time of the battle which was fought in Thessaly, and its predicted outcome, were verified, but all the shifting fortunes of the day and the very conflict of the two armies were represented by the gestures and words of the seer."

Such visions have surprisingly similar analogs across time and space. From 1525, we read Calmet's account of the Duchess Philippa of Gueldres, wife of the Duke of Lorraine, René II, who, having retired to the convent at St. Claire du Pont-à-Mousson, experienced a vision while praying.[50] Then ongoing, the battle of Pavia was the decisive engagement of the Italian War of 1521–1526 between the Kingdom of France and the Habsburg Empire of Charles V. The Duchess cried out suddenly, "Ah! my sisters, my dear sisters, for the love of God, say your prayers; my son De Lambesc is dead, and the king [Francis I] my cousin is made prisoner." Some days later, news of this famous event, which happened the very day on which the duchess had seen it, was received at Nancy.

Similar was another vision of Eugenio Torralva, who, with the help of his "benevolent spirit" Zequiel, was brought in spirit to Rome and witnessed the death of the Constable of Bourbon in 1527 and the slaughter of other citizens as Rome was taken. He returned to himself and his home in Spain to tell of what he had seen.[51] About a week later, when news arrived of the capture and sack of Rome, the court of Spain was "filled with unbounded surprise" at the accuracy of what Torralva had reported.

Then Archbishop of Vienna related that he first announced the 1477 death of Charles the Bold to Louis the Eleventh.[52] "At the instant" that said duke was killed at the battle of Nancy, King Louis had been hearing mass in the Church of Saint Martin, at least ten days distant. At mass, the archbishop of Vienna said to him, "Sire[. . .], Duke of Burgundy is dead; he has just now been killed, and his army discomfited."

St. Nicholas is recorded as having had a vision one night of two armies in a field, the Greeks and Bulgarians, with the entire field soon being filled with corpses.[53] According to Velimirovich, "that which Nicholas saw in his dream, he saw precisely in reality at the time of the battle."

According to French Calvinist Protestant theologian, reformer, and scholar Theodore Beza, one night in December, 1562, Calvin heard "a very loud sound of drums used in war," and although it was stormy at the time, he could not shake off the feeling that they were real.[54] "I entreat you to pray," he told his friends the following day, "for some event of very great moment is undoubtedly taking place." It was: the Huguenots were suffering a catastrophic defeat at the battle of Dreux.

The famed and prominent leader and medicine man of the Ndendahe Apache, Geronimo, once declared aloud to his men that their base camp, over 120 miles away, had been captured by United States troops, which later proved accurate. The author, Betzinez, noted simply that he couldn't explain this.[55]

We might make mention of the "war-dream" of the Makonde, an ethnic group from Southeast Tanzania, northern Mozambique, and Kenya.[56] Regarding distant fighting, in these war-dreams, "the progress of the fight was foreseen, and the result, including the individuals killed, was told to the chief."

In what English author, clergyman, and teacher Montague Summers called "one of the most striking instances of divinely supernatural tele-kinesis," we read that on October 7, 1571, Pope St. Pius V was informed of the result of the Battle of Lepanto and the victory of Don John.[57] This man, at the battle's decisive moment, suddenly rose, left his company, and went to the window, which he opened. For a moment his eyes were fixed on the heavens; then, as he returned to the table, he said, "It is not now a time to talk any more about affairs, however pressing; it is the time to give thanks to Almighty God for the signal victory which He has vouchsafed to the Christians." This fact was later carefully attested to and authentically recorded.

The Mahabharata holds multiple related references and refers to "divine sight" or "supernatural vision."[58] Though far from the battle, wise Gandhari, a prominent princess in the Hindu epic, saw, as if it were right in front of her eyes, the field of battle where certain heroes had fought—a horrific sight strewn with bones and gore, bodies, and death.

During the Indian Kurukshetra War, as described in the Mahabharata, the blind man Dhritarashtra related "all that took place" to his charioteer, with whom he was riding, also using his "divine vision."[59]

In the published life of Vedic scholar Shri Annasahib Patwardhan, it is stated that his mother could describe the battles in the first war of Indian independence from her residence in Poona on their very day, which could subsequently be confirmed by the newspapers.[60]

There is an interesting allusion to the possibility of this kind of vision regarding the 1099 siege of Jerusalem.[61] The genealogist Muhammad-b-Asaa'd an Nassabah asked aloud, "Has thou seen in a dream what I behold with my eyes—Jerusalem captured and the Franks routed?"

A French priest named Stephen once told Frankish military leaders of a vision in which their army had been given a victory during the 1097 siege of Nicaea, the first major battle of the First Crusade.[62]

It is said that Dutch mystic Gertrude of Delft had exactly the same kind of knowledge of a battle being fought some distance away.[63]

Perhaps the oldest recorded account of this kind involves the death of Pelatiah, son of Benaiah, in Ezekial 11:13, which was seen by Ezekiel, a Zadokite priest writing during the Babylonian exile, "in spirit" at a great distance. His death is the one mainly noted, but it comes amid visions of the deaths of many others that were occurring at the time.

Wodrow, in his old study of Scottish Providences, relays that the brother of one John Cameron, while in Kyntyre at the time of the 1679 Battle of Bothwell Bridge, turned "very melancholy" that morning and was seen weeping in his chamber.[64] When asked what the matter was, the man replied, "Our friends at Bothwell are gone." When Mr. Morison told him it might be a mistake, the brother replied, "No, no, I see them flying as clear as I see the wall." And, as near as they could calculate, it was at the very minute they fled that this was seen by Cameron while in the Lochhead of Kyntyre.

Similar was an occurrence recorded around the 1746 Battle of Culloden, which took place across the Scottish Highlands fought between a Scots Jacobite army and the British government.[65] It is said that when the Earl of London retreated to the Isle of Skye, pushed back by the Scottish Rebels, a common soldier there proclaimed victory "at the very moment of success" over them by some magic.

Similar visions have found their way into the romances. At the Battle of Roncevaux Pass in 778, so vividly remembered in *The Legend of Roland*, an eleventh century chanson de geste based on the Frankish military leader Roland, both Marsile and Roland die.[66] At that very moment, the monastic Turpin was saying mass before Charlemagne when he had a vision of demons carrying Marsile to Hell while he saw Roland being borne to Heaven. As he was telling this to Charles, a messenger arrived with the news of their deaths on the battlefield, and they soon found the bodies.

Finally, it is said of John, son of Svojslav, that in the year 1260, while the Czechs were at war with Hungary, he became dangerously ill and fell into a sort of fit.[67] Upon coming around, he described that he had been to the battlefield, where he saw his people and their victory. Later, when news came from the battle, it was apparently shown that the vision occurred at dawn on the very day when the Czechs won their victory over the Magyars.

◆

While up to this point, the apparitions and visions have been relatively mundane, with real emphasis, of course, on that relativity, this is not always the case. Sometimes the visions are rather more elaborate and speak in the language of symbol and metaphor. These will be the subject of the following chapter.

FOUR

Allegorical Visions and Symbolic Apparitions

The chief peculiarity of second sight is, that the visions often, though not always, are of a symbolical character.

ANDREW LANG

In the medieval romance of Guy of Warwick, popular in England and France from the thirteenth to seventeenth centuries, Herhand dreams of his comrade Guy in great danger, being assaulted and chased by wolves and bears; the moment he awakens, he rides with his fellows and finds that Guy is being chased by Saracens.[1]

The late thirteenth century tale "Amis and Amiloun" finds Sir Amiloun dreaming that he saw Amis, his sworn brother, surrounded by foes and other beasts. Amis was indeed in great peril at that time.[2]

Similarly, in the Middle English chivalric romance *King Horn*, dating back to the thirteenth century, we read that Fikenhild was wooing Rymenhild, whom our protagonist loved, and he later forcibly married her.[3] At the same time, Horn dreamed that Rymenhild was taken aboard a ship that began to overturn. As she tried to swim to land, Fikenhild pushed her backwards. Horn awoke, exclaiming, "We must to ship. Fikenhild hath deceived me and now works some hard to Rymenhild. May Christ drive us thither."

In the fourth century verse romance *Erle of Tolous*, the main character, Barnard, dreams that two wild bears have torn his wife in two, and it is written that, "being a man of sense," he immediately knew that she was in trouble. She had indeed been thrown into prison and was potentially facing death.[4]

That a distant crisis, whether in time or space, whether a death or otherwise, might be represented symbolically to the (often sleeping) visionary is long-established and a notion evident throughout the medieval romances and much other literature. Their readers were familiar with prophetic and symbolic dreams, some of which are better known than others. Mordred's dream from the *Legend of King Arthur*, in which a dragon defeats a fierce bear, symbolically foreshadowed his victory. The dream of Iseult from the Chivalric Romance *Tristan and Iseult*, in which a boar's head lies bloody on her frock and from which she awakens very sure of its meaning regarding the morbid fate of her lover, is another example; there are many more.[6]

These visions are basically indistinguishable from the kinds of symbolic ESP-related visions of crisis and death still recorded, and while we'll see that such visions and dreams, which present in symbolic form, are still common, they have a truly ancient pedigree. Far from just the rather versatile literary device that that prophetic or symbolical dream most certainly is, these kinds of narratives also speak to the far broader reality of these visions and dreams, and regarding the human encounter with death and the language of the otherworld itself. While the symbolic dream is found in abundance through time, with the trusted dream interpreter or wizard always at the ready to decipher its contents for men of power, those relating to events occurring at the moment of the vision itself are much harder to find. In the grander scheme of things, however, they are no small aside. In addition, while across the globe, the annals of history tell us that the raison d'être of the dream interpreter lay in the need for the dream, so often symbolic, to be deciphered, this was very often not the case. It is clear from the romances and other sources that medieval intellectuals and poets were aware that while certain dreams might transmit truths under a veil of symbolism and allegory, for the dreamer or visionary themselves, in fact, there was often no such obscurity. The notion, as has been expressed by some, that every dream called for interpretation simply wasn't true. One's dialogue with the divine may be spoken in tongues as far as the listener is concerned, and yet might be perfectly clear for the dreamer.

Just as it was for Guy of Warwick, King Horn, or Iseult of the romances, the meaning of what they see is often immediately known to the visionary. This was true then as it happened to be for Carl Gustav Jung in his own related experience. Jung, in his *Memories, Dreams, and Reflections*, tells us in no uncertain terms that despite the rather indirect and allegorical nature of one of his own particularly affecting dreams in which he saw a figure covered in black symbols floating upward, he had awoken quite sure and convinced of its meaning.[7] In fact, such conviction is a defining feature of the majority of these experiences, and it frequently serves to distinguish them from the more commonplace dreams—those uncountable numbers of them that have no correlation with reality. King Horn, the Earl of Toluos, and Iseult did not, after all, wait for their visions to be interpreted before acting on them but were magically moved to action.

THE ALLEGORICAL BEYOND

That the otherworld may speak and present in the language of metaphor and allegory is clear not just from these romantic and other literary sources but also from an abundance of traditional, folkloric, and related others. As was imparted to Lisa Smartt, author of *Words at the Threshold*, by psychotherapist Marsha Joe Atkins, "the dying commonly speak in metaphors specifically related to travel, which often progress logically as they near the end. Some examples included, 'I need my map . . .' That may change to 'Who has my suitcase? I need my suitcase.' Later the individual may say, 'My suitcase is packed. I am ready to go now.'"[8]* Likewise, Callanan noted that the dying attempt to indicate their oncoming death using symbolic language.[9] Fenwick found the

---

*From the book *Words at the Threshold*. Copyright © 2017 by Lisa Smartt. Reprinted with permission by New World Library, Novato, CA.

same in his British sample,[10] while Pearson noted more pointedly of the dying: "They sincerely want to know where their train tickets or hiking shoes or tide charts are."[11] Far less remarked upon is that the very same often applies to those apparitions and visions which occur in relation to the moment of a distant death. Virtanen, for example, found that a third of all the informatory visions in her rural Finnish sample were of this kind, representing death metaphorically in some way.[12] Long before, Irish folklorist Lady Gregory was told of a vision in West Ireland in which a certain Roland Joyce was seen out and about on the night he died: "He was seen on night of his death in Esserkelly where he had a farm," she explained, "and a man along with him going through the stock, and all of a sudden a train came into the field, and brought them both away like a blast of wind."[13]

Comparably, in Wales in 1910, a man dreamed that he was to go inside the estate of a Lord Kensington and wait for the Lord's wife.[14] He was taken into the living room, and then all the household servants came dressed in their holiday attire and informed him that Lady Kensington was not home after all but had gotten lost somewhere. "When I awoke from my dream," our Welsh informant tells us, "I felt certain that something had happened to one of the Kensingtons." Soon after, a telegram came from Calcutta announcing her death at that time.

According to Scottish minister and historian Robert Wodrow, one night while a Mrs. Gordon, known to the author, was sleeping in Knock in the wild north-east, she dreamed she saw a Mr. Hutcheson come down from a pulpit before seemingly lying half dead over a seat.[15] The place suddenly filled with darkness, and the next day she heard of the man's death, which occurred at the same time as her dream.

More recently, an informant of author Allison Morgan told her that on the same night her grandmother died, she dreamed that her grandmother knocked on her door and came into the room wearing her best navy blue coat and a handbag, saying that she couldn't tell where she was going but had to say goodbye.[16]

The handbag, the coat, the train ticket—the language of the journey is common. The journey, however, is only one means by which a distant death is represented to the visionary; at times the imagery is rather on the nose and direct, being patently death related, while at others it is relatively convoluted and seemingly contrived, even verging on the absurd or humorous. It is with a selection of these kinds of visionary experiences that we now concern ourselves here.

THE VARIETIES OF SIMULTANEOUS SYMBOLIC VISIONS

In a Japanese tale from the Eiroku Period (1558–1570) related to an older Chinese account, a man named Chuta of Noji left for the seaside town of Kamakura on business but was unable to come home for about three years due to unrest.[17] One night, he dreamed he saw his wife standing behind a cherry tree, lamenting the falling blossoms, before laughing and looking into a well. Three days later, Chuta heard that his wife had died. It's also worth noting that he felt moved to write a poem after the experience. As a related aside, Chuta later saw an apparition of his wife and her dead maid, as well as another woman behind them. He asked who it was and learned that she was the wet nurse of his wife's maid; after the maid's death, she had no purpose and so drowned herself on that very night.[18]

In a Chinese tale, at the moment one Chang Shao died, wishing to see his friend Fan Shih, Fan Shih saw him appear at his home wearing a black headdress with a trailing strap and dragging his slippers.[19] The apparition told him that he "died on such and such a day." As in the case of Belasco, a play was based on this old story.

While we will continue to see them so impressively represented, by no means were the mystics and martyrs of the Christian Church the only saints to whom such visions have been ascribed. An Islamic man in 781 CE dreamed of the scholar and Sufi mystic Dawud al-Taz, running at the hour of his death.[20] The dreamer asked him why he was running, to which he replied simply that he had just been released from prison. When the dreamer awakened, he found that Dawud died and heard the lament, confirming the matter.

In 874 CE, nearly a century later, in north-central Iran a dream that was simultaneous with the death of Bayazid Bazmat was said to be indicative of his cosmic importance. In this vision, Abii Misa sees the heavenly throne placed on his own head. When he goes to relate the vision to his master, he finds that the sheikh has died that very same night.[21] During the funeral, his master appeared to him and explained that this death was the meaning of the previous night's dream—that heavenly throne was the body of Bayazid himself.

We read in a medieval Jewish sermon story that a priest was looking after an ill woman who had confessed a number of her sins to him.[22] There was someone in particular, however, that this woman could not bring herself to forgive. This priest had a vision one night in which the devil carried off the lady's soul with a disgusting looking toad on her heart. When he woke up, he was told that the woman had died while he was asleep.

Similarly, again from Caesarius's thirteenth century Dialogues, we read that at the very hour of the death of a cleric named Walter, the canon of the church of St. Andrew's in Cologne was sleeping in the Gate of the Clerics. In a vision, he claims to have seen Walter counting money from a large heap on a board with a devil in the form of an Ethiopian sitting on the other side.[23] As he counted, Walter frequently hid some of the money under his garment. When it had all been added up, the devil exclaimed these words: "Water counts silver and steals it; for that was what he used to be called because of his pride." Having awoken and related this vision, the canon discovered that Walter had died at that very hour.

A later Gaelic manuscript called *The Book of Lismore*, which was originally published in the fifteenth century, explains the providence of two graves at a place called Rudhraighe's Strand.[24] Fionn mac Cumhaill, hunter and hero of Irish mythology, famously dreamed that he saw two gray seals sucking at his breast. His dream turned out to be a vision of the two sons of the King of Connacht, represented in the form of two seals. They were mortally wounded in combat in an effort to protect Fionn and the Fianna (historical Irish warriors and hunters from the Iron Age and early Middle Ages) while they were sleeping.

In a variation on a celebrated Slavic dream from an old Russian oral epic, a tsarina dreamed of a falcon fighting with a black raven, resulting in the killing of the raven by the falcon.[25] The falcon represented a person named Volga and the raven was another named Santal, the falcon being the traditional designation of the Russian warrior, while the raven is that of his Slavic foe.

A poem related to one of the legends of King Charlemagne, *Lady Alda's Dream*, relates that woman's dark dream of her lover and Frankish military leader Roland, who was in Spain, while she lay sleeping in France.[26]

> *I sat upon a mountain shore, and from the mountains*
> *   nigh,*
> *Right toward me, I seemed to see a gentle falcon fly;*
> *But close behind an eagle swooped, and struck that falcon*
> *   down,*
> *And with talons and beak he rent the bird, as he cowered*
> *   beneath my gown.*

Next morning came letters "stained with blood, the truth too plainly tell, How, in the chase of Ronceval, Sir Roland fought and fell."

In the ancient Celtic poem called *Comala*, said to have been written by Ossian, son of Fionn mac Cumhaill and preserved entirely by oral tradition, a man named Fingal, son of Comhal, is killed in battle, and at the very time that he is mortally wounded, a woman called Dersagrena becomes aware of his death by a number of strange signs such as ghostly forms among the clouds and meteors gathering around the head of a deer.[30] She eventually proclaimed aloud, "Ah! hapless sight! These signs too surely tell that mighty Fingal in the battle fell! His foes are trampling on the king of shields, And Caracalla triumphs o'er our fields."

Something similar is said of Icelandic priest and scholar Saemund the Learned (1056–1153), who could discover facts about people through his knowledge of the stars.[28] Once, while looking to the night sky, he exclaimed to his brother, "Bad news! Jon, the foreigner, has drowned my foster-son Kol, for there is water round his star."

Like those shamans we have met with from the South American

rainforests or the Inuit peoples of the frozen north, druids too were said to be able to see over great distances by supernatural means, and symbolic visions are also widely found; indeed, tales that combine the two are recorded in some of the earliest Gaelic texts. In a dream, Eochaid, then High King of Ireland, saw a flock of black birds come from the depths of the sea and fight with all the people of Ireland.[29] Having relayed this to his wizard, he was told that this flock represented warriors that were at that very moment coming across the ocean by the thousands.

While King Eochaid was an accidental clairvoyant, it is again a common story among indigenous tribes that their shamans have intentionally become aware of enemies encroaching on their camps before they arrive. Similarly skilled seers are represented widely in North American traditions. In the old Native American tale of the Modoc tribe, "Thunder and Eagle Boy," five brothers are on the hunt.[30] After encountering the mythical being Yahya'haas and being challenged to wrestle, one brother accepts. He is hurled off a cliff to his death. Indeed, each brother in turn met the same fate. Somewhere distant, in the house of one named Blaiwas, there was an old medicine woman. She woke up and said to a group, "I dreamed that I saw people crying and putting ashes on their heads, our men have been killed. At noon tomorrow we shall get word of it." One of them didn't believe her, saying the brothers were too strong to have all been killed. But at noon the next day, a boy came along the trail, crying and screaming, bringing news that confirmed the old medicine woman's dream.

According to another myth from among the Modocs of Canada, three sisters killed an old man named Kulta.[31] Further away in another village, an old and great *kiuks,* a kind of Indian Medicine man said, "In a dream I saw fresh blood spread on the ground. Kulta is dead!" Again, despite the rather general imagery of blood, its meaning seems immediately apparent to the seer in that a specific individual is construed as the subject of the vision.

Remaining in Canada, although this time from a later French Canadian folklore memorate, we read that in 1956 a man was sitting near a window when he noticed drops of blood falling on a window pane.[32] He immediately recognized it as a warning, assuming someone had died far away. Two days later, he received word of the death of one of his children.

In the Scandinavian *Gísla Saga*, written in the thirteenth century but describing events from between 940 and 980, we come to the story of Gísli the outlaw.[33] Vestein, the saga's protagonist, was slain in his bed after someone stole softly into the room and stood over him in a scene that recalls the previously mentioned death of Thrace; Vestein awakens just as a spear is thrust into his chest. When the news reached Gísli, after traveling some distance, he commented, "I dreamed a dream the night before last, and last night too, but I will not tell it, nor say who did this slaying, but my dreams all point to it. Me thought I dreamt the first night that an adder crept out of a house I know, and stung Vestein to death. And last night I dreamt that a wolf ran from the same house and tore Vestein to death; but I told neither dream up to this time, because I did not wish that any one should interpret them."

Although the man isn't killed, something alike is found in a Jewish folktale collected in Eastern Europe in the nineteenth century. At exactly the time the Duke of the village of Luntshitz in Poland had turned himself into a wolf using magic and entered the bedroom of a sleeping man, Shlomo Ephraim, Ephraim dreamed that the Duke had slipped into his room and was standing over him with a knife in his hand.[34]

In the *Viga-Glums Saga*, it is told that Glum dreamed one night that he was standing outside looking out over the forests.[35] He thought he saw a woman walking up the country road wearing a helmet, her shoulders seemingly touching the mountains on either side. He walked out in an attempt to meet her, but before he could do so, he woke up. Without the need for an interpretor, Glum interpreted the symbolism himself: "The dream is great and mark-worthy, and I read it so, that Wigfus, my mother's father, must now be dead, and this woman that walked higher than the mountains must be his fetch, for he was much greater than other men in honour and in many ways, and his fetch must be seeking to take up its abode here where I am." That summer a ship arrived with news of Wigfus's death. Just like Chuta from the previous Japanese account, Glum was brought to write a verse:

I saw a monster fairy-woman under helm
Faring hither to Eyfnth:
As it seemed in my dream her feet were on the ground,
But her shoulders reached the hills.

Yet another account involving verse was an old story from Eastern Pennsylvania in which the husband of a young woman went to war.[36] She dreamed one night that she was carried off by some sort of phantom while on a white horse. She recognized her absent husband in that ghostly form. In the darkness, the soldier dramatically cried out, "Brightly shines the moon. Swiftly ride the dead!" She awoke the next morning and soon was given the bad news of his death.

More ancient was the Greek dramatist Menander's 323 BCE vision of Alexander the Great's death. During this vision, Menander saw a lion covered in iron being thrown into a ditch.[37] He awoke and told his comrades Selpharios and Diatrophe that he knew this lion was his King Alexander. Just as they were speaking, a messenger came. "Men it was, worthy of death, that laid hands upon my lord, the king, in Gedrosia and have slain him." In this version, Alexander eventually returned to Menander and told him that his life had been restored; regardless, the story, a potentially romantic resurrection, is an illustration of the understanding of meaning in a symbolic dream in its capacity to represent a distant death.

Similarly, in Euripides's last extant and ancient Greek tragedy, *Iphigenia at Aulis*, the mythological Iphigenia dreams of her brother Orestes; she dreams a "strange vision" in which "an earthquake shook the ground," exclaiming then, "I fled, I stood without, the cornice saw of the roof falling—then, all crashing down. Turret and basement, hurled was the house to earth." As professor and theologian E. H. Klotsche noted, "This dream-vision has convinced her that her brother Orestes must be dead."[38] The dream happened to be prophetic; Orestes was rather to die later, and while, as the author again notes, "Iphigenia here makes the mistake of interpreting the dream with reference to the past," it is abundantly clear how seriously she took this possibility with her words and her rituals. Indeed, while recognizing the literary versatility of the dream-vision, Klotsche had previously and importantly noted, with specific reference to a crisis vision, that "Euripides employs such a supernatural element of dreams and visions as a survival of a primitive belief."[39]

Millenia later, in 1603, we have the vision experienced by English playwright and poet Ben Jonson during the Black Plague.[40] During this vision, Jonson saw his eldest son appear to him with the mark of a bloody cross upon his forehead, as if he had been wounded with a sword. That same morning, word came that this young man had died of the plague.

While Jonson's account was widely published in the centuries that followed, another plague-related vision recorded nearly fifty years later by Dutch physicist and anatomist Professer van Diemerbroeck was far less renowned. In his medical treatise *De Peste*, Diemerbroeck wrote of a 1646 vision in a town where the plague raged.[41] A man named Dimmerus sent his wife thirty miles away to safety. When a doctor went to see the gentleman of the house, an old woman fell down weeping as he entered. When the doctor asked her why, she told him, "My mistress is now dead, I saw her apparition but just now without a head." As in those references from the chapter on those who see and those who don't, this woman noted that such visions were a usual thing for her, and it turned out that Dimmerus's wife had died at that very time.

Far older and recorded by Gregory the Great, we read of a man who lifted his eyes up and beheld the soul of his sister in the likeness of a dove ascending into heaven.[42] Of interest here too is the comment in Caesarius's work, which posits the question as to the meaning of the dove in an older crisis apparition for comparison, noting that "it was under the same form that St. Benedict, as we read in his life, saw the soul of his sister Scholastica enter the heavens.[43]"

It should not be surprising that the dove has so often symbolized the soul's ascent throughout the Middle Ages, as there are numerous references to the holy spirit in the form of a dove descending from the heavens in the Bible. This imagery is far older, too. In Egyptian depictions, the soul of a dead person is sometimes shown flying up the tomb shaft in bird form to visit the world of the living.[44]

Many visions involving doves are found not just among the recorded lives of the better-known saints but also of many lesser known. It was said of Spanish saint Eulalia, for example, that when she died after torture, a white dove issued from her mouth and flew to heaven.[45] The origin of this imagery is likely rooted in older folkloric notions, and the dove is still widely reported in comparable accounts. In an American journal of midwestern folklore, for example, one informant was driving with her son to a hospital to see her husband, who was seriously ill.[46] Suddenly a dove hit the windscreen of the car, and the boy turned to his mother and said, "Dad's gone." It was ten-thirty by the mother's watch. When they arrived at the hospital around eleven o'clock, they discovered that Mr. E had died about half an hour earlier.

The soul ascending then takes various forms. Nestor the Chronicler of the Ukranian Church wrote of an experience in which the Grand Prince Svjatoslav of Kiev II, at the death of an important saint, Theodosius, saw a pillar of fire above a monastery. The prince then remarked that he thought it signified that man's death.[47] Many Siberian tribes claim that the shaman dies in the form of fire.[48] The Danish geologist Hinrich Rink gives a more specific instance in which the ghost of a deceased Eskimo appears to another in the shape of a fire.[49] Similarly, at the very hour of Bishop German of Auxerre's death in 448 CE, Benedict of Nursia is said to have seen angels carrying that bishop's soul to heaven in a fireball.[50]

Analogous ideas may be found in Japanese traditions in which fires appearing in unlikely places so commonly indicate the presence of ghosts that Japanese illustrations of ghosts usually have a few tongues of flame somewhere in the picture.[51] Perhaps of relevance, too, within the context of the general mystical experience, fire and light are often indistinguishable descriptors.

Moving onward, in the seventh century, Belgian Benedictine mystic Belinda of Meerbeeke had a symbolic dream.[52] She was looking out at a dark blue sky full of stars, and she heard people singing. Dark shapes flew across the sky, blotting out the stars as they passed, and suddenly an awareness dawned on her they were angels; they seemed to be carrying away her father's soul. Belinda hurried home and found that her father had died in the night.

Much earlier in Belgium, making company here again with the mystic Juliana of Liege, who, while praying, suddenly told those present to do the same for one of her friends who was passing from this world at that moment.[53] When asked how she knew, she said that she felt a special pain in her body, which she only experiences when someone she knows dies. This was said to be a common occurrence in Juliana's life. "At the moment in which a person of my acquaintance has expired," she explained, "I am seized with pains so violent, that it seems almost impossible for me to bear them. I have often found, upon comparing the hour of their decease with that in which I was attacked with these violent pains, that it was exactly the same."

General sympathetic pains in relation to a distant death have been long known to psychical researchers, with the authors of the 1886 *Phantasms of the Living* making a note of such accounts involving "transference of pain."[54]

Moving north and around 400 years later now to the Isle of Man, we read of a Captain Leaths, former chief magistrate of Belfast, who, during a 1609 voyage, lost thirteen men to a violent storm.[55] When the captain made landfall on the Isle of Man, the people there already knew that he had lost thirteen men. Leaths asked a certain man how they could possibly know this, to which he replied that he had known by the thirteen lights that he had seen come into the churchyard.

In a 1911 edition of *The Occult Review*, we read that further north, on the remote Orkney Islands, a woman, looking towards the house of an old man she knew to be ill, stood and saw what looked like a large white sheet rise up from over the roof of the old man's house, hover for a moment, and then disappear. She later found that the strange occurrence exactly coincided with the man's death.[56]

In a compilation of Indo-Tibetan stories that were later brought to Mongolia and translated into Mongolic languages, a girl who was to wed a great lord was killed by her stepmother, who substituted her own daughter to be the man's bride.[57] The spirit of the dead girl is transformed into a white bird. The bird weaves a fine kimono for her younger brother, through which the lord comes to know what happened to his true fiancé.

Henderson recorded a Northern English memorate that makes a symbolic, although again a very clear distinction between the living and the dead.[58] Henderson's informant awoke and told her husband she'd had a very unsettling dream. She had seen him and his two brothers standing in conversation on a grassy plot. A man she knew to be deceased then came towards them with a paper in his hand. The ground opened up, and one of the brothers, James, fell into the chasm and disappeared. Almost right away, a horseman arrived with the news that his brother James had indeed just died.

In the following account, the distinction separating the living and the dead is once again rather stark. A woman dreamed of two old friends, one of whom looked normal while the other looked "see-through." She was awoken by a call with the news that the friend who had appeared see-through had drowned.[59]*

ON-THE-NOSE DEATH IMAGERY

Perhaps the most overt kinds of imagery pertaining to a death are those most archetypally and manifestly related to the very *things* of death. Coffins, processions, and even grim reapers turn up with some frequency, particularly in folkloric memorates. While one may expect apparitions and various death-related visions to present in a patently morbid or symbolically representative manner, when one is unaware of the distant death itself, the content and context become greatly mysterious. That one might experience a vision of a loved one, the one vision of this kind in their life, at the very time of their death, is strange enough, after all. It is much stranger, of course, when those visions seem also to present themselves very clearly in the clothing of death. For one of the oldest of this kind, we read of another Alexander from antiquity,

---

*A special acknowledgment and thanks to the Rhine Center and to John Kruth, whose archives, still being updated, were the origin of this and three other included accounts. They can be found at the Rhine Center website.

this time not a king but a philosopher from Aphrodisias.[60] Alexander reported that, while sleeping one night, he saw the funeral of his own mother being carried out a day's journey from his location. Upon awakening in tears, Alexander shared his dream with friends and acquaintances and observed the timing of the occurrence. Subsequently, word came to him that his mother had passed at the same hour as his dream.

The revolutionary Italian general Giuseppe Garibaldi had what was a profoundly affecting experience in 1852. Basso, his inseparable friend and secretary, noted the extraordinary effect this dream had on him. In the rather solemn words of British historian George Macaulay Trevelyan, "This worst of all terrors came not unnaturally to a man of forty-six, troubled as he now so often was by old wounds and disease, the scars of his conflict with man and nature in two hemispheres; the fear haunted him in the night watches on the broad Pacific. There, too, he was visited by a strange dream—of the women of Nice bearing his mother to the grave—which, as he declares, came to him on the very day when she died far off on the other side of the world of waters."[61]

Pearson relayed a more recent case of a woman whose dream of a funeral appeared to have a prophetic element.[62] Her (already deceased) mother was lying in the casket. "I was shocked," said the informant, "that she was in a casket when she seemed to be so alive." The woman was then awoken by a call conveying the news that a friend had been shot to death. His funeral, held a few days later, mirrored the unusual details in her dream.

Physician Joseph Ennemoser recorded an almost identical instance over 150 years earlier in which a Hanoverian knight was walking in the royal gardens when he saw a funeral procession approaching from the castle.[63] At the same time, he heard the bells ringing. Much surprised, the knight immediately went to the castle and asked who was being buried. They laughed at him, but six days later it was announced that King George of the Hanoverian family had died on that day, at the exact moment the knight had seen the procession.

As recorded in the *Ecclesiastical History of Orderic Vitalis*, one night in 1091 a priest named Walkelin was returning home after visiting with a sick man when he heard what sounded like a great army coming towards him.[64] While initially trying to hide, he was halted by a huge man and watched the army pass. He saw thousands go by—peasants, women on horses, priests, monks, bishops, and knights. Walkelin was disturbed by the fact that some of these figures were people he knew— people who had recently died. At one point, Walkelin, having refused to absolve the sins of a knight amongst the crowd, was set upon. Quickly, however, there came another knight, saying, "Wretches, why are you murdering my brother? Leave him and be gone!" This man identified himself as Walkelin's brother, Robert. Walkelin initially disbelieved that his brother could be among the dead. Robert explained, however, that he had reached his life's end after they last spoke in Normandy and he had left for England.

The authors of *The Phantasms of the Living* recorded a curiously similar account.[65] In a dream, one informant "seemed to be walking in a country road, with high grassy banks on either side. Suddenly I heard the tramp of many feet. Feeling a sense of fear, I called out, 'Who are these people coming?' A voice above me replied, 'A procession of the dead.' I then found myself on the bank, looking into the road where the people were walking, five or six abreast. Hundreds of them passed by me—neither looking aside nor looking at each other. They were people of all conditions and in all ranks of life. I saw no children amongst them. I watched the long line of people go away into the far distance, but I felt no special interest in any of them, until I saw a middle-aged Friend, dressed as a gentleman farmer. I pointed to him and called out, 'Who is that, please?' He turned round and said in a loud voice, 'I am John M., of Chelmsford.' Then my dream ended. Next day, when my husband returned from his office he told me that John M., of Chelmsford, had died the previous day."

The vision of such a processional was remembered in the poem "A Dream" by Irish poet William Allingham, who awoke one night to something rather unusual outside his window. Allingham witnessed a procession of the dead, some of whom he knew were dead, going by "one and two."[66] Of most interest here, the poet clarifies that there were "some that I had not known were dead."

Allingham, as we have seen, was just one of many poets inspired by these visions, with Anglo-Scottish border ballads being particularly rife with such magic and augury. With reference to another Irish example, we read that while sick and bedridden in 1827, Gaelic poet Antoine Ó Raifteirí had a fascinating experience.[67] At night, he heard a noise, which he thought was the cat on the table. He appeared to see Death himself and was told that he or a specific neighbor would soon die. They spoke, and he was also told he'd have a certain amount of time before Death came again for him. The next morning, he sent word to the previously mentioned house to see how the man there was doing. News of the man's death soon came back.

Crossing the Atlantic now to Canada, in an anecdote given again to former Congressman Robert Dale Owen, we read of a ship that was frozen in the upper part of the Bay of Fundy and the dream of its captain, Captain Clarke.[68] That mid-nineteenth century winter, Clarke, who was captain of another ship, although temporarily intrusted to the care of the present one, saw pass before him the funeral of his grandmother, whom he considered to be in good health at the time. This dream made such a deep impression on Captain Clarke that, in the morning, he noted the date of it. Some time later, there came news of his grandmother's death, which, as it turned out, had occurred on the very same day as his dream.

Similarly portentous processions are found as far away as Japan. Through the 1930s, for example, it was widely believed in some areas, such as the island of Oshima, that the sight of a phantom funeral procession with torches presaged a local death.[69]

In a New Mexican account, a relative of our informant was undergoing surgery in Las Vegas. His brother woke his wife and told her that he "knew" the man was dead.[70] This was because he had just had a dream in which he was "digging the grave." The couple stayed up and drank coffee, hoping that word would come telling them the dream was false. The news came, however, that the operation had been unsuccessful and that the man had passed away at the same time the dream occurred.

A man named Harry Kealey from Maryland had similar experiences.[71] Like Juliana of Liege, who felt a certain pain when a friend was dying, this man would dream of a grave or of digging a grave whenever one of his friends was dying. Those kinds of people were known to have been "born with a veil" in Maryland, where, in Hopewell, one Nancy Neilsen's mother, on a winter afternoon at five o'clock, glanced out of her window, and there, over the tops of the trees, came a ship with all sails set.[72] Several hours later, she learned that her husband had drowned—at exactly five o'clock.

We have seen that the woman or man who, by their own personal psychic signs, may learn of the deaths of other family members is a common character of folklore. A woman from a far-west Canadian settlement noted that when she dreamed of fire, she always hears of a death in the direction from which it came.[73] The individual's visions are symbolically specific to themselves. Thus a Copper Eskimo, Ilatsiak, similarly asserted that his familiar visited him in his sleep and revealed what was about to happen, and that whenever he dreamed of small knives he knew that some children were sick.[74] In another of Lady Gregory's memorates from the west of Ireland, her female informant dreamed of being with her daughter and that she was dead and being put in a coffin.[75] She found out later that the time when she was dreaming about her was the very time at which her daughter had died.

One night in Missouri, a woman saw a formation in the clouds over a neighbor's farm that resembled a small, open casket. The next day, news came that the very same neighbor's baby had died at that exact time.[76]

Recorded in a 1905 volume of the *Ladies' Home Journal* was an account from Franc B. Wilkie, an editorial writer for the *Chicago Times*. Franc was asked by his wife one morning in 1885, before they had left their bedroom, if he knew someone named Edsale or Esdale.[77] "No; why do you ask?" replied Mr. Wilkie. "During the night I dreamed that I was on the lake shore and found a coffin there with the name of Edsale or Esdale on it, and I am confident that someone of that name has recently drowned there." They went down to breakfast, and on opening the morning paper, Mr. Wilkie saw the report of the mysterious disappearance from his home in Hyde Park, eight miles away, of that very man, William E. Esdaile. A few days later, the body of the young man was found on the lake shore.

Coffins and their myriad manifestations aside, perhaps no figure is more emblematic of death than the grim reaper. Chaz Ebert, wife of film critic Roger Ebert, told Terkel about waking up to find the figure of death himself at her bedroom door.[78] If this wasn't enough, the figure pointed to a coffin that was lying on her bed and contained her ex-father-in-law, who was not yet known to have actually died that night.

By whatever mysterious means, these distant deaths are often expressed in a culturally recognizable form. We should not be entirely surprised then to find, much further afield, that among the Kaonde of Zambia, to dream that one is hoeing *matumha* or *milala* (the raised beds used for cultivation of sweet potatoes) portends digging a grave, i.e., the death of someone.[79]

The Bori, an indigenous tribe of Arunachal Pradesh in India, believe that if one dreams of a man sitting on a farm alone or in a court-yard surrounded by a ring of friends who do not speak to him, "you will know that he is dying or dead."[80]

At other times, the death imagery is even more culturally specific. Jaffe gives a case from her Swiss sample of a woman who dreamed of her sister around the time of her death, noting that she was holding in her hands a snow-white wreath, a symbol of death "like the ones you buy when little children die."[81]

Another woman reported a very similar experience to Lutheran theologian Hans Schwarz.[82] One night during World War II, she dreamed of being married in a church, and while walking down the aisle, she turned around to look back. Of great interest is that in that particular tradition, the bride should never look behind her while walk-ing down the aisle, as it can mean bad luck. A few days later, a letter came with news of her husband's death during combat, on the same date as the dream.

The vision of Dominican Bishop Guala of Bergamo is comparable in that the figure seen expresses a traditional and culturally relevant death reference to the subject.[83] Having been at prayer and soon falling asleep, Guala saw a friar at the foot of a ladder. His face was "covered with his hood, in the manner in which the friars would cover the face of the dead when carried out for burial." The body was soon received into the company of angels who stood atop the ladder. Guala hastened to Bologna and found that Dominic had died at the very moment of the vision. Just like those Japanese, Chinese, and Scandinavian poems inspired by these experiences, the vision itself is commemorated in one of the many Devotions to St. Dominic:

> *Beheld no more by mortal eye,*
> *He rises from all earthly sight.*

This was by no means the only devotional hymn directly inspired by a crisis vision. Far more ancient was the vision of Hermit Auxentius of Bithyna in 459 AD.[84] When Syrian Christian ascetic Simeon Stylites died in that year, Auxentius, while out of his body during a seemingly induced experience, apparently begins to weep when he sees the soul of Simeon under the stars, as the hymn reads:

> *This night, the Stylite died,*
> *His soul is being ascended to heaven,*
> *Brighter than the stars, a glowing flame*
> *By us, his soul visited,*
> *Me, a sinner, he graciously greeted*

Many nights later, the "truth of the vision" was "all recognized" when the news of Simeon's death came.

◆

In legend and in lore, in letters and in verse, the other world speaks of death symbolically. We have seen examples of the allegorical in dreams, shamanic journeys, visions, and more, some requiring interpretation, and others imbuing their recipients with an immediate knowledge of their meaning, as obvious or obscure as the metaphors may seem to the reader or to those present at the time. If there is a universal language between worlds—between life and death—this mysterious stream of informative allegory is, in fact, exactly that.

FIVE

Magic, Things Broken, and the Legends of the Life Token

The dead man is considered as the inua [soul] of his grave, and of the personal properties he left. It is no doubt for this reason that things belonging to absent persons can by certain signs announce the death of their owners or their being in distress.

HINRICH RINK

Regarding certain Inuit beliefs, Danish geologist Hinrich Rink noted that "things belonging to absent persons can by certain signs announce the death of their owners or their being in distress."[1] This kind of experience is what folklorists refer to as a life index or life token and has a long, mysterious, and most ancient heritage which, despite the often short and repetitive nature of the accounts, deserves further treatment. Furthermore, such experiences continue to be recorded and there has been an unfortunate lack of comparative work in that regard. The idea that a person's life is magically tied up with the fate of an item, often something of their own or to which they might have an affinity, such as a tree, is apparent in one of the heroic poems of the *Poetic Edda*. Atli is warned that his child has been slain when he saw in a dream that the tree he had planted at the latter's birth had suddenly become "red with blood."[2]

TREE OF LIFE

Such "life token" experiences are strikingly similar, ubiquitous in all lands, and qualify as the kind of symbolic crisis impressions pertaining to a distant death, such as was covered in the previous chapter. Regarding the tree as a common token, in her collection of West Sussex folklore Latham stated that dreaming of a tree being uprooted in your garden as a death omen is a common superstition that was commemorated by poet Felicia Hemans in her 1824 poem, *The Vassal's Lament for the Fallen Tree*, in which it is written:

> *'Tis known that ne'er a proud tree fell,*
> *But an heir of his fathers died!*[3]

Far from England, where Latham had collected her folklore, there is much truth to be found in her words, as it is said that even as far away as among tribes of India that "to dream of a falling tree is a death-warning."[4]

In a tale from near the Indian subcontinent, when a barley plant given by a hero to his three friends droops, he is ill. When the plant snaps in half, they will know he is dead.[5]*

In a Japanese example, when a samurai wanted to cut down a tree that had stood for generations, his mother had a portentous dream.[6] A huge monster warned her, "If the tree dies, every member of the household will die." The samurai, being unconvinced, died on the same day the tree was felled.

In an ancient Egyptian tale of two brothers who parted company, the life of the younger brother is tied to a certain tree. That tree is later cut down, and the man, Bata, instantly dies.[7]

Among some tribes of the Niger Delta, whenever the branches of a

---

*See Steel, *Tales of the Punjab Told by the People*, 370–1, for a summary of more examples of life tokens or life "indexes," as the author refers to them.

certain tree were cut off, someone to whom it corresponded died.[8]

The legendary lives of mythological twins Romulus and Remus, too were tied up with a tree, their births being presaged by their mother Silvia's dream of two palm trees shooting up together, overshadowing the Earth, and touching the stars.[9]

These ancient and surprisingly similar beliefs have interesting early Christian counterparts. The Syrian ascetic Simon of Stylites (390–459), had a relatively elaborate vision of a tree, which ultimately concluded in the knowledge that the tree was he himself, and the branch that had been cut off in the vision represented his brother, Mar Shemshi, who died very soon after this vision.[10]

The entire life of the ninth century Norwegian King Harald Fairhair was similarly foreshadowed.[11] Before his birth, his mother dreamed of a tree. The lower part was red with blood; the middle part was fair and green, symbolizing how his kingdom would flourish; and finally, at its head, the tree was white, and they knew then that he would become old and white-haired.

In Madagascar too, a hero setting out on an adventure plants certain trees and tells his parents that if they wilt, it will be a sign that he is sick, and if they wither, he has died, while in a Mongolic Kalmyk legend, six young men go to seek their fortunes and each plant a tree, the flowering or fading of which will be indicative of their being still alive or dead.[12]

In a folktale from the Philippines, a man named Aponitolau, before leaving his wife to go on a long journey, cut a vine and planted it near the stove. He told his wife that if this vine wilted, she would know he was dead. Indeed, in the notes section of the book in which this account was recorded, Cole relates just how common such a belief was in both ancient Egypt and India before expressing rather earnest surprise that the same beliefs should be present in the Northern Philippines.[13] As we'll see, however, not only are they widespread, but they are still commonly reported.

FIRE AND FLAME

First, though, we can note one of the very earliest examples of a life token, found in Sota 13:6 of the Talmud and hailing from 41 BCE.[14]

The Western Lamp was said to be permanently lit as long as the Jewish High Priest, Simeon the Righteous, was alive. When he died, it was found that it had gone out.

In Greek mythology, the hero Meleager's life was also entwined with a flame.[15] His fate was linked to a burning ember in a fireplace, and it was said that it would expire when he did.

Azrael, the angel of death in a Palestinian legend, brings his living son into his abode.[16] His son sees thousands of earthen lamps set on tables, some burning and others flickering out. When he asked what they were, Azrael told him, "These lamps are the lives of men." While Azrael goes to tend some lamps—that is, lives—that have just burned out, his son sees the lamp which is his own life.

In the old Norse tale of Norna-Gest from thirteenth-century Norway, it is dictated that Gest would die by the time the candle lit at his bedside went out.[17]

Such singular tales are complimented by other, more culturally entrenched traditions. It is said of a certain icon on the wall of the Cathedral of Saint Mark in Venice, for example, that one may light a candle in front of it for those they love who are traveling by land or sea.[18] If the flame goes out, it means they are dead. If not, they are still living.

We might also reference Gisli's dream in his saga of the same name, in which he enters a hall full of friends and kinsmen drinking beside a line of seven fires, each apparently representing one of the seven years he had left to live.[19]

That great archetypal mage of Arthurian legend, Merlin, once told his king of certain tapers, "When I am dead these tapers shall burn no longer."[20]

BLOOD, HEALTH, AND THE COLOR OF DEATH

The English antiquary Francis Grose speaks to how ancient these notions were in reference to a token which truly can be called a *life* token.[21] Some children are born with a "caul," the membrane of the amniotic sac, still over their faces. Grose tells us that those in possession of the caul later may know the state of health of the party who was born with it: if the person is alive and well, it is firm and crisp; if they are dead or sick, it is relaxed and flaccid.

In a more specific example, a certain New Mexican family would place a statue of the Virgin Mary in the window to protect a loved one in a storm.[22] "One time," one of the family members related, "we put ours in the window because my brother was out in the storm. The next morning, its head was gone. My brother was killed in the storm."

An Eastern European folktale tells of one man who told another that if the blood in a certain goblet turns black, "do not wait for me, you will know that I am dead."[23]

Comparably, an Italian folktale holds that one of two brothers met a maiden weeping and asked her why she is crying.[24] She stated that she has been unable to find the "dancing water." "Is that all?" one brother replied, "I will go and seek it for you and make you happy again." He then gave her a ring off his finger and told her that if the stone in the ring changed color, it meant he was dead.

In a Portuguese legend, a father and his children entered a forest, and as they approached the base of a tree, the father said, "My children, remain here, and here I leave this gourd: while it continues to sound, it is a sign that I am in the wood; when it stops, it is a sign that I am no longer in the wood, and I am coming back for you."[25]

We read in a Norwegian tale of a man named All-Black who made a hole in a doorsill before he left on a journey.[26] He told his brother, "As long as that hole is full of water, I'm alive. But if it's full of blood, I'm dead." This was later fulfilled as such.

In another Scandinavian tale, a man named Silverwhite told one named Lillwacker that if a certain stream runs clear while he is away, he will be alive, but if it runs red and roiled, he will be dead.[27] While Silverwhite was away, he received a fatal wound, and the spring turned red with blood, letting Lillwacker know he was dead.

Similarly, an East Slavic Cossack folktale tells that one brother said to the other when they had to separate while hunting, "Take thou the road on that side, and I'll take the road on this." The elder brother then took a knife and stuck it into the trunk of a maple tree by the roadside, saying, "Look now, brother, any blood dripping from the blade of this knife will be a sign that I am dying." When the brother returned, he saw the blood dripping and knew his brother's fate.[28]

A Central European Magyar tale has three brothers about to separate for a year, with one of them saying, "Let us stick our knives into the tree, and each start in a different direction; in a year hence we will be back again, and whosoever's knife is covered with blood, he is in danger, and the others must go in search of him." "Agreed," said the others, and, sticking their knives into the tree, they started off in different directions.[29]

In a Georgian folktale, a prince fills a cup with water and says, "When that water changes to blood, I shall be dead, but as long as it is pure I shall be alive."[30]

In a Russian fairy tale, a brother tells his sister, regarding his future adventure, that "I will go forth to get these marvels. And if I die or am killed, this is how you will know it: I will thrust this penknife into the wall; when blood begins to drip from the knife, it will be a sign that I am dead."[31]

In an Armenian tale, a princess had a "necklace of life." When it was taken from her, she would "fall down and seem to be dead." Similarly, in Armenia, only when three birds hidden in a box, which itself is hidden within a certain bull, were killed would a particular old man die. The first bird's death made him ill, the second sicker still, and finally he died with the death of the third.[32]

A tale collected in southwestern Africa has a man named Shalishali taking a stick, placing it in the ground, and saying to his people, "If this stick shakes, take it as a sign that I am coming; but, if it falls, then understand that I am dead."[33]

When a Cahuilla Indian man of California was sick, he told his people that they would know he was dead by the frost around the house. One morning, his sisters saw frost around the house and knew that he was dead.[34]

From the other side of the world, in Indian hero tales, we find a story that seems to combine the symbolic dream elements discussed in the previous chapter with the idea of the life token. It is said that one day one of King Krishna's queens said to him, "Last night, O King, I had a fearful dream. I saw a woman with black skin and huge white teeth enter all the houses in Dwarka and tear from the women's wrists the threads which show that their husbands are still living. Then the dream changed. And I saw a band of vultures descend on the houses and devour the bodies of all the men in Dwarka."[35]

In the legend of U Raitong, from among the lesser-known Khasi, an ethnic group of Meghalaya in northeastern India that Rafy called the "Khasi Orpheus," a man of importance sat in his chamber brooding upon some calamity.[36] Right at the moment when his wife Mahadei had died by fire, her *tapmoh* (headcloth) was blown in a mysterious manner and fell at his feet, though there wasn't enough breeze even to "cause a leaf to rustle." When the man saw this, he said, "By this token my wife must be dead." Hearing further sounds coming from her room, he got up to investigate, but when he opened the door, he found the room empty. He knew instinctively that she must have died and sadly soon found her charred remains.

A fascinating old tale from the Punjab Region has a Princess Aubergine being interrogated by an evil queen whose magic eventually prevails.[37] "Princess Aubergine," said the queen, "in what thing does your life lie?" The princess replied, "In a river far away there lives a red and green fish. Inside the fish there is a bumblebee, inside the bee a tiny box, and inside the box is the wonderful nine-lakh necklace. Put it on, and I shall die." Later, she dies at the very moment the queen finds and puts on the necklace.

After escaping cannibals with the assistance of a dream warning, a Bantu named Sikulume noticed he had left his bird behind.[38] He stuck his *assagai* (a pole weapon used for throwing) in the ground and told his brothers, "If it stands still, you will know I am safe; if it shakes, you will know I am running; if it falls down, you will know I am dead."

In a Lamba folktale from the Congo, a boy named Cow-Child gives a charm to his sister-in-law and tells her he is leaving for five nights and that if his charm dries up, he is dead.[39] Later, when she returned to the charm he had left, it had dried up at the very time of what turned out to be her brother-in-law's death.

A young Liberian man told his mother, when he was about to set off on a treacherous journey, "Mother, don't worry, take this raffia bag," he said, removing it from his neck and handing it to her.[40] This was the first time he had taken the bag off his neck. "When I go into the forest, squeeze it often. Liquid will pour out of it. If it's white, it means I'm still alive. If it's red, it means I'm dead. Don't worry as long as the liquid is white."

In a Mexican tale, Juan, before setting off on a dangerous adventure in a magical wood from which no one ever returned, took his knife and threw it into the ground, burying its blade to the hilt.[41] To reassure his sister Maria, he said, "Check this knife every day. As long as you can pull it out of the earth, you shall know that we are safe. On the day that you cannot pull it from the ground, then you shall know that we are no longer alive."

Similarly, among the Euahlayi of Australia, South Australian born writer K. Langloh Parker heard of a red-painted, tapering pine pole being placed outside a certain abode.[42] Parker was told that if it fell to the ground, it would tell of the death of someone related to an inhabitant of the house. Of interest is also the fact that what came to pass—that is, the death itself being tied to the tapering pole—was the origin of the belief in such things themselves among the Euahlayi.[43]

Before setting out on a perilous journey, two Mohave Indians told their mother, "If we die you will see our dry deer hide, hanging there on the wall, move, and you will know are dead."[44] They further added that "if we die, our flutes will split and scatter over the house and tell you. And our feathers will scatter, and so will the cottonwood tree down, and you will know."

Almost ten thousand miles distant in the frozen north, the very same belief is found among the Inupiat of Alaska.[45] A man named Ayac had a pair of mukluks, a soft boot traditionally made of reindeer (caribou) skin or sealskin, hanging from a rafter in the ceiling. His mother watched them during the night while the rest were asleep. If the mukluks swayed back and forth just a little bit, it meant the hunter was still alive. The mukluks moved, and Ayac survived after being lost for seventeen days in the Chukchi Sea.

In a Coeur d'Alene myth, a woman had a similar understanding with her husband when they first got married.[46] She had told him, "If one of your arrows breaks when you are hunting then you will know I am dead." One day when the man was out hunting, he was warned of his wife's disaster by the breaking of his arrow. He hurried home and discovered she had been killed.

This particular experience of the native peoples of Idaho evokes a certain dream from antiquity regarding the death of Attila the Hun, the infamous ruler of the Huns from 434 to 453.[47] Two nights before his shocking, accidental death in 253 CE, the Roman Emperor Marcian, who had been actively waging war against the Huns, seemed to have known what was to occur, apparently "calmly informing his advisors" of this knowledge upon their arrival at his court in Constantinople. Marcian told them that during that night he became aware of an angel standing at his bedside, who then showed the emperor a broken bow, which Marcian knew to be that of Attila, and that it signified his death.

Not greatly removed from Attila's home comes a Siberian tale in which a mother tells her son that one day he will have to hunt for his own food.[48] "Make yourself a bow and arrow and every night before you go to sleep stand the arrow upright in the ground. When I find it thus I will know that you are still alive but if it is lying flat I will know that you are dead."

In a fairy tale from County Donegal in Ireland, *The Amadan of the Dough*, when the Amadan, or "fool," is about to set off and kill a giant cat, the woman he is staying with tells him that she will watch the well in her garden to know if he is alive or dead.[49] If he is dead, blood will appear and remain atop the water there.

In a Himalayan legend which combines some of the more common kinds of tokens, we read that when Surju and Sidwa were about to leave for Tibet, Surju told his weeping mother to keep milk in a dish, a sword with its blade pointed up, and a garland of flowers.[50] He said if the milk turned to blood, the sword fell, and the flowers withered, she would know he was dead.

TIME AND TOKENS TODAY

Despite little research, particularly of the cross-cultural or paraspycho-logical kind, legend, lyric, and lore agree firmly on the ubiquity of the life token across all continents. As it happens, an impressive number of related occurrences have been and continue to be recorded in more recent times.

Neuropsychiatrist and end-of-life phenomena researcher Peter Fenwick gave us the British case of Jennie Stiles, who described how, when cleaning the apartment of her aunt who had just died, she noticed that all the clocks had stopped at the exact time of her death.[51] Another of Fenwick's informants described how a small battery-operated clock of his father's stopped at the time of his uncle's death.[52]

In Lunenberg County, Nova Scotia, a woman had an alarm clock that was new and supposed to be particularly good.[53] One day it stopped at three in the afternoon, which she thought was very strange, and she started it going again. She learned a few days later that her brother had died at that same hour.

In Virginia, a woman was sitting outside her kitchen door when she heard the refrigerator open and, after a short pause, close.[54] When she went inside, the room was empty. An hour later, she received a call that her youngest son had drowned, and as she thought back on it, she recalled that whenever he came home, the first place he always went was the icebox.

Falling picture frames, too, relating to or owned by the person in crisis, appear in uncountable numbers. In one account from a 1939 issue of *Psychic Science*, we read of a Mr. T. who, when he was eight years old, was sitting alone with his mother by the fire and heard three great bangs that set three pictures violently vibrating.[55] His mother turned to look at the time: ten minutes to ten. "That's a death token," she said in a frightened voice. "Your grandmother must have died and given me this warning as she was going." Two days later, a letter reached them announcing the passing of his grandmother, which had occurred exactly at the time of the knocks.

Drawing again from the collection of prominent Canadian folklorist Helen Creighton, we read of a *forerunner*, the likes of which, the author states, could be replicated almost anywhere in the world.[56] A calendar had a picture of a vessel on it, which a family remarked looked exactly like the one that one of their sons was currently on. It fell from the wall at the very moment he drowned at sea. Another informant told Creighton that the same night her son died, the front door opened. "He always used to take the key with him and when he opened it, the key always made a noise. I heard that as plain as anything just the time he was washed over going to the Gulf Stream."[57]

One can easily imagine, in another time and place, that these individuals might have suggested, for example, before setting out on some perilous journey, that, "If my picture falls, you will know I am dead" or "if you hear me come through the front door, etc.," just as had those protagonists we have seen in the legends and romances of old. The stories remain fundamentally the same. If any phenomena related to and coincidental with death deserve further scholarly and comparative treatment, the life token has, perhaps, one of the strongest claims.

POETRY AND THE SACRED

As a final note, the life token has made its way into some of the most popular Anglo-Scottish ballads, and a more exhaustive study would doubtless discover the same much further afield. While in his work on related border ballads, Lowry Charles Wimberly merely speculates that their presence in those works might be a relic of the belief in the life token; considered in our broader context here, his suggestion seems to be a firm reality.[58] Wimberly noted especially the ballad *Bonny Bee Hom*, wherein the discoloration and bursting of the stone are seemingly concomitant with the death of one of its protagonists. He even references a folkloric parallel to the ballad omen as reported by William Henderson, where it is known that "The breaking of the ring forbodes death."[59] Wimberly noted that this belief held ground as far south as Essex, where, in 1857, a farmer's widow, on being visited after her husband's death, exclaimed, "Ah! I thought I would soon lose him, for I broke my ring the other day; and my sister, too, lost her husband after breaking her ring—it is a sure sign."

Just as we have seen the ring turn up in legendary tales, it makes appearances throughout these ballads. In *Bonny Bee Hom*, as well as in *Hind Horn*, Hom's lady gives him a chain of "gowd" and a ring with a ruby.[60] Should this ring fade or fail, as it was written, or should the stone "change its hue," Bee Hom is to know that his lady is "dead and gone."

A diamond ring in *Hind Horn* has similar prognosticative powers. One version reads, "She's gien to him a diamond ring, With seven bright diamonds set therein. When this ring grows pale and wan, You may know by it my love is gane."[61]

In the Motherwell text of *Lamkin* too, we find one of its characters exclaiming, "I wish a' may be weel with my lady at hame; For the rings of my fingers they're now burst in twain!" While similarly, buttons flying off the coat of Lord Montgomery warn him that things are "undone" at home.[62]

It is not only the old ballads and rhymes that remember these things. The lyrics of "My Grandfather's Clock," a Johnny Cash song originally written in 1876 by American composer and songwriter Henry Clay Work and which went on to sell over a million copies, also speaks to this phenomenon, having been directly inspired by an experience echoed in the song's contents.[63]

> *My grandfather's clock was too large for the shelf*
> *So it stood ninety years on the floor*
> *It was taller by half than the old man himself*
> *Though it weighed not a pennyweight more*
> *It was bought on the morn of the day that he was born*
> *And was always his treasure and pride*
> *But it stopped, short never to go again*
> *When the old man died*

◆

It is fitting that we end this chapter with a discussion of rhyme, given its intimacy with allegory and metaphor. The allegory lends a certain mystery to otherwise less complicated and familiar things, although, in some ways, that mystery may be closer to the strange truth! It may shake the reader or listener out of the trappings of mundanity, as do the experiences upon which the verses are so often based. That romances and tales across the world make use of these stories as a versatile literary tool, then, should come as no surprise. More than this, though, these experiences are a very real, ancient, influential, and ongoing kind of magic.

SIX

Messengers, Tokens, Angels, and Totems

It seems to be assumed in the sagas that disaster and death are frequently revealed beforehand in dreams, and that this knowledge is brought either by some supernatural power from the Other World or by the dead.

HILDA DAVIDSON

According to the Gospel of Matthew (2:19), in a well-known and widely reproduced vision, after King Herod had died an angel of the Lord suddenly appeared to Joseph in a dream and said, "Get up, and take the child and his mother with you, and go to the land of Israel; for those who were seeking the child's life have died."

Accounts such as these are an interesting and well-attested variant on the majority of apparitions and visions presented so far, in that a third party brings the news of a distant death on behalf of those in crisis. While a useful and often rather impressive literary device, accounts in this form are nevertheless widespread in both the mundane memorate and the magical myth alike. From that shimmering angel who so famously appeared to Joseph or the brilliant white horses with messengers gracefully astride from a later account of Didymus to the wailing banshees of the Celts or the Yamadoots of the Indians, supernatural messengers are widely reported as bringing news of death. Regarding appearance and form, these heralds run an impressive gamut: animals, voices, lights, shadows, shapes, and the dead themselves. Indeed, sometimes the living are employed to convey the morbid message. Despite the messenger often appearing in a culturally relevant context, the fundamental reality that a non-ordinary third party is experienced as bringing accurate news of a distant death is perennially clear.

In North German folklore, *gongers* are the ghosts of drowned seafarers who visit distant relatives to announce their deaths.[1] This is, of course, quite a common kind of spectre; notably, however, the gonger only tells the news to a relative in the third degree. Calmet heard similar about the ghosts of Hungary, who came not to announce their own deaths but those of their "near relations."[2] Regarding these more general observations, we can also note, for instance, that in Sri Lanka, it is understood that spirits might whisper news of the death of a child's mother or father in his or her ear while they sleep.[3]

One of the most valued and commonly recorded dreams in the ancient world and among many indigenous cultures across the globe are those in which divine or supernatural messengers deliver general counsel or warning.* During the previously mentioned vision regarding the fate of King Herod, Joseph is also given a warning as the course of those events unfold, specifically that he should avoid Judea. Such warnings are found in abundance in the literature of antiquity and beyond. We begin proper, however, as far from those sources as one might imagine, aboard the famous HMS Beagle, with an unusual event which occurred while a young Charles Darwin was en route to Tierra del Fuego.

Yamana native Jemmy Button, while aboard the HMS *Beagle*, returning from a much-publicized stint in England to his people on the

---

*In Felton, *Haunted Greece and Rome*, 30, for example, the author notes that accounts involving messengers of this kind occur "so frequently in classical literature that any discussion of ghost stories in antiquity" would be "negligent" in omitting them. Similarly, with reference to indigenous tribes, for example, in *The Chippewas of Lake Superior*, 17, Danziger made an observation which might be extended to many comparable cultures when he noted that "Benign guardian spirits acquired during a youthful vision communicated warnings and advice directly to individuals via dreams."

islands around Tierra del Fuego, dreamed that a man came to his bed and whispered that his father had died.[4] When they arrived, they found that he had indeed passed in their absence. One of his shipmates commented that "poor Jemmy looked very grave and mysterious at the news but showed no other symptom of sorrow." He had first mentioned this dream to another named Bynoe, who tried to laugh him out of the idea. FitzRoy noted: "He [Jemmy] fully believed that such was the case and maintained his opinion up to the time of finding that his father had died." After hearing the confirmation of the sad news, Jemmy gathered some branches, made a fire, and solemnly watched them burn.

In this experience, even when an otherworldly stranger delivered the news, it was not thought of by Button as a particularly unusual occurrence but received with a somber acceptance. In a more recent experience, however, and in speaking to the varying ways in which different cultures respond to and integrate the non-ordinary, the same could not be said.[5] In this case, the informant saw a man standing in her doorway who told her outright that her grandmother had died, causing her great fear; she even called the police about potential home invader. Her father later told her that her grandmother had passed.

Sometimes the messenger is not initially identified, though they may nevertheless have a relationship with the informant. This is brought out in an even more recent account, in which once again, a man appeared in the doorway of the informant's kitchen with the message that her mother had become gravely ill.[6] Her mother, as it happened, had suffered a heart attack. Interestingly, upon describing the messenger, the informant was told emphatically that this was her long-dead uncle, whom she had never met.

The following early seventeenth century example recorded by English antiquary John Aubrey, whose much-quoted miscellanies regarding British traditions were one of the earlier tracts compiling such accounts in number, takes on new meaning in this context.[7] Roger L'Strange, in 1617, dreamed that while he was walking in a park, a servant came to him and brought him the news that his father had passed. The next day, according to Aubrey, after going to his usual recreation, "he was resolved for his dream's sake to avoid that way; but his game led him to it, and in that very place, the servant came and brought him the ill news according to his dream."

A similar incident related to World War II was printed by botanist and parapsychologist Louisa Rhine in her classic volume, *Hidden Channels of the Mind*.[8] We read that the husband of a Pennsylvania woman was the pilot of a B-17. One night, she had a dream that a strange soldier in an Air Corps uniform approached her on a beach with a letter from her husband. The man then tells her that her husband died two nights ago. The telegram came two weeks later with the news that he had died on the exact date indicated by the dream.

Another stranger delivers the news in the following poem of obscure origin found in the old Icelandic *Njals Saga*.[9] The text tells of an Earl Gilli in the Hebrides, an archipelago off the west coast of Scotland, who dreamed that a man came to him and gave his name as Herfinnr. The Earl asked him for tidings from Ireland, where the man said he had come from. The man replied in the following verse: "I have been in Ireland where heroes were fighting and many a sword was clashing as shield met shield—the steel was clashing as shield met shield—the steel has shivered in the crash of armour. Fierce I know was the encounter of the warriors. Siguror fell in the crash of spears, but the blood was already pouring from his wounds. Brian fell but won the victory." In this way, the man acts as a messenger, the supernatural bringer of the news of two deaths, of which Gilli was otherwise unaware.

The sagas hold numerous such references; in *The Saga of Olaf Tryggvason and of Harald the Tyrant*, Throndhjem slays Erling. Later another, named Kark, while sleeping in a cave, dreams of a man "black and ill to behold," who tells him that "Ulli" is dead.[10] "Erling must have been slain," was Kark's conclusion.

In another ancient poem, *The Birth of Saint George*, the knight Albert is told by a rather prototypical "magical woman in the woods" that his wife must die before his son is born.[11] The moment he returns, he finds the castle gates "hung with black" and discovers that his wife has died in his absence.

Abd al-Muttalib, fourth chief of the Quraysh tribal confederation and grandfather of the Islamic prophet Muhammad, had a dream between waking and sleep in which a man came to him on a horse and told him all who were slain during the Battle of Badr in 624, including specific people known to him.[12]

From a collection of North Carolina folklore, a state where Green noted there to be "innumerable" related incidents, we read of a family living near the Fort Bragg military reservation.[13] The father and sons went away to fight and were tragically all killed. Before that news reached the family, a man named Nicholas had a vision of the killing. This man was a runaway slave just passing through the neighborhood. Looking for a place to eat and sleep, he came into contact with that family and, the morning after he had first spent the night there, told the woman who lived there, "Missus, the Lord's done come to me in a vision last night, and the Lord said to me . . . the good lady's husband and six sons has been killed."

One of the more widely known archetypal death messengers is the Irish banshee, whose cry is said to herald a death either about to happen or, as is more our concern, one that has just occurred. Folklorist and Professor Emerita of European Ethnology Patricia Lysaght gave multiple examples. In County Cork, Ireland, in 1967, a man was walking home from work with his coworkers Jim and Tom when they heard a cry down in Riordan's Glen. Initially, they thought it might be a dog. That same night, they heard the "latch of the room rattling," though when they went to check no one was at the door. This was about twelve o'clock. Soon after, news came from America that Lizzie Carey had died, and they found out that it "twas the same time the same evening an'all" that they had heard the cry.[14]

Another of her informants told Lysaght that in 1996 she heard the cry; a cousin of hers had died up in Dublin, and he "must have been dying at the time we heard the banshee down here."[15]

Returning to Switzerland and the work of Aniela Jaffe, a girl living in Solothurn dreamed that she met her cousin on the Bahnhofbrücke bridge in Zurich.[16] In the dream, the cousin told her that their grandmother had died. In the morning, the girl received the announcement of the passing.

At times, the messenger appears in close proximity to the individual for whom the notice is intended, despite the news being intended for

another. In 1884 an informant told French astronomer and avid collector of such tales, Camille Flammarion, that when she got out of
bed, she saw a figure standing upright, surrounded by a circle of light.[17]
Gazing upon the form, it soon became clear that it was the brother-in-
law of the informant's husband, who said, "Warn Adolphe, tell him I
am dead." The woman immediately called to her husband, who was just
in the next room, and told him, "I've just seen your brother-in-law; he
announced his death to me." The next day, a telegram confirmed that
he had died unexpectedly from cholera.

In a unique variant reported again in a North Carolina folklore
journal, the sister of a Mrs. Green was in bed when she saw a neighbor
of hers, someone who visited almost every night.[18] They didn't know,
however, that he was sick at that time. Mr. Hopkins seemingly came
and stood by her bed that night and told her that Nell, her housekeeper,
was dead. But the next day they heard that it was Mr. Hopkins himself
who had died.

Lady Gregory noted in her classic study of beliefs in western Ireland
that shadows may deliver such warnings, and she gives this example,
told to her by a man named Steve Simon: "I will tell you what I saw the
night my wife died. I attended the neighbours up to the road, for they
had come to see her, but she said there was no fear of her, and she would
not let them stop because she knew that they were up at a wake the
night before. So when I left them, I was going back to the house, and I
saw the shadow of my wife on the road before me, and it was as white as
drifted snow. And when I came into the house, there she was dying."[19]

Much removed from the Emerald Isle, Espinosa noted that, among
other New Mexican omens, a distant friend or relative may receive warning of the death of someone by a passing shadow.[20] Related examples are
widely found. Among the Bondo from southwestern India, for example,
the word for the dead is *sairemtl*, which appears to mean shadow, and
we need not mention the very "shades" of antiquity.[21]

In the seventeenth century, according to Wanley an English gentleman living in Prague had a vision one morning of a shadow passing
by that told him that his father was dead.[22] He then wrote down the
day and hour of the incident in a paper book, which he sent home to

England. Later, while in Nuremberg, a family friend told him that his father had died some time ago—the very same time, in fact, that the note had been written and so carefully stowed away.

More recently, one informant told Heathcote-James that after she fell asleep one night, she suddenly became conscious of something "dark" in front of her and felt a light touch on her head. She learned later that her father had died in the night and became convinced that this was a messenger with that news.[23]

MYTHS OF THE MESSENGERS

The next encounter comes from over eleven thousand kilometers away and is taken from the folklore of the Ainu, those indigenous peoples from the lands surrounding the Sea of Okhotsk between Russia and Japan.[24] Told in 1886, though in reference to a time much longer ago, a certain wizard attempted to kill a man by telling him if he jumped from a cliff he would "ride about" on those cliffs "as on a horse, and see the whole world." The man, tempted by such wonders, did so but survived, having been saved by the god of the mountain. That same god revealed to him in a dream that night that the wizard had attempted to replicate the same feat and had been dashed to pieces on the rocks below.

In a Hawaiian folktale said to have been known from the most ancient times, a man named Ku-ula, when he and his wife Hinapukuia were living at Leho Ula, devoted all his time to fishing.[25] During this period, the wife of Ku-ula gave birth to a son, whom they called Aiai-a-Ku-ula. Ku-ula noticed that an eel, or *puhi*, was the cause of his pond's fish loss, and while he initially planned to kill it, his wife convinced him to grant the task to their son, who devised a plan and killed the puhi. After this event, a man came over from Wailua, Molokai, who was a *Kahu* (keeper) of the puhi. He dreamed one night that he saw its spirit, which told him that his *aumakua* (god) had been killed at Hana, so he came to see with his own eyes where this had occurred. Arriving at Wananalua, he was befriended by one of the retainers of Kamohoalii, the King of Hana, and lived there a long time, serving under him, during which time he learned the story of how the puhi had indeed been caught and killed by Aiai, the son of Ku-ula and Hinapukuia, just as he had been told in his dream.

In another Hawaiian legend told to Westervelt, two gods deliver the news of a son's death to his father, but only after they have been unintentionally come upon. A young boy, tired and hungry, passed the temple of the gods, and in his hunger, he ate all the bananas there. The gods became enraged and killed the boy, leaving his body lying beneath the trees and throwing his ghost into the underworld. His father, returning home, met the two gods, who told him of the death of his son and that he was now in the underworld. He searched for the body of his son and, at last, found it. According to the tale, "he saw too that the story of the gods was true, for partly eaten bananas filled the mouth" of the boy."[26]

The British philologist Walter William Skeat heard of a Malaysian woman whose son had disappeared.[27] Three days of searching turned up nothing; soon, however, she dreamed that a certain deity, the Toh Kamarong, appeared to her and told her he had taken her son and where to find his footprints, which she found where indicated. The boy's fate is not confirmed; death, however, seems to be the implication.

Far removed, from amongst the Buryats of Mongolia, comes a tale in which the supernatural messengers are again accidentally come upon by a shaman.[28] He was very much known for being able to see the dead, having what the author referred to as "second sight." The shaman was passing through a large field around dusk when he saw coming towards him three men whom he knew to be dead. One of them was carrying a small box. "What are you carrying?" asked the man. "We are carrying the soul of an infant, one of the dead," came the answer. The shaman knew that the son of a rich Buryat was very sick, and in a manner that recalls Jemmy Button, he made up his mind that the child must have indeed died, and the dead were carrying its soul away. It turned out later that the child had died in his absence.

Returning to the native people of the North American continent, we find a tale from the great and widespread Orpheus tradition. Those tales, so well represented among, though not limited to, Native Americans, are stories in which a bereaved person specifically seeks to bring back a loved one from the underworld. As these stories fundamentally involve certain knowledge of death at their outset, many of them do not meet the definition of a crisis apparition, which typically notifies someone who does not know that another is dead, something Ake Hultkrantz addressed in his seminal study.* There are exceptions, however, some of which we have seen. One of those is an old Ntlakyapamuk Indian folktale from Southern British Colombia in which two brothers learn of a death by means of a supernatural guardian spirit before setting out to the underworld to retrieve the soul.[29] These men, who had sought in vain for their missing mother, had traveled for four years, passed through all countries, gone to the edges of the Earth, and had yet to find her. Finally, however, one of the brothers was told by his guardian spirit in a dream that his mother had indeed died and was in the land of the dead. With this knowledge, they then set about their attempt to retrieve her soul.

Resembling the previous case, in that the death was considered a possibility but not known until a messenger brought and confirmed the news, is a story told by a Tatar man to August von Haxthausen, a German collector of folklore. He described the capture of a certain Ali and his sons by the Yezidis and how an angel came to the former as he lay in chains.[30] After the death of Ali, his sister wandered the world seeking him, then spoke of her bitter grief when she was finally assured of her brother's death by a vision of a prophet in the night, who told her outright that her brother was indeed in Paradise.

Author Michael Wells gives a case from Africa in which his interpreter, having dreamed the previous night of a man who informed him that his mother would die, meets a woman while in church.[31] This woman, a stranger to him, says, "Your mother has died." Later that day, he called home and found she had indeed died at the "exact hour" that this woman had spoken to him.

---

*In Hultkrantz, *The North American Indian Orpheus Tradition*, 66, Hultkrantz noted of another tale, which turns up in this work in the chapter about *Veridical Voices*, that it was the fact that the protagonist was unaware of the death of the person whose voice he hears coming from the woods, which is why it cannot be considered part of the tradition of Orpheus-type tales. The distinction, of course, is not relevant here, as we are only interested in supernatural knowledge of a distant death by any means.

It is written of fourth century bishop Martin of Tours, as it is of many mystics, monastic or otherwise, that when anything happened, he learned of it by revelation and announced it to his brothers.[32] According to legend, the devil once rushed into Martin's cell, holding a bloody ox horn and making a loud roar. He showed him his blood-stained hand and boasted that he had just killed one of Martin's men. Martin ordered a search and eventually found a peasant, who had been hired to haul wood, almost dead, not far from the monastery. Just before his last breath, the man revealed that an ox had turned its head and driven its horn into his groin.

ANIMAL MESSENGERS

In one South American tale of the Colombian Cubeo Indians, the messenger imparting the news of a death is neither man nor deity but a reptile. Many indigenous tribes in the Americas believed that animals could serve as death messengers or heralds in general, and similar beliefs are still prevalent. The Cubeo tale, of which there are multiple versions, tells of a certain woman who went to a river to fetch water.[33] Each day she went, an anaconda would come and copulate with her. A man named Kuwai notced this and killed the anaconda. This woman was waiting for the return of her anaconda lover at the river when a different, smaller anaconda appeared to tell her he had died.

It seems important to note here that the Cubeo Indians have traditions in which humans may specifically exist in the form of the anaconda and origin tales in which they are descended from one.* Shamans as far distant as Japan also believe that a number of deities prefer to manifest themselves in snake form to the ascetic.[34] Many Central American peoples share similar beliefs.

Among many Peruvians, but particularly the Chacra farmers, it is similarly held that an evil bird announces a person's death by singing from the rooftop of the unlucky person's house.[35]

---

*As the author notes in Goldman, *The Cubeo: Indians of the Northwest*, 101, "Their first male ancestor was called Oiobakii. According to one version of the origin tale, he was the head of the anaconda from which all Cubeo are descended."

Something similar was recorded in the North regarding the death of the legendary Germanic hero Sigurd in a fragment from the Lay of Brynhild.[36] There it is written that a raven sitting atop a tree sang out loudly, "Sigurd has fallen south of the Rhine."

These references are truly widespread. It is said in Syrian literature that two birds who looked strangely like humans and spoke like humans told a man of the death of King Alexander along with some information regarding other things yet to come.[37]

In a "typical" Oaxacan myth from southwestern Mexico, Sun and Moon killed their father, who had taken the form of a deer, and proceeded to cook him. They later served this to eat with their mother.[38] Just as she was about to take a bite, a frog came and told her that she was eating the flesh of her husband. Her sons denied their part in it, so she went to see if it was true. Along the way, a crab told her too that this was so, and she flattened it. She eventually found the hide of the deer that was her dead husband, just as the frog and the crab had told her.

While tales barely distinguishable from the kind above are indeed typical in that region, conspicuously similar is a Vietnamese narrative in which Tam, a young woman, is tricked into killing herself by jumping into a cauldron of boiling water.[37] She jumped right into the pot and died while a trickster ordered her body to be cooked and sent to her mother to eat. A crow sat in a tree and cried, "The crow knows, you are eating your daughter's flesh: isn't it crisp and gamy?" Tam's mother couldn't believe it, but when she was almost done with the meal and saw her daughter's face, she realized Tam had died. One morning a Hopi Indian man, while on the way to a doctor, saw a dead horned toad before him.[40] He stopped and said to it, "Well, you have told me that the little boy whom I have left behind is dead, but I will go on and get a doctor to discover who killed him." It turned out the baby had died soon after he left for the doctor.

In a Russian folktale, one named Lyubim asks a wolf for tidings of his brothers, and the wolf tells him that they have "long ago been slain."[41] Likewise, in the Italian tale "The Nightingale," a lamb informs a princess that her lover, a certain young knight, has died. In the form of a nightingale, the princess flies away and discovers this to be true.[42]

In the following well-known and widely reproduced account, the messenger is again an animal. According to the legends, though, many people had different visions of this death, which occurred in 1100 CE, and those covered much of the ground in terms of the kind of informatory experience reported, from the allegorical to the visionary or apparitional, etc., in their manifestation of that information to those individuals, although in this case we are examining the "animal as messenger" variant.[43] We read of Robert, the Earl of Cornwall, a special friend of William Rufus, King of England between 1087 and 1100, who was hunting in the woods around Bodmin, a town and civil parish in Cornwall, England. After pursuing an old red deer, the Earl came through the woods and up to the moors. There he was surprised to see a large black goat coming over the plain. As it came closer, he saw that on its back was King Rufus, black and naked and wounded through his breast. The goat, upon questioning, replied that he was carrying the Earl's King to judgment, soon after which the apparition vanished. Robert related the circumstance to his followers, and shortly after they learned that at that very hour William Rufus had been killed in the New Forest by the arrow of Walter Tirell.

In a Basque legend collected in Spain, Webster writes of a young boy who had become a monk against his adoptive parents' wishes.[44] At the moment he was saying mass at the monastery, two men were passing in front of the garden at his biological father's house when they began to fight. One became so enraged that he killed the other man and threw him into the garden. While the young man was saying mass, a white pigeon had come and informed him of the killing of the man in his father's garden.

A goat was also seen as a messenger of death in the following New Mexican account given to Robe.[45] In Las Tablas, 1957, there was a lady who was very sick and needed medical assistance. A boy who was sent for a doctor was returning to the scene, when along the way he kept seeing a black goat. The goat would just look at him and laugh, and then disappear. This happened repeatedly until he arrived home to find that his grandmother was already dead.

As opposed to being told directly, in a South African Kaffir folktale, the idea that an animal may deliver the news of death is uniquely

presented in that a man who owns an ox, a jackal, and a cock specifically asks each, in turn, to deliver the news to the parents of someone
who has just died.[46] While the jackal and ox refuse, the cock takes on
the task of returning home to deliver the message.

More pointedly, among the distant Ge tribes of the Brazilian highlands, a man died in a fire after he ignored his wife's warning not to
poke its embers.[47] The next morning, his wife sent an owl to give this
news to his mother. The owl delivered this message, carrying the man's
bones with him.

Likewise, in a rare Hebrew manuscript, the animal is told to have
spoken directly of another's death.[48] In the house of Rabbi Elazar, a filly
was born which killed everybody who came near it. He presented it to the
king. It was used by the king in battle and helped him to victory, but later
became unmanageable. He, therefore, returned it to Rabbi Elazar. The
horse suddenly spoke with a human voice and told its story, relating the
fact that a certain man named Abiathar had died, giving more details of
the man's death, and saying that his soul now possessed the horse.

Of interest also, in the Acts of Paul, taken from the Hamburg papyrus, Paul speaks to a lion, who tells him how many distant people were
killed in a heavy hailstorm from heaven.[49]

In a related tale, we read that when the Muslim monk al-Mutharram
died, the uncle of Muhammad, Abu Talib, waited to see if he was really
dead, and eventually a *hitan* (big fish) emerged and told him that the
monk was really dead.[50]

The same was true in a tale from the Wyandot Indians, indigenous
peoples of the Northeastern Woodlands of North America. A hunter
who stayed in a cabin out in the woods during the winter returned earlier than usual from a hunt and found that one of his young dogs was
missing.[51] The hunter, being able to speak with animals, was advised by
the mother dog that he was being hunted by an *uki*, a kind of monster,
and that he should leave the cabin and return to his home village. Taking
heed, the mother hound was telling him on the way that another dog
had lost its life just at that very moment. When he reached the village, he
induced himself into a trance to find the dogs and discovered they had
indeed died.

The deaths of animals themselves are often discovered in this way too, as opposed to an animal being the messenger. In an Albanian folktale, chosen specifically for its representative qualities and wide circulation, the death of a horse in a distant forest is revealed to a man named Visojidha in a dream by "three tall women, with faces as white as chalk and long black hair."[52] Visojidha got on his horse and rode for fifteen hours before he discovered the corpse that he had seen in his dream.

In the following Islamic account from the early Middle Ages, it is a deceased friend known to have passed who brings news to the subject regarding the distant death of an animal—in this case, a cat.[52] The Islamic scholar Ibn Abi al-Dunya tells of a man who dreams of his deceased friend; in the course of the conversation with him, the deceased man informs the living man that his family's cat died a few days ago and that the living man's daughter will die in six days. The dreamer then goes to check with the family of the dead friend, and they tell him about the death of the cat.

Of some similarity, and returning to *Njals Saga*, at the moment that his loyal Irish wolfhound Sámr dies, tenth century Icelandic chieftain Gunnar Hámundarson awakens and proclaims, "You have been harshly treated, Sámr, my fosterling."[54] While some suggest he was awakened by Sámr's distant cry, others convincingly offer that Gunnar learned of the wolfhound's fate in a dream.[55]

Such accounts recall one widely circulated from 1904 in which adventure novelist Rider Haggard awoke from a dream in which his daughter's dog was dying.[56] Haggard sent the account to the *Times* himself. He saw the dog lying in some rough brushwood, and the dog seemed to transmit mentally that it was dying. The dog's body was later found floating in a river near some reeds, in a place that seemed to be that of the vision.

TOTEMIC MESSENGERS

As alluded to, sometimes these messengers are taken to be quite literal and independent entities, the individual's tutelary spirit or guardian perhaps; at other times the individual is openly aware that the messenger is simply representative of the message itself, in an allegorical or symbolic form, such as in the following instance from an Aboriginal Australian community. A tribesman, Harry Monsell, was sitting outside his home one night talking about the "old times" when he suddenly heard a crow cawing.[57] He was convinced the crow was telling him something bad about his people and discovered the following day that his friend's wife had died at that very moment. Interestingly, Harry noted specifically that he knew the crow, his totem, generally a sacred object or being important to the individual and often symbolic of their wider people, wasn't real as such; he saw it in his mind, and it was simply mediating the reality of the crisis to him in this particular and appropriate form.

Worlds away in a small English village in Western Sussex, a man known to author Charlotte Latham had "perfect faith that the thrice-repeated caws of a carrion crow are a token of death; and one day astonished all his family by announcing to them that they had lost a near relation."[58] On being asked how he had become acquainted with the fact, he said a carrion crow had just told him so by flying over his head and uttering three dismal caws.

Similarly, among the Indians of the Colombia Plateau in South America, a man named Smohalla was claimed by informants to be able to communicate with animals such as the crow and coyote, whose howlings might warn him of the death of a tribesman.[59]

A relevant story comes from a native of Duke Island, off southeast Alaska.[60] While at sea, Natsihalne, the man said to have carved the first blackfish and brought them to life, called one of them to him. He instructed it to find and destroy his brother-in-law's canoe and drown those in it, but to save the youngest. Some nights later, the blackfish appeared to him in a dream, although now in human form, telling him that the canoe had been destroyed and that all but the one, as he had requested, had been spared. This was later confirmed.*

---

*An interesting aside here regarding the Norse *fylgja*, (a sort of personal guardian spirit or follower) is that its appearance and shape were often specifically related to the mental state of the individual to whom it appeared. See Lecouteaux, *The Return of the Dead*, 164.

Similarly, Shirokogorov noted that the shamans of the Siberian Tungus might receive the news of distant events in the form of an animal and that these animals are "not understood as physical animals."[61] A medicine man among the Kiowa Indians of the Great Plains also clarified that when receiving messages from his spirit owl regarding distant facts, this was his deceased ancestors speaking to him *through* this bird.[62]

In an Okanagan Indian tale from "long ago," the Shuswap tribe came down the Kettle River in British Colombia, killing old women and children.[63] Two brothers from the village were hunting in the mountains at the time. While they were placing hot stones in a sweat house, as the smoke began to rise, the spirit of one of them informed him, "Can't you see: your father and mother are dead, and there are your enemies right at the camp?"

Historian Ernest Wallace documented that among the Comanches of the South Texan Plains the seer is specifically called upon in order to ascertain the fate of absent war parties.[64] In one instance, a ghost, in the form of a bird, was questioned by this medicine man as to the health of a certain party. "They are all killed," came the reply.

Regarding the death of the Aboriginal man Billie Combo, a certain person noted that another named Danny Sambo came over to his house that morning.[65] They both agreed that Combo had died, apparently intuiting this in some way. When asked for further particulars, the man said, "I bin told by my black crow that tells me these things."

Among another indigenous Australian tribe, the Euahlayi, Parker, who lived alongside them in the Australian outback most of her life, wrote that "one of the greatest warnings of coming evil is to see your totem in a dream; such a sign is a herald of misfortune to you or one of your immediate kin."[66]

Something similar was recorded in as dissimilar a context as one might imagine by twelfth century historian William of Malmsbury, involving a so-called witch from Berkeley, a woman "addicted to witchcraft and skilled in ancient augury."[67] One day, as she was dining, a little crow that she kept as a pet uttered a cry that sounded like human speech. This startled her so much that she dropped her knife. Groaning

with sorrow, her face suddenly growing pale, she said somewhat cryptically: "This day, my plough has completed its last furrow; today I shall
hear of and suffer some dreadful calamity." At that very moment, a messenger arrived and hesitantly gave her the news of the death of her son.

In a Hopi Indian tale, the sister of a young boy, Joshokiklay, killed
one of his eagles in a fit of rage.[68] When he returned from the hunt, one
of his other eagles told him, "Your other eagle brother is dead." After
the eagle described the location and where the body was, Joshokiklay
went and found the dead eagle.

In a life token-esque Naskapi Indian experience from Eastern
Canada, a man named Big One, one of two brothers, slips a raven's
head charm into his brother's pocket and tells him that if anything
were to happen to him, the raven would send a sign.[69] Many months
later, Big One had a vision. He saw a large raven carrying a man's man-
hood in his beak. As the raven was flying over the lake, the penis fell
from its mouth and disappeared into the water below. When the raven
attempted to retrieve it, the water swallowed him too. When he awoke,
Big One knew without doubt that his brother had died, and this was
later confirmed.

American anthropologist Leslie Spier noted relatedly that among
the Sinkaietk Indians of Washington "if an owl talked to a person, it
might tell him which member of his family would next die."[70]

On Papua's Rossel Island, a mother who died appeared to her son
as a small bird; this was the "usual way in which ghosts appear to their
friends and relatives" there.[71] Those who have "just been eaten" appear
in this way to announce their death.

In the following anecdote written in a letter to author Elliot
O'Donnel, one could imagine that the bats might be construed as messengers in another culture. They might be considered to be this man's
own totemic being or guardian spirit, particularly considering this
wasn't a once-off incident in the informant's life.[72] The man in question, Major Roper, wrote to the author from India and relayed that he
had twice dreamed of bats, and on each occasion the dream was followed by a calamity. "In the first instance, I thought I was sitting in my
bedroom in my old home in Bedford," the man related, "when six bats,

one after the other, flew in at the window and, after whizzing round the room, vanished in the marvelous fashion that seems so natural in a dream. The next day I had a cablegram from England to say my brother was drowned while bathing in the sea."

The other dream, more recent than the former at the time of writing, had Roper on a bus in London when a bat flew past him, after which he awoke repeating the words, "How remarkable! A bat!" Roper put this to paper and heard of his father's death a week later. The events are not said to have occurred simultaneously, but this seems to be indicated.

Virtanen spoke to differences in cultural dynamics regarding the case of a Finnish man receiving a warning or being told by "someone" that his animal was in trouble.[73] The author noted that in the past, such experiences would be explained as being related to the guardian spirit of that animal.

Rose explained that the totem is an "appropriate mediating vehicle" for tribal natives but that the Christian might find the angel performing a similar function.[74] This is apparent in numerous accounts. Lambert of Maastrich, Bishop of Maastrich-Liege, was assassinated by the followers of Pepin the Short c. 705 CE. This was said to have been revealed by an angel to Frankish statesman and military leader Pepin Herstal "at the same hour" as the killing.[75]

Such traditional understandings are by no means relegated to indigenous communities, legendary sagas, shamans, or saints. As Bäckman concluded upon studying the helper spirits of the Lapps, while these spirits appearing in dreams were traditionally restricted to the shaman, "common people could sometimes also receive messages from the powers."[76]

In a first-hand account given to pioneering folklorist Mary Fraser, two young girls in Nova Scotia were out swimming when they saw a big bird come in from the sea and alight on the shore.[77] One of them came ashore and tried to catch it. Her companion, who was older and knew more about such things, shouted to her, "Leave it alone, don't touch it, it is a *taibhs*." The younger girl, asking what that was, received the answer. "It's a spirit. We're going to get some bad news." The next day, news arrived of the accidental drowning of the younger girl's uncle. These are the kinds of supernatural messenger animals that, if encountered among the numerous tribes of that continent, might be carved into crests or other important items, as, for example, do the Gitxsan Indians of the upper Skeena River.[78]

Much farther south, there is the belief among the Lenguas of Paraguay that the soul of someone dead may temporarily take the form of a fox.[79] One day, while a woman of those people was talking to a Catholic missionary, she became startled by the sight of a fox passing nearby. Having left her daughter in a neighboring village, she exclaimed, "May it not be my daughter who has died?"

More recently, Carey gave the case of a Maryland man who, while on his way to work one morning, had a strange dog follow him for some distance and suddenly disappear.[80] When he arrived for work, he learned that his employer had died that very morning. Such ongoing experiences might speak to the origin of beliefs like those of the former Lengua.

NEWS FROM THE DEAD

Commonly, the dead themselves are the harbingers of death. This is widely found, and it may be more widespread than the accounts even suggest. We have seen, after all, multiple examples of a spirit taking the form of an animal in order to deliver the news. The dead offering information to the living is not just the purview of the ancient necromancer who might conjure him or her for that very reason, nor is it only the concern of the shaman who travels to other worlds. The dead are still commonly reported to convene with the living.

As related by author Susy Smith in her book *Life is Forever*, there was the unusual case of a woman who lived in Anaheim, California.[81] Having regained consciousness after delivering a child, Maxine saw her father in the upper corner of the room, holding a child in his arms. The form spoke to her: "Don't worry. I'll take care of this baby." Then he disappeared. She soon discovered the baby had been stillborn and, furthermore, her father had died suddenly while she was in the hospital.

In an old Scottish tale it is the mother, rather than the father, who brings the news, though a little more directly this time. In *The Tale of Good Bess*, a man named Lowry was "fairly convinced" that his lover and sister had both been murdered.[82] The reason for his suspicion was that he dreamed that night that the spirit of his dead mother came to him and told him as much: that they had both been killed by a certain lord and sunk with a sackful of stones in a lake called Acremoor. Lowry and another man eventually went to the spot pointed out in the dream and, to their horror, located the bodies exactly where the spirit had shown them to be.

That one's previously dead relatives become the messengers for later deaths is common among native groups and clearly continues, cultural context notwithstanding. These experiences persist. The present author's own late grandmother related just such an experience some years ago. Around the time her daughter, Holly, was involved in a car accident, she was paid a visit by her long-deceased brother. This man, apparently as solid as anyone or anything she had ever seen, simply looked at her with a somber gaze, tipped his hat, called her by her nickname, and gave her the simple message, "It's Holly." Seconds later, the news came, confirming the tragic event.

Regarding a more well-known instance, the case of John Donne certainly deserves mention. In his biography, *The Life of Dr. John Donne*, English writer Izaak Walton shares an account in which the wraith of Donne's wife brings news of his child's death.[83] One night in 1612, while staying in Paris, Donne was discovered in a deeply disturbed state. "I have seen a dreadful vision since I saw you: I have seen my dear wife pass twice by me through this room, with her hair hanging about her shoulders, and a dead child in her arms," Donne reportedly said to a witness. "I cannot be surer that I now live than that I have not slept since I saw you: and am as sure that at her second appearing she stopped and looked me in the face, and vanished." It is then claimed that a messenger was immediately dispatched to check on Donne's wife, returning with the news that she was in very poor health after losing their child.

One such story, in which again a dead wife brings the news of another person's death, comes to us from the haunted north of

England.[84] The informant, a chaplain in America at the time of the Revolutionary War, took refuge in England but returned to his home and family after the re-establishment of peace. When he was halfway across the Atlantic, he dreamed one night of home. His door appeared to be open, so he ran into his study and found his wife sitting there in his chair, wringing her hands and seemingly lamenting the death of their favorite son. This experience made such a big impression on him that he wrote a full account of it and apparently had his fellow passengers and captain sign the record in attestation. On his arrival in Philadelphia, he rushed to his study and found his wife sitting in his chair. In an agony of grief, she told him of the death of their beloved son, which had taken place at the very time of the dream.

In a related account from Africa, Parrinder told of a hunter who, one evening while out hunting, heard voices shouting and singing, eventually sounding like they were very near.[85] Thinking that they were fishermen, he returned to his camp, where an old friend awaited and explained that after eleven at night, the spirits of the departed go to meet one who has just died. "Certainly, somebody has died today or yesterday," he said. The next morning, on returning to their village, they found that a young man of sixteen had died in the neighboring village.

As previously demonstrated, the dead frequently enlist the living to deliver the news of their deaths to those still alive. In these instances, a crisis apparition proper often appears and reveals their death to a percipient, but the message is meant for another. Bill and Judy Guggenheim had a case in which a young informant noted that around the time they were drifting off to sleep, the room lit up and their grandmother was there, standing under a trellis with roses around her and a clear blue sky at her back.[86] Her grandmother then said, "Marilyn, tell your mom that I'm at peace now." After her mother came in and found her crying, the child told her that she had to call grandma and that something had happened. They then discovered that her grandmother had died just ten minutes before.

We read in a 1953 issue of *Midwest Folklore* of a woodcutter named Tom who died in 1877.[87] Tom's wife and child bought their food at the store of an old woman called Miz Schmidt, whom they paid every

Saturday night like clockwork. One night, Miz Schmidt was sitting by the stove, dozing a little. Suddenly the bell on the door rang, and Miz Schmidt awoke, looked up, and saw Tom coming in as usual. Then she saw that he looked tired and worried. "Anna," he said, "you and me has been friends for a long time and now I'm asking you a favor. I want you should let my wife and young-ones have whatever groceries they need, and not lack for anything." Schmidt had no doubt that Tom's visit was a token of his death. Tom was discovered early the next morning, alone in the forest, under a fallen tree. Miz Schmidt, according to the piece, spoke about the experience before Tom's body was ever found.

MYSTERIOUS MESSAGES

While we have seen that the message might come from someone or something unknown to the percipient, at other times the message itself seems to have no particularly definable source. Many cases are reported in which there is a simple yet often overwhelmingly powerful sense or feeling that something has happened. The message might seem vague when relayed, but often the meaning is clear. As one informant told Heathcote-James, "It wasn't just a feeling; it was utterly and completely a feeling of certainty."[88] Founder and director of the Division of Perceptual Studies at the University of Virginia School of Medicine, Professor Ian Stevenson referred to these case types as incredibly important, with surveys suggesting that upwards of 31 percent of all telepathic impressions have been of this kind.[89]

When news reached Italian Carmelite nun and mystic Mary Magdalen De-Pazzi of her mother's death in 1590, she said that she already knew, as when her mother breathed her last, she felt an unusual pain in her heart and a strong inclination to kneel and say a prayer.[90]

In a recently published case, one morning a woman felt as though some disturbing message was trying to get through to her. By afternoon, she became aware that it was "a death message."[91] She waited for news all evening. Because she didn't have a phone, she asked her upstairs neighbors to answer their own phones if they rang in the night. News of her father's suicide arrived at two a.m.

Again, in some cases, the experiencer ends up being the bearer of bad news, though from whom or what they received the information, and whether or not it is an actual message as such, remains unknown. "We were sitting on the couch when the strangest feeling came over me," a source told American author Doreen Virtue.[92] "I told him that my grandmother had just died." This was soon confirmed to have happened around that time.

It has similarly been said of the ancient legend of Osiris, in which he was killed by his brother Set, that Isis "knew as soon as her husband was dead, though no one told her."[93]

Louisa Rhine gave the case of a salesman in Arkansas who suddenly had an overwhelming sensation that he "must return to St. Louis."[94] When he arrived, his brother met him in the yard, saying, "I am glad you got my telegram." Rhine's informant had no idea what his brother meant and asked what happened. His brother then told him that their father had died just an hour ago.

Richard Grattan wrote of a similar occasion in his *Considerations on the Human Mind* that, upon his arrival in Dublin, he "anticipated evil," going on to add, "Why I could not tell. Instead of driving up to the house, I left the carriage at a distance, walked slowly towards the door, and then heard, for the first time, that my wife had died the morning before, and was buried."[95]

While Grattan was unsure, Native Hawaiian cultural historian "Kepelino" wrote of his own understanding of these very same intimations as they occurred in his own land.[96] He wrote that one might weep for their mother and feel a sudden pang of dread, and not long after, they would hear of their mother's death.

Similarly, regarding the inmates in Bomana, a Papua New Guinean prison, it is believed that when someone outside its walls worries about a prisoner, the person is said to literally "send thoughts" (*salim tingting*) to them. This may cause the inmate to display symptoms such as itching, sneezing, headaches, or ringing in the ears. Numb limbs or certain reflex kicks of the legs, in fact, are said to indicate a distant death.[97] Among the prisoners there, in fact, dreams are commonly believed to facilitate thought-transference. One inmate, Peter, claimed to have learned of a death outside of the prison in this way.[98]

Regarding such capacities similarly recognized among the Yauelmani Yokuts of Central California, we read that when a man called Prairie Falcon died, another named Coyote, far away, knew that he was dead.[99] He knew it because he had a supernatural power called *Tipni*. He simply "felt bad." "His heart came out of his mouth," and he "felt so sorry." He soon went and came upon the body.

◆

That a third party in the form of a messenger has, among many other things, announced the distant death of another is widely apparent in the myriad memorates, myths, and legends from which we have drawn. These messengers take the form of strangers, animals, the dead, shadows, and lights, as well as angels, devils, creatures, and more. In their interpretation and imagery, these accounts sometimes vary between cultures; one man's totem is another man's angel. It is clear that there can often be room for such interpretation and perhaps later derivation. What seems clear, however, is that people have reported experiences of certain third parties bringing accurate news of a distant death and continue to do so, whatever their later interpretations.

These magical messengers might be said to be heralds of the news that no one wants to hear. What is apparent in the accounts, however, is that they also bring, by means of some strange mediary, the sacred above and the profane below into contact and communion. For many, they bring with them not just morbid messages of dying and death but glimpses of something far greater.

SEVEN

Veridical Voices and Supernatural Noises

I heard a voice, that cried,
Balder the Beautiful is dead, is dead!
And through the misty air
Passed like the mournful cry
Of sunward-sailing cranes

HENRY WADSWORTH LONGFELLOW

We have long passed the age when "hearing voices" was considered a solely pathological occurrence, at least as far as the research has borne out. In the healthiest populations, rather than being seen, apparitions and visions of the dying have often been heard. Voices and sounds, both recognized and unfamiliar, may be perceived and directly related to a distant death. Some of the earliest accounts of the kind we are looking for are of this type, and they can be found in a wide range of often unrelated literature. Sometimes, the message is quite pointed and seems to be the very words spoken by the distant person at their last. At other times, an unknown or non-specific voice or sound appears to announce the death of one or more people, rather unceremoniously.

In a North American case from the nineties, for example, a woman traveling with her adult son in Europe is abruptly awoken by a voice with a message: "Your brother will not live." She soon returned home on a ship, only to learn that her healthy younger brother had died in a car accident.[1]

Oceans away comes an Angolan tale from a village in the lower Kuanza River region.[2] While on a journey, Ngunza, one of two Bantu brothers, had a dream about Maka. "Maka, your dear younger brother, is dead," an anonymous voice told him. Ngunza returned to his village, went straight to his mother, and soon learned that Maka had died while he was away.

From the most venerated religious texts and their tales to the memorates of geographically separated collections of folklore, the impressive variety of sources from which these accounts may be drawn becomes quickly apparent. One of the oldest written examples of a voice announcing a death comes from the ancients of Babylon.[3] Berosus, a Hellenistic-era Babylonian writer active at the beginning of the third century BC, gives the following account of an ancient flood: Xisuthros, the last king of Sumer prior to the Great Flood, built a ship to save his family and dearest friends after being warned of the coming deluge. When the flood ended, Xisuthros came down to the Earth, erected an altar, and seemingly "disappeared." Whatever happened to him, those who remained on the ship did not witness this and were thus very surprised when he did not return. When they went to look for him, a "voice from heaven" informed them that Xisuthros had "received the reward of piety" and had been taken up to dwell with the gods. That is to say, of course, that he was dead.

Another ancient example comes from Sotah 33a of the William Davidson Talmud and involves the death of the infamous Roman Emperor Caligula in 41 CE. Based on an earlier stratum from a lost Aramaic chronicle, the incident involved Shimon HaTzaddik, who heard a divine voice emerging from the House of the Holy of Holies that was saying: "The decree that the enemy intended to bring against the Temple is annulled, and Gaskalgas, Caligula, has been killed, and his decrees have been voided." It was particularly stipulated that certain people had written down the time that the divine voice was heard and later found that it matched exactly the moment Caligula was killed.[4]

There are numerous deaths accompanied by a heavenly voice in the Talmud, including those of Raban Gamliel in Taanit 29a, R. Hanina b. Teradion, and an executioner, in which a heavenly voice invited them to the next world, in Avodah Zarah 18a:13.[5]

As it is in the tribal communities or among the selected mystics, the voice as messenger is remarkably prevalent in ancient religious texts. The rather simply expressed experiences allow the similarities between disparate sources to be easily appreciated. One example comes from the second century apocryphal gospel The Protoevangelium of James.[6] When a group of priests was awaiting the return of one Zacharias, they went to greet him with prayer. One of the priests heard a voice pronounce, "Zacharias has been murdered, and his blood shall not be wiped up until his avenger come." They soon entered the room where Zacharius had been and saw what had happened. As the text makes clear, "the sons of Israel did not know that he had been murdered."

Similarly, in the apocryphal Acts of Andrew, the earliest testimony of that apostle's acts and miracles, is the account of an old man, Nicolaus, who had died.[7] Andrew heard a voice address him directly: "Andrew, Nicolaus for whom you interceded is become mine," and he quickly informed his brothers that Nicolaus had died.

A comparable and significant story comes to us from the apocryphal Assumption of the Virgin.[8] According to this text, Peter, who was staying with Mary as she was on her deathbed, heard a knock on the door and found many virgins who had come with incense and lamps. They had apparently been warned by a voice to come to Mary, who was soon to die. There is also a reference in this text to a voice eventually welcoming her soul to heaven.

This is very similar to the voice that, at the death of Sufi mystic Rabia of Basra in 801 CE, exclaimed, "O soul at peace, return unto thy Lord, well-pleased!"[9]

According to Jewish legend again, when the time of Moses came to an end, a heavenly voice "resounded throughout the camp of Israel." "Woe, Moses is dead; woe, Moses is dead."[10]

Another ancient record comes from Plutarch, who wrote of a person who was "neither fool nor knave" named Epitherses, the father of

Aemilianus the orator.[11] Epitherses told that on a voyage to Italy, the ship was at one point carried towards the Isles of Paxi, where immediately a voice was heard calling for one named Thamus, a mariner from Egypt. This name was apparently "scarcely known on the ship." That man eventually replied and was told by this divine voice that when he arrived at Palodes, he should "take care to make it known that the great god Pan is dead." It was said that Christians took this episode to be simultaneous with the death of Christ.[12]

Returning to the north, an unrecognized voice was there involved regarding the death of the man Thorstein Codbiter from the Icelandic *Eyrbggja Saga*.[13] Once, while Thorstein went out to fish, a shepherd he knew was looking after his sheep north of Holyfell. The shepherd saw a mountain open on the north side, within which he saw great sights and sounds. He heard the words proclaimed that Thorstein and his crew were being welcomed there. The shepherd told this to Codbiter's wife that evening. The next morning, men arrived to inform them that Thorstein and his crew had indeed drowned while fishing.

The mountain, hill, cave, or cairn as an entrance to other worlds is a common and geographically widespread motif. Caesarius gave a number of notably similar accounts in his *Dialogue on Miracles*.[14] In one of those, we read that once upon a time, when some Swedes who had been on pilgrimage to Jerusalem and were on their return sailed near a volcano, they heard these words issued from it: "Welcome, welcome, our friend the Steward of Kolmere; it is cold; get ready a blazing fire for him." These men noted the day and the hour and discovered that he had died at that time.

In one of the other stories recorded there, a priest named Conrad, once crossing the sea with some others of his province, heard the words coming from that same mountain: "Here comes Bruno of Flitert; take him." When they returned, he immediately noted the date and hour on his tablets and discovered that this man, Bruno, had indeed died while they were at sea.[15] Of great interest, too, is the implication that Conrad later became a monk due to this experience.

In 1962, an informant of Dr. Melvin Morse was similarly affected by such an auditory experience.[16] Just as had been the likes of Zacharias or Nicolaus from those apocryphal gospels, the death of the informants' father was announced. After the informant's room had been filled with light, she heard a voice saying, "I'm going to take him." Soon, news came that her father had died at that time.

Returning to the realm of the fairytale, from a collection of legends from around a historical region of the Alps we read of one Lorenz Mayrhofer, a friend of a farmer named Seehaus.[17] He stopped at a house on his way home one day and told the man who lived there, "One sees most wonderful things in these times. On my way here a voice called out to me from the height of the mountain." That voice exclaimed, "Tell Hitte Hatte that she can now go home, for Jordan [a giant known for devouring children] is dead," which was true, as he had been drowned in a lake a couple of days before.

An old Eastern Norwegian folktale tells of a boy from Eldstad who was coming home from a wedding and, as he passed over a moor, heard a voice shout clearly, "If you're driving over to Eldstad, then go tell Feliah that Fild fell in the fire." The boy drove away so fast that the wind whistled about his nose. When he arrived home and told of this, someone shouted, "Oh, that's my child," and rushed off home.[18]

In a Salish Indian folktale from the Canadian coast, three of four brothers are drowned by some being who resides there.[19] In succession, each brother wonders what happened to the last, goes searching, and suffers the same fate. A voice, however, reveals their fate, including that of the most recently drowned brother, to the fourth and youngest. "All of your brothers have been drowned in that lake. There is a dangerous being (*pa'sa*) there, who puts an elk in the lake to entice them to swim out after it, so that he can eat them."

A related folktale from Zanzibar has one Al Faan trying to steal a ring from a king's finger. During the attempt, a great cry arose and he was thrown a great distance by some unseen force.[20] While another who was with him, called Bolookeea, was "looking at all this," a nondescript voice confirmed to him, "Go your way; this wretched being is dead."

Among the Liberian Sapa, such warnings of approaching death are firmly believed in. "Whenever the plaintain-eater (*Turacus turacus*) is heard talking at night," they say, "we know that a chief is to die."[21]

With its often obscure source, the divine voice lends itself particularly well to the interpretations of the listener and, therefore, to their ascription of its source. Of course, even with its potential literary versatility, these accounts should not, of course, be mistaken for having their source solely there.

In his early work on apparitions and related phenomena, Thomas Bromhall relayed an incident involving the Baptista of Cardanum.[22] Once, while studying at Papia and having awoken in the night, he suddenly heard a voice, accompanied by a great brightness, announcing, "Go, my son, go to Rome." Upon questioning by his roomates later, he was sure it meant his mother was dead. While they didn't take him seriously, the next day, despite being unaware that she was sick, he was notified of her death and that she had breathed her last in the hour in which he had had his strange experience.

American abolitionist and native American rights activist Lydia Maria Child relayed in her biography of Isaac T. Hopper a tale she had heard him tell "often."[23] His mother had preserved the experience, along with a number of related ones, in her diary. On the occasion in question, her other son, James, tragically drowned while attempting to save the life of a friend. A messenger was sent to inform her of this news, but when he stood in front of her, he couldn't tell her. At that moment, she heard a voice proclaim, "James is drowned." Of great interest is that Child spoke of hearing "many such stories of Quakers, which seem too well authenticated to admit of doubt."[24] They call this capacity the "inward light." More fascinating still and of great relevance here, the author later noted, is that "[t]hese strong impressions on individual minds constitute their only call and consecration to the ministry, and have directed them in the application of moral principles to a variety of subjects, such as intemperance, war, and slavery. Men and women were impelled by the interior monitor to go about preaching on these topics, until their individual views became what are called 'leading testimonies' in the Society."

The voice is not always unrecognized. In a much more recent Icelandic memorate, one morning the informant heard somebody speak behind their shoulder: "I am Thorbjörg's husband, I was here yesterday." And that was all. Later that day, it was discovered that the informant's great-grandmother had died in the night. His great-grandmother was Thorbjörg; her husband was called Thordur; and he had died in England when he was in his prime, apparently murdered. The informant later told Haraldsson that "I did not recognise him; I had never seen him or spoken to him."[25]

In Finland, 1944, a sleeping mother heard her son's voice shouting "Mother Mother," to which she responded that she is coming.[26] In the morning, she told her husband something had happened; their son was at Kalevi in northwestern Estonia, and they later got the news that he had been wounded in battle at that moment.

THE OLD MAGIC IS THE SAME AS THE NEW MAGIC

Reaching back in time once more to 774 CE, the following event comes from the Korean history *Samguk Yusa*, first compiled by the Buddhist monk Il Yeon in 1281 CE, and tells of a message regarding the death of a key political figure from the eighth century Silla Kingdom.[27] We read that on a certain day at the home of Prime Minister Kim Mullyang, a voice from heaven was heard. "The boy Taesong from the village of Moryang will now be born in your house." Because everyone in the house was astonished by this voice, Kim Mullyang sent someone to investigate. As had been anticipated, Taesong had died at the very same time that the voice from heaven had spoken. The connection made between birth and death is related to Korean reincarnation beliefs; the idea that Taesong was about to be quickly reborn. This, in fact, is later confirmed when the child is born with that very name on his hand.

One account, rather similar in that it happened to involve both a political figure and a voice announcing a distant death, came over a millennium later in 1766 and involved Pieter Nieuwland, a former minister of the Hague.[28] Nieuwland told that on a certain night, a Mr. Laan, afterwards Professor at Franeker, while studying in Utrecht, dreamed he was at the Court of Ispahan in Iran, where he heard two words spoken in a strange language, which, despite not recognizing them, he clearly remembered upon awakening. He inquired with another professor as to their meaning, and the words in Persian meant, "He is dead." As it turned out, this man's brother was strangled at the very time of Laan's vision, as was confirmed by his own written notes.

Nearly one hundred years earlier, in 1671, an account was recorded by French aristocrat Madame de Sevigne, who was remembered for her vividly written letters. She writes of a certain poet who was known as something of a "ne'er-do-well" and who was fascinatingly "converted" by a vision in which, on the night of the death of his physician and friend Theophile, he heard the man's voice calling him several times.[29] That his servant, who was with him at the time, seemed to hear the same voices, was apparently the factor that most moved the man.

Much earlier, from France, was another experience of Dutch mystic Lutgardis of Aywières, with whom we have also previously met, in which she was supernaturally informed of the death of her own sister.[30] Suddenly, one day, in the air above her head, she heard a terrible, resounding cry, the voice of a woman in great anguish: "Have mercy on me, dearest sister! Have mercy on me and pray for me, and obtain mercy for me, as you did for all those other souls!" Soon after, the news of her sister's death reached her by ordinary means.

On the day that Spanish military commander, diplomat, and author Don Bernardino de Mendoza was taken ill and died in 1557, Roman Catholic Saint Teresa of Avila noted that she knew he had died despite being "far from the place" where he was.[31] She had heard a voice, which she interpreted as being that of the Lord, who informed her of Mendoza's passing.

The highly venerated Arab poet Umar b. al-Farid provides a noteworthy example in a story he narrates in his hagiographical account of his own grandfather.[32] He tells how Ibn al-Farid met with a greengrocer in Cairo, a man he later came to recognize as one of God's saints. The greengrocer informed him that he must travel to the Hijaz because he would not become enlightened in Egypt. After spending fifteen years in the Arabian wilderness, Ibn al-Farid heard the greengrocer's voice telling him to return to Cairo, that he was dying and to pray for him. He obeyed the voice and returned to Cairo, where he discovered the greengrocer right at the point of death.

At times, the apparitional or visionary experiences are comple-
mented later by a clarifying voice. In 357 CE, it is said that while
St. Antony was living on a certain mountain, he looked up and saw
what appeared to be a soul ascending.[33] Amazed by this sight, Antony
specifically asked about the nature of this phenomenon, to which a
voice replied that this was the soul of the monk Ammon, who lived at
Nitria. Ammon was a very old man, and the place where Antony lived
was a thirteen-day journey from Nitria. In another attestation to the
power of these kinds of experiences on the individual, when the monks
who had come saw Antony in a "state of wonder," they asked him to
explain the cause of his joy. He told them that Ammon had just died.

Of interest too, in W. K. Lowther Clarke's translation of Christian
chronicler Palladius of Galatia's *Lausiac History*, the author, similarly
to classicist Collison-Morley six years prior, makes a reference to *The
Phantasms of the Living*, noting that the reader should see that work
for what were then modern accounts that parallelled Antony's vision.[34]
We read in the *One Thousand and One Nights*, a collection of Middle
Eastern folktales compiled in Arabic, of a man named Camaralzaman
who dreamed that he saw his father on his deathbed and heard him
say, "My son, whom I so tenderly loved; my son, whom I bred with so
much affection, so much care; he abandoned me, and is himself, by that
means, the cause of my death." Camaralzaman awoke in great distress.
"Ah!" cried the prince, "at this very moment my father is perhaps no
more!"[35]

The extent to which the individual might take these voices seriously
remained as apparent in the twentieth century as it had been in the
poetry of al-Farid or by the readers of the miracles of Vitalis. In one of
those cases, told to Frank Podmore, a woman heard a voice telling her
to go to a certain town because a friend was in urgent need of her.[36] The
effect was so strong that the informant bought a fresh train ticket and
changed her route there and then.

Similarly, in a Portuguese folktale, a young woman heard a voice
that told her, "Your father is dying, and does not wish to die without
taking leave of you." When she returned home, she found her father at
the edge of death, and he died just after they said their goodbyes.[37]

Whether in the oldest religious texts, the folktale, the memorate, or in romance, the veridical voice is there to be found. Quoting from another case out of the Rhine Institute collection, and in the informant's own words, we read that, "On the morning of April 22, 2010, while standing in my home office, I began to feel as though something was physically wrong. I wasn't dizzy or nauseous but I felt odd and became slightly concerned." Several seconds later, a voice told her that so and so was dying. The informant went on: "I was amazed and remember thinking, How can I know when he—or anyone else—is dying?" Soon came the word that so and so was indeed dead, and some weeks later, she learned that this person had had a heart attack on the day of her experience.[38]

WHAT'S IN A NAME

Rather than hearing a voice informing them directly or giving a clue of the passing of someone distant, it is not uncommon for individuals to hear their own names or other similarly specific information as if spoken by another. From folkloric sources, when one hears their name called by someone in need, it is often heard three times. A Bordeaux woman was awakened three separate times by the sound of a voice calling her name, Jeanne, in what sounded like anguish.[39] Later, she was informed that her former lover had died that very night on the other side of France and had several times called out her name.

Originally given by French physician and psychiatrist Brière de Boismont in the nineteenth century was the dream of a young lady who saw her mother before her, pale and disfigured.[40] She heard her mother call her name multiple times, which apparently she had done aloud as she died at the very time of the dream.

In a North American memorate, a man driving a truck suddenly heard his sister's voice saying, "Oh, no, Mamma!" In a quandary, he got in touch with his sister as soon as possible, only to find that he had heard the exact words she spoke when she realized their mother was dying.[41]

These cases where a voice is heard—either that of the dying or dead or from another messenger—and the passing confirmed are particularly convincing for the observer; as Brian Inglis[35] noted, the likelihood that coincidence might be a sufficient explanation in these cases seems to be a particularly wanting one. Another example comes from the Denham tracts, a series of fifty-four pamphlets and jottings on folklore collected between 1846 and 1859 by Michael Aislabie Denham, from which even Tolkien is said to have drawn.[42] In what Denham calls a "good description of a warning" from Northumberland in North East England, the informant tells that an aunt of theirs was very ill and far away in Liddesdale, clarifying that they had no idea of the illness at the time. One night, this man was riding alone along a long and lonely road, far from any house, when he suddenly heard his name called three times— "Matthew, Matthew, Matthew"—in a voice he concluded was "so like my mother's or my aunt's that I thought it was one of them." A few days later, this man got a letter from Liddesdale with a black seal and saw that his aunt had died at the time at which he had heard the voice.

Scottish writer and poet James Boswell once said of another biographer, the distinguished English polymath Samuel Johnson, "An acquaintance, on whose veracity I can rely, told me that walking home one evening to Kilmarnock, he heard himself called from a wood by the voice of a brother who had gone to America, and the next packet brought accounts of that brother's death."[43]

We find something similar in the indigenous *Legend of Qu'Ap'elle* from Canada.[44] An Indian man was on his way to claim a bride when he passed a small wood by night in his canoe and heard a voice repeat his name. Upon asking who called, the voice repeated his name again. He then recognized it as that of his future bride. Early in the morning, he drew up his canoe and saw a number of people gathered around her lodge. Hearing the death songs, he had no doubt that she had died while he was away. He specifically asked the time and circumstances of her death, and he was told that on the preceding evening she twice repeated his name and then her spirit fled.

Among the Ojibwa Indians is a tale in which one brother, Wisa'ka, is separated from his younger brother, Kyapata, while one walks toward dawn and the other toward the sun.[45] Later on, from a distance apparently much too great to have been heard by ear, Wisa'ka supernaturally heard his younger brother calling him, "Oh my elder brother, now I am dying!" The ominous feeling that something was very wrong increased each time he heard this voice. When he returned home, he asked everyone for information about his brother, but there were no reports. Soon, however, he discovered that his brother had indeed died.

From the Santee natives of Nebraska, we read that while a man named Chaske was sleeping, he suddenly heard the voice of his friend, whom he had previously left at the river to drink, calling, "Behold me." When Chaske reached him, he had transformed into a fish.[46]

In a tale from the Quinault Indians of Washington, a man, while hunting near the Raft River, heard a voice that sounded like that of his brother's wife crying for her children.[47] It turned out to be a strange creature, which he killed. When he came to the mouth of the river, he saw his eldest brother on horseback, and he looked up and told the man that both boys had died, and the man knew exactly why the animal's voice had sounded like that of his sister-in-law.

Among the West African Yoruba, the voice of a dead man named Shango clears up the ongoing controversy as to whether or not he had actually died.[48] His body at one point looked as if it had been hanged, but when the news was returned to his village and they came to take the body, it was gone. Finally, Shango's disembodied voice confirmed his fate: "I, Shango, do not hang! I have merely returned to my place in the sky!"

While not a voice, the following account is still a heard message that goes beyond the noises, knockings, and so forth that we will explore in the next section, and illustrates the impact these experiences may have, despite often seeming relatively mundane. Charles-Camille Saint-Saëns, French composer, organist, conductor, and pianist of the Romantic era, told Flammarion that on the last day of the Franco-German war he and his fellow soldiers at the front had been able to dine unexpectedly well and were feeling well-satisfied with themselves when, as he went on to say, "suddenly I heard, running through my head, an unusual dirge of melancholy chords"; a profound sadness overcame him, with the certainty of some misfortune. Later, he heard that his close friend Henri Regnault had been killed at that very moment: "I experienced, therefore, the reality of telepathy before the word was invented." The dirge he heard would become the opening movement of his celebrated requiem.[49]

That something so tangible might come into the world in this way was also the case again among the Yoruba of West Africa in a tale in which the body of a man named Orunsen was missing and for which a search party had been gathered.[50] That group was similarly informed of his fate: "Abandon the search," a voice in the sky said to one of them, one named Renrengenjen. "Where I am now, you cannot find me. I have gone into the sky to live under the protection of Olorum." This particular instance in which a disembodied voice informed of a death was how the *Igogo* festival began, in which the long search for Orunsen's body is reenacted.

POTS, PANS, AND CROSS-CULTURAL CLANGS

While voices that convey messages of death are a common occurrence, from a folkloric perspective, it cannot be overstated the extent to which knockings, rappings, falling picture frames, domestic consternations, sounds in general and other things that go bump in the night have widely been observed as occurring simultaneously with a distant death. These occurrences have been noted in every country and county where omens have been collected. While more recently such things are considered incongruous with what is "normal," American Unitarian minister, psychical researcher, and author Minot Savage, in a less quoted 1899 volume of anecdotes and musings upon life after death, observed the following with something of an elegant economy regarding these phenomena: "It seems," he wrote, "to be the simplest and most natural method of announcing one's presence in this world, and why it may not be as simple and natural in the case of some invisible person who wishes to make his presence known I have never been able clearly to understand."[51]

The noisy ghost, with his or her rappings around the house, was of particular interest to nineteenth century spiritualists. The Welsh founder of utopian socialism, Robert Owen, is even said to have been "converted" to a belief in a spirit world and future state after just such an experience.[52] Often sounds of this kind were linked to the deaths of particular families and bloodlines; this was most famously true of the Irish banshee, which may vary in its manifestation between each bloodline. In one Irish family, for instance, the Banshee was said to be a semi-supernatural being and daughter of a fairy queen, while in another Welsh family, the Banshee was said to be a deceased and restless member of the family themselves. Often there is nothing specific to separate the way the banshee acts between familes. The important distinction is that the banshee is tied to certain families and not to others. With that said, one relevant example could be that German botanist and physician Rudolf Jakob Camerarius wrote in 1621 that specific rappings and noises were associated with the days of deaths of certain Princes of Germany.[53] Regarding how old the idea that the ghost might affect the material world in this way is, the most ancient Assyrians believed that if the spirit of an unburied body made sounds, the owner of the house in which this occurred would die.[55]

The Greek sophist Philostratus wrote of a demon knocking over a statue, while the house in which Emperor Augustus was nursed as a baby was said to be home to such a force that when a new owner moved in, he might find himself ejected from his mattress.[56] Indeed, the slave Tranio in antiquity claiming that it was a ghost causing certain knocking sounds speaks to the phenomenon as much as did Camille Flammarion in nineteenth century France, who told us he could have filled a volume rather than the chapter he had done with the number of instances which came to him.[57]

While supernatural noises and rappings have been fairly well considered across Europe, here we can get an even wider feel for just how disparately these traditions can be found. Again referring to Lavater, he noted in his treatise regarding psychokinetic activity that "[i]t has many times chanced that those of the house have verily thought that somebody had overthrown the pots, platters, tables, and trenchers and tumbled down the stairs, but after it waxed day they have found all things orderly set in their places again."[58] He also wrote of these rappings that they "happened the very same hour that our friends departed in." This was to hold true across greatly separated lands.

This situation of "nothing disturbed" despite an obvious din is a common one. A related tradition in Rose Bay, Nova Scotia, specifies that if dishes are heard falling and they don't break, something is going to happen.[59] More specifically, from Mahone Bay, within hours of the death of the informant's father, his nurse and then "all in the house" heard a sound as if china had fallen from a shelf, though they found nothing disturbed.[60]

Robe provides an example of two women in New Mexico.[61] When one of them died, the other one heard a clatter of dishes in the kitchen, as if they had all fallen to the floor. She went to see and found that all the dishes were still in the cupboard. That day, she found out that her friend had died at the moment of the sound.

Sometimes the sounds are followed directly by an apparitional encounter. The notion that such sounds indicate death would have clearly gained a stronger footing in certain communities when followed by such a bolstering vision. One Finnish woman heard the sound of saucepan lids falling in the kitchen.[62] Soon after turning off the lights and going to bed, she saw her father standing at the end of the bed and heard the death rattle in his throat. They later discovered that he had died at that time.

It becomes clear that at times both the legends and the memorates also point to *actual* disturbances. From farther west, and far earlier, comes a memorate from a selection of legends collected in northern Norway in 1870.[63] We read of Jacob Nilsen Tjern, who, sitting with his parents one evening, heard the carpentry tools being disturbed on a shelf above his head. Both Jacob and his parents noticed the noise from the tools, and it repeated itself several times. "Let the tools lie," said Jacob. "When we have occasion to use them, then we will use them." Straightaway, it fell quiet, and the tools were left alone. But before Jacob got up the next morning, he received a message saying that his son was dead and that he had to make a coffin for him. Such phenomena are well known in Norse countries, and it might be said that such a thing was similar to the *vardøger*, where the spirit of a living person arrives and is seen by others in advance of their actual arrival.

Summers related an early nineteenth century French case, apparently "rigidly documented" in those years, involving John Baptist Vianney.[64] John spoke of a demon who seemed to hammer nails into the floor, cleave wood, or make other sounds like a "busy carpenter at work." The idea that a coffin will have to be built can also be found in North Germany, where the carpenter generally knows when a death is about to occur because he hears movements and the cracking of boards, which are directly related to the wraith of the dying person.[65]

Similiar beliefs are found among the Alaskan Inupiat. In 1949, three men drifted out from King Island, and only one returned.[66] One of the men who was lost was this author's third cousin, Pahina. His grandparents heard a loud crack underneath their house, and they knew therefore that he was dead.

The notion of these "undisturbances" also extends beyond the house. From Oklahoma, where, just as in remote Norway, such tokens and omens are often received as familiar things, an informant told that while their friend's mother was in the hospital, his relatives, while at dinner, heard a terrible sound at the front of the house as if a tree had blown over, although when they looked out, nothing was wrong or disturbed.[67] Soon they received word that the mother was dead, and the informant "naturally believed in that token."

In a similar memorate collected from Indiana, we read that at two o'clock one morning, a farm family was awakened by a knocking sound.[68] Having thought it was a tree branch, they investigated and found nothing, only to hear the next morning that their grandmother had died.

The similarities between these disparate occurrences are again striking. The Aboriginal Australian Jimmy Barker told Matthews that one night, while some men were camping, there was a loud noise like a tree had fallen.[69] The men walked around the camping area in the morning, gradually extending their search. Their real concern, however, came specifically because no fallen tree could be found; they seemingly understood the meaning of this token clearly, and indeed they soon learned that a young child had died.

It is clear that while in some cultures the potential connection between the sound and a distant death is either unrecognized or dismissed as superstition, in others, such as those as far apart as Finland and Aboriginal Australia, they are recognized for what they might represent and taken rather more seriously. Johnson had noted, for example, that New Englanders were "scared to death" by such synchronicities.[70]

Rose gave another example from Aboriginal Australia in which, on a still night, an awful bang was heard on a roof, as if a "big stone come down from long ways."[71] The informant said to the others present, "By golly, something's wrong. Something's gonna happen by'n'by," noting that this had happened before and that bad news followed every time.

Much removed, Lavater again gave us something similar, relaying the words of Italian Renaissance polymath Gerolamo Cardano, who wrote of a parish priest who "could tell beforehand when any of his parish should die. For in the night time, he heard a noise over his bed, like as if one had thrown down a sack full of corn from his shoulders, which when he heard, he would say, 'Now another has bid me farewell.' After it was day, he used to inquire who died that night or who was taken with the plague, to the end that he might comfort and strengthen them according to the duty of a good pastor."[72]

Thousands of kilometers away, among the Blackfoot Indians of Montana, McClintock was told of a ghost that kept two families up one night, announcing a death with its din.[73] "It came from the trees and roused the dogs. They gave the ghost-bark; they growled and sniffed the air. That ghost cried like an owl and pulled their door open." The next morning, they found a dead body in a tree close to their camp. It had been the unhappy spirit of a man who was apparently murdered by his jealous brother.

Indeed, among Native Americans such references are widely found. Regarding the Cheyenne, it is said that the *mis'tdi*, or ghost, is very rarely seen but is often felt or heard, and that sometimes when one is walking at night through the woods, where it is very dark, a ghost may tug on a robe or blanket. Ghosts may scratch or tap on the lodge skins, as well as make strange and mysterious noises just outside the lodge.[74] In a more specific Cheyenne example, a ghost is said to have thrown open the doors of multiple lodges.[75] The ghosts of the Gros Ventre Indians are similarly "never seen, but only heard."[76]

Among the Ecuadorians, the Secoya Indians echo the words of the distant Lavater in that the *bai hoyo* of a dead man may appear as a vision to a member of his household, but he may also "rattle the cookpots" in the night to make his presence known.[77]

Returned spirits show themselves to the Mapuche of Chile in a number of ways besides their appearances in dreams.[78] People may become aware of their presence through unexplained noises, household objects found out of place or knocked over, or whisperings in the rafters at night. Among the Tukanoans of Colombia, a man's spirit might be heard "pounding on coca" of his enemy's house.[79] In Peru, a ghost caused a great quantity of tiles and bricks to be thrown down with great noise in a house.[80]

While such domestic disturbances are most commonly associated with tales from the likes of Victorian England or wider Europe, it is clear that this is a far more widely known phenomenon. Many Jamaicans believe that if a jalousie window drops unexpectedly at night, there is a duppy in the house.[81]

Hobley noted of the East African A-Kamba that "[s]ometimes at night the people will hear a child crying in the road outside the village when they know it is impossible for a child to be there, this is a sign that Azzmu (ancestor spirits) are passing."[82]

Among Sindh Hindus, the ghost of the dead man "not unfrequently" causes "violent disturbances."[83]

Like the apparitional and dream encounters, the references here among the New Guineans are myriad. Rogers noted that among the Keraki, a ghost is sometimes overheard by solitary travelers in the bush.[84] Landtman found among the Kiwai Papuans that sometimes a whistle from outside or tapping noises on a wall signal a spirit's arrival, while Newton noted very similarly of the New Guineans who lived in Wedau that after a death, they might "sometimes say that they have heard the spirit scratching along the wall trying to find its way into the home."[85] As an interesting aside, this is similar to the belief in the state of Illinois that a spirit might knock on the wall when one in the house is to die.[86] Among the Kosi of the Melanesian Trobriand Islands too, the wraith might be heard "knocking at the houses of his friends and relatives for a few days after death."[87]

SAINTS, SOUNDS, AND BOOTS ON THE GROUND

In certain accounts, legendary or otherwise, sounds heard on a larger scale with multiple witnesses are frequent and linked to the death of someone often though not always renowned. From a legendary Australian Aboriginal tale, we read that, at the time of the "mother doctor's" death, there was a beautiful, dazzlingly bright falling star, followed by a sound of a sharp clap of thunder, and all the tribes around when they saw and heard this said, "A great doctor must have died, for that is the sign."[88]

The young mystic Fina, patron saint of San Gimignano in Tuscany, Italy, left this world similarly.[89] It is written that this poor girl, who endured much suffering from disease in her short life, was first warned of her oncoming demise in a vision, a common motif in the life of the mystic, saint, or hero. Importantly here, it is said that when she died in 1253, all of the town's bells rang on their own.

The same is said of Brittany's Saint Jorand. At the hour of her death, certain men on horseback heard the bells of the church ringing without anyone there to set them in motion and exclaimed that someone holy must have died.[90]

At the death of Francois de Sales, Bishop of Geneva, in 1622, it is said that a bell hanging in one of the windows of the chateau tower began ringing loudly.[91] Those inside initially assumed that someone had arrived, but they were surprised to find no one there. After around seven minutes, the bell rang again, but they found no one. When this had occurred several times in the same way, one of them understood that something extraordinary was about to happen. Orders were given to detach the cord from the bell, but the bell is said to have rung without it and the sound lasted so long that the whole family, in great terror, began to pray. It was later found that the Bishop of Geneva had died that very night.

Much earlier, in 1123, at the death of Robert, bishop of Lincoln, there was heard in the air a "wonderful and most agreeable kind of sound," a kind of melody.[92] After a while, Faulkes, bishop of London, asked the people nearby if they had heard the same thing. He told them, "I hear a supernatural sound, like that of a great convent bell, ringing a delightful tune in the air above." Though they replied that they'd heard nothing of it themselves, Faulkes was certain of the meaning, noting specifically that he believed his beloved father, brother, and master Robert was passing from this world and that the noise he had heard was intended as a warning of this news. He also understood that there was no convent anywhere nearby with such a loud bell. Upon inquiry into the matter, he found that his father had indeed departed the world at that very time.

While those with Faulkes heard nothing, on that same night, some brothers of the Order of Minorites were traveling themselves to where the bishop was staying and, in passing through the royal forest of Vauberge, lost their way. At one point while wandering about, they heard in the air the ringing of old bells, among which they clearly distinguished one bell of a most sweet tune, unlike anything they had ever heard. When they arrived in Buckdon, they learned that Robert, the bishop of Lincoln, had died at the same time they heard the bells.

The ruins of Scotland's Kirkmaiden Church, one of its oldest, are home to the graves of many from the McCullock and Maxwell families. In a manner that recalls the life token, its bell is said to ring whenever someone from one of those families dies. In a more specific, related legend, when one of the McCullocks disappeared into a stormy night to fetch something for his comrades, the ringing of that "wraith-bell" was what soon told them of his fate and that he had passed on to the next world.[93] We might also mention a certain old Japanese Buddhist tradition, again from the village of Hamanakamura, where it was thought that a person who had just recently died would appear to ring a certain bell at the Myoho-san temple.[94]

From another time and place, in 1933 Missouri, it was reported in an issue of the *Springfield News and Leader* that a number of Springfieldians heard loud death bells at the time of a Dr. A. J. Croft's death.[95]

Alexandre Dumas, one of France's most widely read authors, related that as a child, he and his cousin heard a loud blow upon their bedroom door.[96] He then got down from his bed and, with his eyes "full of tears," and told his cousin, who was mystified, that he was going to say good-bye to his father and that he was going to open the door for him before going back to sleep. They found out the next morning that his father had died exactly at that time.

Another notable French example involved Carl Linné, better known as Linnaeus, generally regarded as the founder of modern botany.[97] One night in 1766 he and his wife were awoken by the sound of someone in his museum walking up and down with heavy steps. He knew nobody could be there, as he had locked the doors and had the key with him. He recognized the sound of the footsteps as those of his dearest friend Karl Clerk: "it was his step, undoubtedly." A few days later, he heard that Clerk had died "at precisely the same hour."

The number of instances involving footsteps, whether made by the revenant or the wraith, is impressive. Famously, in *Grettir's Saga*, one of the fundamental texts involving revenants and their lore, we read that shortly after Glam dies, his footsteps are heard upon the roofs of Thorhallsstead.[98] Similar activities, which seem to merge with those of the poltergeist or warning ghost generally, are ascribed to the revenant or wraith in many regions. Among certain Yugoslavians, for example, it is believed that when a woman becomes a vampire and rises from the grave, she stalks about in attics and across roofs.[99] In East Africa, if a person dies in a village nearby, the footsteps of the deceased are seen the next morning leading into the cave.[100]

Ronald Rose related the case of an Aboriginal Minyung man, Frank Mitchell, from northern Australia whose son, Billie, was in the hospital, though, as far as he knew, not remotely in danger of dying.[101] One morning, Mitchell came rushing to Rose's residence and told him that Billie had died in the night. How did he know this? According to Mitchell's explanation, he and his wife heard the "spirit footsteps" of his dead mother on their veranda, followed by the familiar tapping of her walking stick. They interpreted this specifically as a sign that Billie had died.

In a memorate collected in Ireland by Irish Anglican priest John Seymour, a man was preparing to sleep in 1879 when he heard, with "the most unquestionable distinctness," footsteps move from the hall door and traverse the hall before hearing an agitated hand searching for the handle of the door.[102] He was sure his wife wanted to speak to him, so he called her name, but no answer came. He checked the areas and was greatly puzzled to find nothing. Soon after, the entire performance was repeated, but the handle this time seemed to partially turn. On Friday, he received a letter saying that someone he knew had died at about the same time that night.

Finally, here we end this chapter with an account from among the Californian Cahuilla Indians. While August Lomas and his wife were in bed one night, they heard someone come in, walk around the room, and then leave again, despite being sure the door was locked.[103] A few months later, their uncle died, so they knew then that it must have been his *telewel* (a spirit or soul Among the Cahuilla) that had been wandering around.

◆

While it is fairly well known among occultists and parapsychologists that voices and sounds are often tied to a distant death, it has been less explored just how widely this is believed and how ancient an idea this is. Just as we have seen with the primarily apparitional and visionary accounts, the folklorists, hagiographers, anthropologists, ethnologists, and others, independently of each other, have collected innumerable and often rather idiosyncraticly similar accounts that speak firmly to this reality.

EIGHT

Making the Rounds and Collective Accounts

> *The very existence of collective cases is on the face of it a grave difficulty for any telepathic theory of apparitions. Surely a telepathic hallucination ought to be a purely private phenomenon, experienced only by the person for whom the telepathic communication is intended? But in fact it is sometimes experienced by indifferent bystanders as well.*
>
> HENRY HABBERLEY PRICE

At certain times, more than one person is a direct witness to these apparitions and visions. The subjects are sometimes together, and other times they are far apart. While the former, the *collective apparition*, has been well considered and will be further represented here, some of the following experiences are of a particularly unique category in which the departing person appears to multiple witnesses either simultaneously or consecutively, though in different locations both parties often later confirming the event and its timing with one another. Authors Bill and Judy Guggenheim, in reference to this kind of behavior on the part of the deceased, described it as "making the rounds."[1] Others, such as Mesegeuer, noted that in these cases, it seems the dying person themselves "take the initiative" and visit multiple far-off relatives.[2]

These kinds of experiences were described before they had been specifically classified by some of these authors in the 1871 book *Spiritualism and Animal Magnetism*.[3] Magnetism, being essentially a term for and encompassing telepathy, was popular before the kinds of words used today replaced it. The author, Hungarian journalist Gustavus George Zerffi, described them as follows: "These visions of absent persons in great danger, struggling with death, or dying, have taken place; such visions of the same person were often seen in different places, by different people."

Longer ago still, Martin, from Duntulm on the Isle of Skye, in his classic study of the second sight in Scotland and its western isles, noted that "the seer knows neither the object, time, nor place of a vision, before it appears, and the same object is often seen by different persons, living at a considerable distance from one another."[4] Furthermore, the possibility of such visions is clearly implied in the belief systems of cultures worldwide regarding the general behavior of the departed after death.

MAKING THE ROUNDS

In beginning, we may draw again from antiquity and an account which comes down to us from a Galatian monk, bishop, and chronicler known primarily for his widely translated and read *Lausiac History*, Palladius of Galatia. Writing about the experience of a friend of his, the early Christian writer Didymus of Alexandria, Palladius tells us that he had once decided not to accept an invitation to pray with Didymus, who then proceeded to relate to him the following story: "As I was thinking one day about the life of the wretched Emperor Julian, how he was a persecutor, and was feeling dejected—and by reason of my thoughts I had not tasted bread even up to late evening—it happened that as I sat in my seat I was overcome by sleep and I saw in a trance white horses running with riders and proclaiming: 'Tell Didymus, to-day at the seventh hour Julian died. Rise then and eat,' they said, 'and send to Athanasius the bishop, that he too may know.' And I marked," he said, "the hour and month and week and day, and it was found to be so."[5]

Sozomen, in his *Ecclesiastical History of the Church*, also makes note of this particular account and tells us that the death had also been witnessed during a sleeping vision of a friend of Emperor Julian around the same time.[6] This man had traveled into Persia with the intention of making acquaintance with the emperor. One night along his way, he had a vision in which the emperor's death was announced just after it had occurred, by two figures who were apparently his killers.

When the Italian saint Benedict died, a particular note was made of this kind of vision.[7] When one of his servants was in "devout prayer," he saw a vision of Benedict yielding his soul to heaven. Another of his followers, in a place "distant," had a similar vision, seeing Benedict adorned with gorgeous tapestries and shining with a multitude of "unnumberable lamps" as he proceeded to heaven. Some particularly beautiful artworks have been created in relation to these experiences around the life and death of Benedict.

Very similar are the visions related to the death of St. Honoratus in 429 CE, who was born in France about 350 CE.[8] Hilary of Arles, in his Sermon on the Life of Honoratus (c. 430), describes how, when Honoratus died, more than one person had miraculous visions at the time of his death and that "the sleep of many was disturbed by various visions, all according to the same form: namely, that the saints came to meet this saint."

Something related is said of the early Egyptian Muslim mystic and ascetic Dho 'L-Nun Al-Mesri. On the night of his death, seventy different people saw him in a dream.[9]

Upon the death of St. Jerome in 420 CE, he is said to have appeared to both Severus and Augustine at the same hour.[10]

According to one story, at the death of a ninth century hymnographer named Joseph, a certain pious man heard a voice that told him to look outside.[11] He saw the heavens part dramatically, and all the saints that ever lived leading a soul to heaven. When he asked who this was, the voice told him that it was Joseph the Hymnographer. Furthermore, according to some versions of the Synaxarion notice for Joseph, a man who was trying to locate his escaped slave went for help to the shrine of St. Theodore Phanerotes. After three days and nights, the man was about to give up and go home when St. Theodore finally appeared and told him that Joseph the Hymnographer had died just last night.

It is written that at the time of the death of the fifth century Welsh saint named Brioc, two people in distant places had visions of the event at the time it occurred.[12] Brioc fell ill and died at the age of ninety. At the time of his death, a priest named Marcan saw a vision of angels bearing his soul to heaven, while another monk named Simaus dreamed that he saw Brioc ascend a ladder into the heavenly land. Similar to the visions of Benedict, the fact that both saw different visions nevertheless tied to the same event speaks strongly to the almost personalized allegorical nature that some of these visions take.

The idea that such visions may present differently to separate people far apart despite representing the same event is reflected by something that comes to us from the Western Highlands of Scotland and was recorded in a late nineteenth century issue of *Folklore*.[13] When the death of a laird who was about to step down had occurred while he was away from his home, in which a relative was staying at the time, a servant there dreamed she had seen a *dreag*.* She was "quite sure" the new, incoming laird had died on his way there. "At the same time," his relative dreamed that a large river was running past the house and that the new laird was on the opposite side of it. It turns out a son of the laird had died "just about the date of the dream."

Author Allison Morgan received something related from her informant, Rachel.[14] On the night that her grandfather died in 2009, her grandmother told her that she was sure he had actually died around 4.30 a.m., as opposed to 5.30 a.m., as the hospital had told her. She was sure of this because that night she had woken up and seen him in her bedroom. As it happens, Rachel's aunt told her that she too had woken up at the same time and heard him saying goodbye to her, as opposed to an apparitional experience, even looking around and noting that she couldn't see him.

---

*A dreag is a kind of portentous meteor, falling star, or fireball that, among the ancient Britons, was a vehicle by which the soul of some departed Druid would make their way to paradise.

While the crisis apparition of Sulpicius Severus regarding the death of Martin of Tours was previously detailed, he was not the only one given notice of that bishop's death. St. Ambrose was also said to have been informed of Martin's death, this time in a dream, but this very moment is depicted in a beautiful piece of fourteenth-century art, *The Vision of St. Ambrose.*

Rose of Lima, native to Peru, was the first person born in the Americas to be canonized. When she passed away on her deathbed in 1617, two separate people living in the city were informed of her death as it happened: one saw angels singing around her coffin; another, a close friend of hers, saw her in the presence of "saintly and angelic heavenly hosts."

The fact that a simultaneous vision might present variously to each individual yet still represent the same event is brought out strongly in the life of revered Welsh saint Illtyd. When he was on his deathbed, he specifically told two abbots, Athoclus and Isanus, that when he died, one of them would see him borne to heaven by the hands of angels, while the other would see him carried away by their entire form. And "as Illtyd foretold," so these things respectively occurred.[17]

Returning to Irish saint Columba, an account given to Adamnan, abbot of Iona Abbey and hagiographer, tells of multiple distant witnesses who were a party to a phenomenon at the time of his passing.[18] On the night of 597 CE, when Columba died a "happy and blessed death," the informant told Adamnan that "while I and others with me were engaged in fishing in the valley of the river Fend [the Finn, in Donegal]—which abounds in fish—we saw the whole vault of heaven become suddenly illuminated: struck by the suddenness of the miracle, we raised our eyes and looked towards the east, when lo! there appeared something like an immense pillar of fire, which seemed to us, as it ascended upwards at that midnight, to illuminate the whole Earth like the summer sun at noon; and after that column penetrated the heavens darkness followed, as if the sun had just set." Later the man noted that it was not only he and his acquaintances who saw this, but that "many other fishermen also, who were engaged in fishing here and there in different deep pools along the same river, were greatly terrified, as they afterwards related to us, by an appearance of the same kind."

Similarly, in a Middle Indian myth from the other side of the world, we read of the son of a Chamar (a kind of Indian leatherworker) and the son of a Raja, who were friends.[19] When in time the Raja died, he was carried off by the monstrous "Death Chaprasis." The Raja's daughter-in-law saw this in a magical mirror; in addition, as he was being carried to the otherworld, he passed over a river where a rich man was catching fish when he, along with his wife, looked up and saw the Raja take his leave of this world.

It is unsurprising that the death of great men should be so well represented in these accounts. When King Conrad III of Germany died, a bright star appeared in broad daylight over the place of his passing and was seen throughout the whole province.[20]

In a Hungarian Magyar folktale, a man named Paul the Handsome and a maid staying in the same town, though unaware of each other's presence there, had similar and related dreams.[21] Paul dreamt that a bay stallion had died, and this ladies' maid, at the same time, dreamt that a mare was dying and soon died. When they met, they told each other their dreams, and they "knew" that those royals, her father and mother, were represented by the mare and stallion and must have died the previous night. Next morning, an official proclaimed that the king and queen had suddenly died; the tale specifies this occurred "at the very moment they had their dreams."

A related occurrence was referenced in a Mohave Indian myth from the southwestern United States.[22] When a certain man was killed and his body lay stretched over the earth, it was said that several tribes dreamed about this killing, including the Yuma, the Maricopa, the Kamia, the Valapai, the Halchidhoma, and others, all the way down to the mouth of the Mohave river.

A tale from Calmet was recorded in the year 1330 regarding the apparition of a spirit at Lagni sur Marne, about six leagues from Paris.[23] It was that of a woman who, after her death, apparently spoke to more than twenty separate people, including her father, sister, daughter, and son-in-law.

From the Navajo Indians, Walking Thunder once awoke at the same time as her husband, both exclaiming, "Mom is dead."[24] They ran to her house and found her dead, just as they had pictured it in their dreams.

In *The Epic Histories*, P'awstos, an Armenian historian and the one to whom the work is generally attributed, wrote that at least three separate people had visions of Nerses I, the eighteenth Armenian Catholic Patriarch at his death in 373 CE.[25] On that day in the mountains, though they were a far distant from one another, two clerics named Shaghitay and Epip'an both saw Nerses appear as though he were being taken upward to the clouds. Each man descended their mountain where they investigated and found that Nerses had in fact died at that time.

Around a millennium and a half later, an account involving a colonel serving in Canada who appeared to two of his officers in London on the night of his death was published.[26] While chatting in the morning, one said to the other, "Did you see anything remarkable last night?" "Yes," he said, "I did; did you?" The first man said, "Assuredly. I saw the apparition of Colonel B." The other man asked, "Did he say anything to you?" "Yes," came the reply. Then the second man said, "So he did to me: we will not tell each other what it was, but we will make a deposition of it, and see if our two accounts agree." They subsequently did so, and both accounts agreed exactly.

Revisiting the pseudepigraphal *Assumption of the Virgin*, we read that John hears a voice telling him Mary is about to die before being magically set at the door of the house as she is in her throes. Peter, Thomas, and Mark described hearing the very same message while being in different places.[27]

In another vision by St. Lutgarde, in 1216 Pope Innocent II appeared "wrapped in a great flame" to the mystic.[28] Lutgarde announced to her sisters of the Pope's death, which had actually taken place. Not only hadn't the news reached Belgium, but Lutgard is said not even to have known what the Pope looked like as they had never met. Of interest here is that another mystic, A Cistercian brother and a contemporary of Lutgarde, Simon of Aulne, is said to have had a "similar vision" of Innocent's death.

While at prayer in the ancient Basilica of Saint Peter, St. Catherine of Sweden saw before her a woman dressed in a white robe.[29] This woman asked her to pray for someone who was dead. "It is one of your countrywomen," the woman said, "who needs your assistance." Catherine asked who this person was who needed prayers. "It is the Princess Gida of Sweden, the wife of your brother Charles." When Catherine went to tell her mother, she told Catherine that the apparition was actually Gida herself and that she had come to her too, revealing her death. A few weeks later, an official from the court of Prince Charles arrived and confirmed Gida's passing.

St. Louis Bertrand of the Order of St. Dominic wrote that in the year 1557, while Louis resided at the convent of Valentina, a pestilence broke out.[30] During a time of great plague in 1557, a certain man, wishing to prepare himself for what he considered an inevitable death, confessed all his sins to St. Louis Bertrand of the Order of St. Dominic and suggested he would return to him and explain his fate after it came to pass. As those purgatory-bound souls were so often inclined to do, this man did appear to the saint. Of greater interest here, however, is that six days later, another man of the town who "knew nothing of what had passed" at the convent came to Louis and told him the same man had appeared to him, eventually ascending towards the sky like a "resplendent star."

The literary utility of such accounts is also clear. The fact that multiple people who had seen the same vision later confirmed the details with each other is an impressive kind of veridicality. Such a less intimate account type with its shared and communal aspects being found so commonly among the lives of the saints should not, perhaps, be entirely surprising, though of course, they are also found much further afield.

Returning to the revenant and wraith-filled landscapes of Peru, in a folktale there, a young boy suffering from unrequited love drowns himself.[31] He later appears to his father in order to explain his fate, as we have so often seen. Additionally, he appears separately to his mother and further explains where his body might be found.

Recorded in the seminal *Legends of Tono*, Kunio Yanagita's cornerstone of Japanese folkloristics, comes a tale in which the master of a wealthy family in the town of Tono was on the brink of death.[32] One day, he suddenly visited his family temple and drank tea with the priest there. Feeling like something was not right, when the man was about to leave the priest sent his younger disciple to follow him, though he soon disappeared around a corner. That man greeted many others along that street, despite the fact that, as it turned out, he had been dead at the time.

A similar account comes to us from twelfth century China and may be found in the *Record of the Listener*, a work which contains a number of apparitional encounters.[33] A girl of seventeen sacrifices herself so that bandits will not kill her father. She promises to leave with them and fulfill their every wish. The bandits agree, but when they reach the East Market Bridge, the girl jumps into the water and kills herself. Her brother, several days later and entirely unaware of her fate, dreamed that she appeared to him. She told him, "Thank goodness you and father are alive, I have died. And so I've come to say goodbye." Come morning, his wife told him that she had a very similar dream in which the girl came looking "just as she normally looked." They said a hurried goodbye before departing. It wasn't until the following day that they had news that she had drowned herself.

English clergyman and writer Nathaniel Wanley recorded a like anecdote from the eighteenth century.[34] The author was told by a man that, in his youth, he dreamed that his mother passed by him with a "sad countenance" before telling him she would not be able to make his graduation. When he woke, he went and found that his brother had had the very same dream. The news of their mother's death came very soon after.

We may return again to the ancient world for a surprisingly comparable account related to the death of Emperor Julian in 363 CE.[35] Julian had locked up two men, Basil and Liberius. Liberius saw a vision in his sleep in which Mercurius appeared to him and told him, "Verily I will not permit this infidel to utter blasphemies against my God," "infidel" being a reference to Julian and some sort of seemingly obligatory punishment for the man. Liberius woke from his sleep and told St. Basil of the vision he had seen, which turned out to have been the very same.

Basil evidently "rejoiced with very great joy" at his vision. Soon afterwards came the news of the killing of Julian by Mercurius.

Regarding the death of Italian Dominican sister Catherine De' Ricci, the following was recorded: A nun at a convent in Prato, while spending the night in vigil, suddenly saw a vision of a magnificent procession of saints accompanied by what she construed as Christ bearing a soul to heaven. While gazing "in delight" at this apparition, she heard the death bell at San Vincenzio ring for Mother Catherine and immediately realized what this affecting vision had meant. The very same sight had been seen in another town by a man named Baccio Verzoni, who himself instantly recognized Catherine.[36]

Alfred Montoya, a native of Taos Pueblo, had a very unusual experience in 1974 in which, while nearing sleep in the woods, he noticed Indians dressed in the old Taos manner emerge from the darkness.[37] They danced in a blur, ethereally, for some time before retreating to the south. When he met with his friends, from whom he had previously been separated, they told him they had the very same experiences. When Montoya reached his grandmother's house, she told him that his other grandmother had died at the exact time as the vision and that this was her way of letting him know she was fine.

Once more from the English monk Bede's *Ecclesiastical History of the English People*, we read of the handmaid Begu, who, having been resting, saw the soul of St. Hilda carried among lights towards heaven at the time she had died. Of most interest, according to the historian, "it pleased Almighty God, by a manifest vision, to make known her death in another monastery, at a distance from hers." All the sisters were roused to long-lasting prayer and devotion at this vision, and when the brothers arrived to announce the death officially, they answered that they already knew.[38] According to Bede, "it was found that her death had been revealed to them in a vision at the very hour at which the brothers said that she had died."

On the night that al-Mutawakkil, the tenth Abbasid caliph, died, venerated Islamic intellectual Ibn Hanbal wrote that he was "wakeful one night but afterwards fell into a slumber and in my dream I saw, as it were, a man ascending to heaven, and a speaker," who said the following:

"A King who is led to a just king, Eminent in mercy and not an oppressor." Hanbai went on, "Afterwards, when I awoke at dawn, there arrived at Baghdad from Surra Man Raa a messenger announcing the death of al-Mutawakkil." A'mrf-b-Shayban al Jubnan, then Arab leader of the Shayban tribe, noted similarly that he too had learned of the death of al-Mutawakkil during a dream on that same night.[39]

Gunnlaug, from the circa thirteenth century Icelandic saga of the same name, was killed by Raven the Skald.[40] Before the news could reach Iceland, Illugi the Black dreamed of Gunnlaug and his wounds. It is said that on the same night, Gunnlaug also appeared to another named Onund, far away at Mossfell.

Journalist and revolutionist Gustav Zerffi relayed a case from many ages later that occurred around the time of the death of a woman in a Jewish hospital in Frankfurt.[41] The woman's sister and niece both lived five miles apart. The morning following her death, they realized "she appeared to both of them during the night, whilst she was dying." Interestingly, the superintendent of the hospital who recorded the incident noted that such cases occur often.

COLLECTIVE CRISIS APPARITIONS

While these previous accounts of spirits or other messengers "making the rounds" are less formally studied, the phenomenon in which there are multiple witnesses, the collective apparition, is a well-established variant about which significantly more has been written.

Although the recorded incidence of collective apparitions are plentiful, those tied to a distant death make up a relatively small percentage of assembled research. However, their uniquely evidential value in the eyes of the experiencers and indeed in the eyes of hagiographers and other writers warrants the provision of a few examples. Much has been made of their enigmatic nature, particularly as it pertains to their contribution to the hypothesis that these are objective and external phenomena related to the survival of consciousness. As Tyrrell wrote of a related sample. "It is obvious that the probability of two or more percipients having similar hallucinations at the same moment corresponding to the same distant event and being very closely, if not exactly, similar to one another is enormously less than the probability of one percipient having such a hallucination alone."[42] With Tyrell's words in mind, it seems that such collective experiences, particularly when they occur in the same vicinity, might greatly affect those involved. This very kind of impact was noted in a related third century vision regarding the French Christian martyr Valerie of Limoges.[43] When she died, a crowd nearby saw a "dazzling light" and Valerie herself flying away in it. According to the legend, those present were so affected that they all converted to Christianity that very day.

An account from much later had a similar effect on one of the men who saw their own vision.[44] In 1817, Methodist preacher Thomas Savage and three others were sitting down one night when suddenly a light came through the windows. They saw the spirit of one of their brothers. The form waved a hand, smiled, and bid them goodbye. Savage's sister then cried, "He is dead, he is dead!" Soon came a letter saying that the man had died on the island of Minorca. Savage noted the following about this experience: "Before this event I was an Atheist, though a boy. By this circumstance I was convinced of the certainty of another world, and by the solemn impression it made upon my mind."

Returning to China, with reference to a tale from renowned writer Pu Songling in the eighteenth century, the mother of a man named Song passed away.[45] When her funeral rites were concluded, Song retired to his chamber, laid down, and died himself. His wife's parents lived further within the town's western gate, and at the very moment of his death, they both saw him approaching their house riding a richly decorated horse. He came walking into their main hall, made a formal bow of farewell, and went on his way. Not realizing that he was a spirit, they rushed out in confusion to see what it could mean, only to be informed that their son-in-law had just died.

A ninth century collective apparition proper was recorded in *Old English Martyrology*, in which the simultaneous deaths of Sicilian martyr St. Vitus and former patriarch of Jerusalem Modestus were marked by a "public vision" of their ascent.[46] It is said that as an angel led both Vitus and Modestus into the vicinities of the River Siler, "Christians there watched their souls fly to heaven like doves, which were whiter than snow."

There is a reference in the life of the Franciscan St. Anthony to a vision of passing souls that he himself had witnessed.[47] He saw a towering figure reaching for the clouds, allowing some souls to pass as opposed to letting others fall. Of interest is that this vision was brought to Anthony's attention by an unnamed brother, who himself was clearly a witness to the spectacle of passing souls at the same time.

A somewhat dark account given by Caesarius involved a woman who asked a priest, "O Sir what will become of the concubines of priests?" He, knowing the woman to be of an apparently "simple nature," replied playfully, "They can never be saved unless they pass through a burning furnace." This woman later hurled herself into a flaming furnace and died. At that hour, there was a group nearby outside her house who saw a snow-white dove come forth from the chimney of the furnace and pass away into the sky in a flood of light.[48]

From Gregory's dialogues comes a more traditional collective account in which a group of religious men and another of "great credit" were sailing from Sicily to Rome.[49] While they were in the middle of the ocean, they both "beheld the soul of a certain servant of God carried to heaven, who had been an anchoret in the land of Samnium." Soon after making landfall in that same place and making inquiries, they discovered that the man had died and departed this world on the very same day upon which they saw their visions.

Again of St. Benedict, it is written that one night in 541 CE, he was watching at his window and praying when he saw a great light and the soul of Germanus, bishop of Capua, being carried up to heaven, and he learned later that at that same hour the bishop had died.[50] Servandus, a deacon and abbot of a monastery in Campania, was visiting Monte Cassino at that time and was in a room in the tower of the monastery just below that was occupied by the saint. When Benedict saw the vision, he called Servandus so that the latter might be a witness to the marvelous sight. Servandus came but saw only a little part of the great light. Benedict sent word to Capua and found that Germanus had died at the moment of the vision.

The following 1856 account comes from a group of Maori men who were on a hunt.[51] They were seated at night in the open air around a blazing fire, talking over the events of the day. Soon after, they saw the figure of a relative, who had been left ill at home, approaching. The apparition appeared to "two of the party only" and vanished immediately upon their surprised exclamations. When they returned to the village, they inquired about the sick man and found that he had died about the time he was said to have been seen.

A Mr. Justice Norman of the Calcutta High Court saw his mother while sitting in court one day, although "others saw her too."[52] A few hours later, he received a telegram informing him of her death at the moment when he had seen her in court. This was in broad daylight, and he had "no idea of her condition."

Similarly we read in an Irish memorate of a former Dean of Cashel (in Country Tipperary) who was staying with a friend in Dublin.[53] One day they were engaged in needlework in a front room when they heard the gate opening and saw an elderly gentleman they knew coming up the path. As he approached the door, they both exclaimed, "Oh, how good of him to come and see us!" As he was not shown into the sitting room, one of them rang the bell and said to the maid when she appeared, "You have not let Mr. So-and-So in; he is at the door for some little time." The maid went to the hall door and found no one there. The next day, they learned that he had died just at the hour that they had seen him coming up the path.

As with all of our accounts, they may be found either filling the pages of folklorists or in the most legendary of tales. Returning to the Icelandic *Njal's Saga*, Svan was driven ashore while fishing by a great storm, and he and his men were soon lost.[54] The fishermen back at Kalback, however, said they all saw him seem to enter a hill at Kalbackshorn around the same time.

Centuries later, former Icelandic Professor Emeritus of Psychology Erlendur Haraldsson gave the interesting case of a nationally renowned Scandinavian lawyer from 1939.[55] While coming home from a dance, he saw a woman wearing a shawl walking towards him. The informant bid her a good morning but got no reply, soon becoming anxious as she seemed to be following him. When he arrived home, she had "disappeared," but his brother woke up and said, "What is this old woman doing here? Why is this old woman with you?" The following day they spoke about it, and their father noted, "That is strange, around three o'clock this morning old Vigga died." The figure looked exactly like her.

At the very moment British lawyer, politician, and legal reformer Sir Samuel Romilly, anguished at the death of his wife, cut his own throat in 1818, Lord Grey, and his son-in-law, Sir Charles Wood, walking on the ramparts of Carlisle, saw a man pass them, return, then pass them again. They both exclaimed that it was the image of Samuel Romilly.[56]

A young Oraon lived in the village of Harti-Tangar Noa-toli in the Barway Pargana of the Ranchi District in Eastern India.[57] His parents-in-law always rebuked him for his laziness, so he resolved to leave the house and asked his wife to bring him his *ghilnsi* (waist-string). As soon as his wife put out her hand to take it, a cobra bit her, and she died. Neighbors assembled after hearing the wailings of the family. One of the neighbors exclaimed, "I have just seen the very couple with a bullock on the boundary of the village." Hearing this, they all proceeded to the boundary of the village and saw the two walking hand-in-hand with a bullock in front of them. Although it is not specified in the tale, it seems the man may have killed himself in order to join his wife.

Another interesting collective apparition comes from the incredibly rich folklore of Edward Island off the Canadian coast.[58] In 1858, a captain on his way to the stables heard the tolling of a bell. It seemed to come from the St. James Church belfry so he headed there. At the door appeared three women in white who seemed to take no notice of him, all soon disappearing from sight. An acquaintance came along just then, and they unlocked the door intending to follow the figures, but they were gone. That very afternoon, the steamer boat *Fairy Queen* went down in the Northumberland Strait. Several had drowned, including women who had been members of that very church.

Recorded by French explorer and writer Adolphe d'Assier was the case of one Madame D., who was still a young girl at the time and shared a bed with her elder sister.[59] One evening, to her "amazement," she saw a priest by the fire at night who looked exactly like one of their uncles. She brought it to the attention of her sister, who also recognized the form. The next morning, a letter was received informing them that their uncle had died the previous evening.

At the 1893 sinking of the HMS *Victoria* of Britain's royal navy, two guests staying at a Lady Tyron's house in Eaton while she entertained them were both surprised to see what they thought was her husband simply walk across the room without saying a single word.[60] Knowing he was in the Mediterranean, it happened that he had already been drowned at the moment they saw him.

Folklorist and historian Ernest Marwick, who refers to such stories on the Orkney Islands as *foregings*, gives an account from there in which some children saw a woman they clearly recognized standing in the water with a child in her arms.[61] According to Marwick, at almost the very same time this occurred, that woman died in childbirth.

In what Scottish explorer and fur trader Alexander Mackenzie called a "very remarkable instance of supernatural vision" in an 1877 issue of *The Celtic Magazine*, we read that on a certain evening on the island of Skye in Scotland's Inner Hebrides, a large party had been invited to enjoy New Year's festivities at a neighbor's house.[62] At some point after dinner, the figure of a lady was seen gliding along the side wall of the room, from end to end, observed by "several of those opposite it." "My mother! My mother!" screamed one of the young ladies of the family, who then fainted. The vision brought a sudden end to the festivities, and apparently "the most surprising fact was that, at the very time of the vision's appearance, the lady of the house had died in a city in the south."

In all times, the pages of the folklorist brim with these accounts. Of the more modern kind, Gillian Bennet had a story that she called a "neat example of the type" from Manchester at the end of the First World War in which the informant's husband appeared in the bedroom of his sister while her fiancé was there.[63] Both saw the apparition "as plainly as anything in his uniform" before finding he had died at the same time.

From the folklore of Wiltshire in southwest England, a prolific author of that region, Ralph Whitlock, was given an example from around 1946 in which an old man, Joshua Cowdry, went to Devizes Hospital, and one afternoon, multiple of his neighbors were surprised to see him walk up his garden path and go into his cottage.[64] Later, they learned that he had died in the hospital at the same time as he had appeared to them,

Margaret Coffin relayed a similar American memorate, a type that she too calls "rather common," in which some people were getting ready to receive a guest from out of town.[65] At one point, they saw her walking down the street carrying her suitcase and dressed for the train trip she would have just finished. They waited expectantly for a knock on the door, but it never came. What did come was a message that the would-be guest had died earlier that day.

From the truly rich body of supernatural folklore from Illinois, an informant told folklorist Harry Middleton Hyatt of something that, at the time of writing in 1935, apparently occurred "years ago."[66] The informant went to get water, but when he got there, he saw his mistress's sister in her nightgown sitting on the crossboard over the well. He dropped his basket and ran back to his house, knowing from this token that his mistress' sister must be dead. He, his mistress, and his master returned to the well, and all saw the form there. That day, word came that she had died, just as our informant suspected.

In an earlier account from that state, we read of the son of a clergyman who was playing on the floor with his father when he suddenly pointed to the ceiling and said, "Dada, look there!" The man looked up and saw, with "perfect clearness," his own father looking back at him. The author noted that "a comparison of times showed that this was three hours before the death of the elder father in Kentucky.[67]

In West Virginia, as recorded by that region's premier folklorist, Ruth Anne Musick, a man and his son went to hoe out a neighbor's corn field as he was quite ill.[68] After stopping for a drink in the shade, one of them suddenly said, "Look, there comes Ef in his shirttail." Ef came onto the spring, laid down on his stomach, and then seemed to vanish. Both men stared before one of them finally said, "Ef will not get well. That was a token of his death." When they returned home, they found that Ef had died in the middle of the afternoon, just when they saw him drink. Folklorist Ruth Ann Musick noted later, as do most folklorists collecting memorates of this kind, "I have pages more of these token-tales, at least five times as many more as these given here."[69]

In Arizona, a Mr. B and several friends were sitting on the front porch one summer evening.[70] As darkness fell, they saw a man walking along the road and soon recognized him to be a neighbor who had left for Texas to get work. The next day, notice came that he had been killed in an automobile accident.

Having just recently arrived at their new home after leaving her father in Washington, a mother and her fifteen-year-old daughter were therefore greatly surprised to see him standing in their new house one day.[71] "Why Dad, when did you get here?" she exclaimed. At that point, her daughter turned around, and she, too, saw the figure of her grandfather, his hand apparently raised in some sort of gesture, before he slowly faded away. Shortly afterward, they received the news that he had died.

Some of the best-known of all apparition accounts are of this kind, and we will end here with a couple. We can mention "Old Booty's Ghost," a popular story in its time which recalls some of Caesarius's accounts.[72] An 1867 entry in the journal of a Captain Spinks gives an account in which that captain and his men were sailing to the Isle of Luciera. He and his crewmates went ashore, and soon, to their surprise, they saw two men run by quickly. Captain Barnaby remarked, "Lord bless me, the foremost man looks like my next-door neighbor, old Booty." He was dressed in gray clothes, and another was behind him in black. They were both seen running into the burning mountain in the midst of the flames, upon which they heard a "terrible noise, too horrible to be described." Barnaby and his men then looked at their watches, penned down the time in their pocket books, and entered it in the journals. When they made landfall back in England, they found that Old Booty had died during the time they were at sea.

Famously too, from 1694—though again more impressive in this broader context—a Mr. Brown's phantom appeared to both his sister and her maid in London's Fleet Street around the time he was killed far off in Herefordshire.[73]

◆

If, as we have seen, apparitions and visions that appear to the individual might greatly impact them and those around them, apparitions and visions at the moment of death that occur with multiple witnesses are perhaps of even greater evidentiary value to the community or those individuals involved. The fact that they are so frequently cited in the lives of the saints may speak to this understanding. They are widely found among the work of both parapsychologists and particularly folklorists and continue to be recorded in numbers.

NINE

Alcyone's Tradition and the Veridical Appearance of Apparitions

There are very frequently other circumstances accompanying the appearance, which not only show the form to be spectral, but also make known to the seer the nature of the death that has taken place.

CATHERINE CROWE

From some of the most ancient written and literary sources up to the present, apparitions of the dead and of the dying have sometimes conveyed the particular manner of their deaths. These forms frequently include not only wounds but also details such as facial hair changes since the subject last saw the object of the vision or even the exact garments worn at the time of death. When employed by artists and authors, the meaning of these apparitions has regularly been debated; however, little heed has been paid to their ongoing and impressively documented analogues.

Regarding the spectres and shades of antiquity, Professor of Ancient History at the University of Exeter Daniel Ogden wrote that the appearance of apparitions often reflects the state of their bodies at death.[1]

Examples of this include the murdered Tlepolemus from *The Golden Ass* appearing to his wife with a bloodstained visage and the shade of Sychaeus in the *Aenid* specifically pointing out the dagger wounds he had suffered when revealing his murderer.[2]

In Ovid's *Fasti* the gory ghost of Dido herself appears dramatically covered in blood with filthy hair.[3] During one of her famous visions, Dinocrates crawled out of the darkness in front of his sister, the early Christian martyr Perpetua, bearing the wound on his face from which he died.[4]

One of the earliest instances of wounds being observed on unknown deceased persons came when Odysseus famously sacrificed two sheep, spilling their blood so that he might bring forth the souls of the underworld. Those shades "gathered, stirring out of Erebos, brides and young men, and men grown old in pain, and tender girls whose hearts were new to grief; many were there, too, torn by brazen lanceheads, battle-slain, bearing still their bloody gear."[5]

So famously too, the ghostly form of Shakespeare's Lord Banquo appeared "gory in death," bearing his wounds during a banquet.[6]

From the Norse sagas, we are spoiled with examples. The revenants of the frozen north, where deaths at sea were so common and where the closure of a body found and buried was never guaranteed, seemed particularly willing to appear in this manner. When the maid of Sigrun, the Valkyrie of Norse mythology, saw the shade of the saga hero Helgi among a throng of other warriors visiting his own gravestone, she noted that "his wounds bled ever because of their tears."[7] As an interesting aside, the sagas also often represented future wounds in dreams—wounds that the dreamer was later to suffer, represented in varying symbolic ways.[8]

On the opposite side of the planet, among the Tucano of the Northwest Amazon, it is believed that the victims of bloody murders are doomed to stand forever outside their dead-spirit house (otherworldly abode), with blood continually flowing from the wounds that had killed them, while further north in Jamaica ghosts were often likely to appear "just as they were put in the grave."[9] As far away as Melanesia, too, a ghost revealing itself to a person walking alone in the forest frequently appeared in the state in which it had died.[10] Iwasaka noted a certain group of Japanese Buddhists who believe that the ghost of a recently deceased person can be seen going to a particular temple "in the everyday clothing that he wore when he died."[11]

While a clearly dramatic touch for the legendary or literary ghost, such accounts were far more widely recorded than the epics of antiquity and their predecessors, and importantly, they continue to be. Of particular interest and concern to us here are those apparitions which display the manner of their death at a time when the person encountering them was unaware they had died and therefore unable to have known the details of their death, including clothing or wounds, etc. These tales hence provide a powerfully veridical corroboration. These are less represented in antiquity and relatively less common when set against apparitions generally, though they have nevertheless been recorded in impressive numbers in the last two hundred years or so and are notably represented in many of the most well-remembered memorates and traditions. Furthermore, where they do appear in older and particularly Roman sources, they are some of the better-known shades. These constitute the continuation of a greatly mysterious phenomenon, one with an impressive legacy and even a very particular capacity to impress the experiencer and the reader.

PORTENTOUS DISPLAYS, TRADITIONS, AND AGE

That apparitions sometimes display the manner of their death or other aspects of their appearance to those who have no way of knowing their situation is one of the more compelling and well-established veridical elements of these encounters. In fact, in certain recent cases, the percipients' reports of the apparitions' appearances were found to more accurately reflect the cause of their deaths than what had initially been assumed or known by the attending investigators. As opposed to those ancient sources which might reference a more magical or mythical context, many of these are impressively, robustly, and soberly documented. One example was given by Gurney, Myers and Podmore.[12] The mother of a lieutenant in the army dreamed, on the night of the storming of the Redan, that her son was wounded in the left arm. The subsequent newspaper account described him as having been severely injured in the right arm, but his mother persisted in her view that the dream was correct, and it proved later to have been so: it was indeed the left arm that had been injured.

Rather than pertaining specifically to wounds or ailments, the idea that the appearance of the apparition in a general sense relates to whether or not its presence means death and what manner often turns up in traditions around the globe. Perhaps most famously, in the highlands of Scotland, Scottish folklorist John Gregorson Campbell tells us that "the manner in which the apparition was clothed afforded an indication to the skilful seer of the fate then befalling, or about to befall, the person whose taibhs it was. If the apparition was dressed in the dead-clothes, the person was to die soon."[13]

In a later, and far more specific description, Norman Macrae tells us that "if a man's fatal end be hanging, they'll see a gibbet, or a rope about his neck; if beheaded, they'll see the man without a head; if drowned, they'll see water up to his throat; if unexpected death, they'll see a winding-sheet about his head; all which are represented to their view."[14] Similarly, in the North East of Scotland, to dream of seeing one smeared with blood is looked upon as a warning that an accident is either about to occur or that death has already occurred.[15]

When the likes of Gregor and Macrae wrote these words, it was at a time of high intellectual interest in Scottish second sight, though even then most serious scholars realized that these were not capacities or experiences relegated to those highlands, however strongly they may have seemed to exist there. Macrae, then, was in fact speaking very pointedly, if incidentally, to a most ancient idea. From Apuleius's second century CE *Metamorphoses*, we read that a miller's daughter, who lived in a village near where the suicidal death by hanging of her father had occurred, arrived at the scene in mourning, tearing her disordered hair and beating her breast.[16] She already knew the whole story, but not from just any messenger; her father's ghost had appeared to her in a dream (occurring just after the time of his death)—with the noose around his neck.

Thousands of years later, in rural Finland, a certain person fell asleep during the day and dreamed of a neighbor, Antti, wearing his best shirt and a black beret.[17] It was found that, at that same moment, Antti had hanged himself while wearing those very clothes. In Polynesia, the native peoples of Kiwai have a name for the spirit of one who has hanged themselves: the *iviboro*, which appears carrying a rope around their neck.[18] These accounts are, again, found in both legend and memorate, each sometimes influencing the other at different times. Thus from a journal of North Carolina folklore comes *The Dream That Hanged a Man*, a story widely known in the county where it happened and surrounding areas.[19] While sleeping, a man named Reid Quinn saw a vision of a girl dressed in black, her head hanging against her chest. Quinn fell back to sleep but was soon revisited by the vision, this time the girl pleading with him to "stop them," which woke him up. He felt he knew her but couldn't be sure. Having attempted to calm down and laugh the matter off, he fell asleep again, but again she appeared. This time Quinn recognized her as Kathy Richards, his former pupil. "Mr. Quinn," she said, "I beg you, sir; you must hurry. My husband killed me; he broke my neck; and I shall be buried soon. No one will ever know I was murdered if you don't stop them." Quinn quickly dressed and rode off in the darkness. It was mid-morning when he arrived at the home of the girl's parents, but there was no one there. A neighbor explained: "They're burying Kathy Fever. Don't reckon that they'll even open the casket." When he caught the procession and the coffin was opened, they saw that the girl's neck had been broken and the prints were on her back, just as the apparition had told.

For a much older account, Claude de Tisserant, author of *A History of Prodigies*, wrote that the wife of one of the chiefs of the Provinces Parliament, somewhere around 1555, dreamed that her husband was executed, which, it turned out, he actually had been, in another city.[20] She had awoken to the image of her husband with his head cut off and bloody.

WATERY GRAVES AND SHIMMERING SHADES

Perhaps no kind of death is as widely represented in these encounters as those of persons killed at sea. Daniels spoke to this regarding particular

North German traditions of Grongers, the ghosts of people who have been buried at sea and come to the most distant parts of the Earth to warn their friends and loved ones of their death, appearing "at twilight in wet clothes."[21] The idea that the apparition might appear in a manner that clearly suggests a watery death can be found in traditions across the globe. There is, however, a far older example that seems not to previously been referenced in relation both to the crisis apparition and regarding the extent to which it reflects the same kinds of encounters which were to come later.

From the depths of Greek mythology we find Ceyx, ruler of Thessaly, who, after dying at sea, appeared to Alcyone, his lover, with water "dripping from his locks and beard," just as did the saga revenants, the Celtic wraiths, and even the Polynesian spectres.[22] While it has sometimes been suggested that this element was later added by Ovid for a specific narrative purpose, it becomes clear that apparitions of this sort have long appeared and continue to appear far and wide.[23] Scholars, in fact, often seem entirely unaware that parapsychological and folkloric material contains hundreds of basically indistinguishable cases.

As the tale goes, then, Ceyx, perturbed by events in his kingdom since Apollo transformed his brother into a hawk, decided to seek out the oracle of Delphi. Despite the pleading of his wife, Alcyone, not to make the trip, Ceyx nonetheless took to the seas. Every night afterward, Alcyone would pray for her husband's safe return, which tragically was never to be, at least not in living form, as Ceyx's ship was destroyed in a terrible storm. In the words of Fantham, "Ceyx did indeed die in that storm, but Alcyone, not knowing that her husband was dead, continued to pray to Hera."[24] Hera later decided that Alcyone should know of the death of Ceyx, and so she dispatched Iris to Hypnos in order that the news could be passed on in a dream. This came in the form of the man's apparition, dripping and clearly indicating the manner of Ceyx's death, providing one of the earliest examples of an apparition displaying the manner of death to someone who did not know of their passing.

Relatedly, in the oldest cultural travel guide that there is, *The*

Description of Greece by Pausanias, written between the 150s and 170s CE, the author describes a painting depicting ghosts in the underworld, in which the Greek mythological hero lesser Ajax, who had drowned, is shown in the "color of a drowned man with sea salt still on his skin."[25]

While we might more easily look to the anecdotal wraiths of English novelist and playwright Catherine Crowe and find a number of apparitions presenting similarly, dripping, indicating a drowning, or to the annals of the Society for Psychical Research, where so many were also documented, here instead we come to an account recorded in a nineteenth century Chinese newspaper of a man who met his death in a collision between the steamers *Fusing* and *Ocean*.[26] This man's ghost appeared to his wife, who was living in Soochow, streaming and dripping with water from head to foot. If it wasn't clear from his presentation, he told her that, unfortunately, he had drowned. He also stated that he had sent a certain friend some money for her use before he took passage in the *Fusing* and that the friend would arrive with it shortly. The wife was left in a state of bewilderment and did not exactly know what to make of it. A day or two later, the friend named John actually came with the packet, his arrival shortly followed by the intelligence of the *Fusing*'s disaster.

Scottish metaphysical writer and philosopher James Frennier gave an experience of his own. He heard it that on a stormy night, an old gentleman was sick in bed, and an officer was reading to him. That old man's fishing boat was out at sea, and he several times expressed concern for his people. Suddenly he had cried out, "The boat is lost." The Colonel asked how he could know this. "I see two boatmen, who carry a third drowned; they stream with water, and now place him close beside your chair." That night, the fishermen returned with the dead body of their comrade.[27]

These kinds of encounters are remembered in one version of an old and popular folk ballad of American origin, *Lowlands Away*, where the singer dreams their love is "drowned and dead," noting that he was "green and wet with weeds so cold." One of the common refrains among these versions is that the protagonist "now knows" that their lover is dead. This was apparently a shanty known to every sailor down to the time of the China Clippers.[28] The dead lover appearing in the night to the sailor, or they themselves to their loved ones at home, is a ubiquitous theme.

The apparition coming to the individual is not the only way in which the information is discovered; clairvoyant viewing of the scene itself often furnishes similar details. In his own very early work on apparitions, Ferriar gives us a case from the middle of the preceding century, around 1750, in the north of Scotland, in which an officer was quartered in near the castle of a gentleman supposedly gifted with second sight.[29] One stormy night, the latter, while confined to his bed, expressed great anxiety for the safety of his fishing boat, then at sea, and at last he exclaimed, "My boat is lost!" "How do you know it?" said the stranger. "I see two of the boatmen," he replied, "bringing in the third drowned and all dripping wet, and laying him down close by your chair." In the course of the night, the fishermen returned with the corpse of the drowned man.

An account from 1763 involved a woman named Elizabeth, who had been interviewed by the founder of the Methodist movement, John Wesley, who gave multiple related accounts.[30] She told him that her brother George Hobson, who was, she noted, "a good young man," set out on a sea voyage as a member of a ship's crew. The vessel sailed just before the Christian feast of Michaelmas. "The day after Michaelmas-day, about midnight," she went on, "I saw him standing by my bedside, surrounded with a glorious light, and looking earnestly at me. He was wet all over. That night the ship in which he sailed, split upon a rock, and all the crew were drowned."

Traditionally, seeing features such as dripping water upon a figure was often the final straw for the individual in assuming this might indeed be a revenant or a wraith. In the *Laxdaela Saga*, we read of Gudrun's vision. After arriving at a church ground and coming up towards the doors, she sees men standing outside; she immediately recognizes them as her husband and his crew, but does not at first realize that they are dead.[31] Gudrun doesn't begin to suspect this until she notices the water dripping from their clothes. This is her tip-off.

When it is revealed that her husband and his man had not arrived home from an errand to Bjarney Island, Gudrun becomes almost certain of the deaths, which are finally confirmed by those who witnessed it from both the mainland and the island itself.

While often it might be presented with something of a fearful or dramatic backdrop, death at sea was nevertheless considered a good death in Iceland and other sea-bound regions, such as certain Polynesian islands. One account from the Icelandic "days of yore" describes a king who, having bid farewell to his children, set sail out of the country on important business.[32] Later, his ship and crew were caught up in a wicked and unprecedented hurricane, which tragically killed them all. The king's son, Sigurdr, is said to have dreamed that very same night that his father came "all wet into the bower," took off his crown, which he laid at Sigurdr's feet in what seems a relevant symbolic gesture, and soon silently departed. Sigurdr told his sister this dream, and they both grew sure of their father's fate.

A similar case was narrated by one Archdeacon Farler, who, one night in 1868, saw a friend of his, a fellow student, sitting at the foot of his bed, dripping water.[33] Realizing it was a hallucination, Farler told the family with whom he was staying in Somerset what he had seen, and a few days later they heard that his friend had drowned while swimming off the Kent coast.

FOLK AND LORE, GHOULS AND GORE

While Dinocrates had so famously pointed out his wounds to Perpetua, she had already known that he was dead; Cambrensis, in his famed Welsh chronicle, noted that on the very night that Welsh Bishop Morien Ap Morgeneu was killed in the year 999 by Danish pirates, he showed himself in a vision to a bishop in Ireland, pointing to his wounds and telling him, "because I ate flesh, I am become flesh."[34] It should also be noted that in Cicero's famous accounts from Megara, one presented in a previous chapter, the apparition there also pointed out their wounds at a time when the observer was unaware of their death.

In 1128, William Clito, former count of Flanders, while engaged in battle, was wounded by a pike.[35] Within five days, his arm swelled and became gangrenous, leading to his death. It is said that his aged and blind father, Duke Robert, while prisoner in England, awoke from a dream in which a soldier appeared to him, wounded his own arm with a pike, and explained that his son was thus slain.

Chemistry professor and author William Gregory gave a comparable account from decades before they had been collected in numbers.[36] A certain gentleman of "rank and property" in Scotland had served in the army of the Duke of York in Flanders in his youth. He was staying one night in the same tent as two other officers, one of whom had been sent out on service. During that officer's absence, this man, while in bed, saw the figure of his absent friend sitting on the vacant bed. He called to his companion, who also saw the figure, which soon spoke to them, telling them that he had "just been killed at a certain place," and pointed to his wound. He then went on to make certain requests of them. The next day, it appeared that the officer had been shot, in the manner and at the time and place he had told them.

Much earlier, Sacheverell gave an account related to the 1690 Battle of the Boyne. There, a young boy spoke frequently to two people only he could see, who informed him on various matters. One day he came and told Captain Stevenson that one of the two came with his hand bloody and said he had been in a battle in Ireland.[37] The captain marked the day, and though they had no news for nearly a month after that, it]corresponded "exactly" with the time Colonel Woolsley had given the Irish a considerable defeat.

Somewhat more obscurely, when the dead Heraclius, Eastern Roman emperor from 610 to 641, appeared to a certain Bertrand, who at the time was deathly ill, he bore the "jagged" wound which had been the cause of his death on the battlefield.[38]

In the Icelandic *Svarfdæla Saga*, Klaufi, a powerful man brought from Norway to Iceland as a child, was killed by the sons of Asgeir; his head was chopped off and laid down beside his own feet.[39] The next evening after this, and far away, while Karl the Red, Klaufi's foster father, was sitting by a fire with his followers, they heard something scraping on the house, followed by the voice of Klaufi. One man pointed out that it sounded like him and suggested he may be in trouble. Stepping outside, they saw Klaufi, his head in his hand, presenting himself just as he had been killed, displaying not just the fact of the death but the manner.

From *The Saga of Gunnlaug the Worm-Tongue*, we read again that Raven kills Gunnlaug by driving a sword into his head and leaving a great wound.[40] Before this news came to Iceland, Illugi the Black dreamed that Gunnlaug came to him, all bloody. This was expressed in verse as follows:

> *Knew I of the hewing*
> *Of Raven's hilt-finned steelfish*
> *Byrny, shearing, sword-edge*
> *Sharp clave leg of Raven.*
> *Of warm wounds drank the eagle,*
> *When the war-rod slender,*
> *Cleaver of the corpses,*
> *Clave the head of Gunnlaug.*

Long after those old sagas, similar encounters were still being collected in those same lands. In a later Icelandic tale, a farmer appeared to his lover in a dream, all covered in blood and terribly bruised.[41] He told her straightforwardly of his condition: "Thus I have been dealth with." Later, a search party found the man, just as his appearance had indicated, bruised and torn beneath the sheer cliffs.

Far more recently, this time again in Finland, a North Karelian informant had a dream in which she saw her brother in a big open place with a lot of soldiers.[42] The brother's right leg was broken at an angle, which corresponded to what had actually happened to him.

We read something very similar from the African Bambara, an ethnic Mandé group native to much of West Africa, relayed by Parrinder.[43] A workman named Agosu, the younger brother of Dansu, was sent away from the informant's farm. Several days later, on the way to Porto Novo, the farmer overtook Dansu, the elder brother, who was walking slowly and limping on his left foot. The following week, the farmer returned to the village where the brothers lived and discovered that Agosu's brother had died some time before. He was also told that Dansu had suffered from a bad left foot and had not stirred from his bed for two months. From another time and place, on a night in late July 1813, the Duchess of Abrantes awoke and saw distinctly, near her bed, her husband, Marshal Junot, who was in Geneva, dressed in the same grey coat he had worn on the day of his departure; his face was pale and profoundly sad.[44] According to the Duchess, "what terrified me most was to see the apparition walking round my bed, and yet—heavens!—one of its legs was broken." Junot, as it happened, was depressed by the defeat of his army in Spain and by Napoleon's consequent coolness towards him. He had gone to stay at his father's house, and in his depression, he had thrown himself out of a window, breaking his leg.

From Bennett's 1987-published British sample, her informant, Phyllis, reported that in a dream, she saw her brother with his leg all shriveled.[45] Soon she discovered her brother had died in the war (presumably World War 1 or World War II) after his leg was wounded on a landmine.

A more recent account in which the manner of the apparition's death is made apparent and which was particularly well documented, comes again from the late and brilliant Erlandur Haraldsson's seminal work *The Departed Among the Living*. Like his Scandinavian peer Virtinan, Haraldsson was not at all shy about making direct comparisons between the contemporary apparitional experiences he and his colleagues had so assiduously studied and those of his own Iceland's rich and still greatly untapped folklore.[46] He gives the account of Jacob, a sanitorium patient, as told by someone who had worked with patients there for years.[47] She often tried to brighten his day, as he frequently got depressed. One day she told Jacob that he should come to visit her because he came from the same village as herself and her husband, and they would enjoy talking about the people from there. He said "yes" to that and was glad, and she said to him, "You promise to come tomorrow." "Yes, yes, I promise," he said. That night, this woman woke up and felt like all her strength had been taken away from her. She was unable to move, when suddenly she saw the bedroom door open and there stood Jacob, his face all covered with blood. She looked at this for some time, unable to speak or move. Then he disappeared, and the informant felt as if he had closed the door behind him. She awoke her husband and told him, "I can swear that something has happened at the sanatorium." She telephoned in the morning and asked if everything was all right with Jacob. "No," said the nurse, "he committed suicide last night."

The author goes on to note that: "our percipient hadn't known about the manner of death, which was later confirmed to the investigators by her husband along with the details of her account." The authors later followed up on the postmortem report of Jacob, having successfully identified him, and concluded that the report declared the cause of death as suicidum submergio, that is, suicide by drowning. In the report, it is written that he was seriously injured, with "two large cuts on the head and the skull is very badly broken." This fit the percipient's description of the manner of death.

British physician and writer Charles J. S. Thompson gives a Japanese account and notes that "the ghosts of Japan are much the same as those seen in similar conditions in western lands."[30] A woman fell into a river on a dark and moonless night and drowned. As her son lay dozing at home, he felt a tugging at his hand and thought the touch felt like his mother's hand. After calling his father, they both saw that the boy's hand was covered in blood. The woman's body was discovered the next morning, and it was found that she had made a wild grab at a stone or tree while falling, tearing her hand open before she drowned.

In Taichung, Western Taiwan, there is an interesting and previously referenced case in which someone went to the Sheng Ming Temple and, as soon as they walked in, saw a man standing under the black temple flag with blood stains on his neck and his head twisted to one side.[49] The man had just died in a car accident somewhere far off.

In 1863, and in an "unusually well-documented" case, the Belgian noblewoman Baroness de Boisléve gave a dinner to, among others, General Fleury, Master of the Horse to Emperor Napoleon III, and two judges.[50] Her son, Honoré, was in the expeditionary force in Mexico.

At nine one evening, when she went to the drawing room to see if the coffee was ready, she gave a loud cry and fainted. She had "seen" her son, she explained when she recovered, in his uniform but without his cap; his face was "a spectral pallor" and from his left eye, "now a hideous hole, a trickle of blood flowed over his cheek." A week later, the news came that Honoré had indeed been killed by a bullet through his left eye at the same time as the apparition.

English writer, philosopher, and clergyman Joseph Glanvill gives an account from around 1690 in which, after a Mr. Bower was found murdered near a highway outside the English town of Guildford, his throat slit, two men were arrested and imprisoned.[51] That night, a third prisoner, who "knew nothing" of the murder, saw a ghostly figure enter his cell with a "great gash cross his throat, almost ear to ear, and a wound down his breast." Regarding these wounds and the man himself, it was later said that he "could not have given a more exact description" of the man who had died.

Speaking rather explicitly to apparitions of this kind, in the Icelandic *Eyrbyggja Saga*, Thorod famously entered a banquet hall with his men all soaked through.[52] Thorir Wood-leg and his men followed, all six of them covered in dirt. They sat down by the fires and started to wring out their clothes. Those who died at sea were dripping; those who died on land were covered in soil. While the authors of *Islanders and Water-Dwellers* speculate that this particular aspect might have been influenced by folk legends, other accounts bear similar characteristics, such as this much later memorate recorded by St. Clair in Ulster, Northern Ireland.[53] In 1954, St. Clair's elderly informant told of a childhood friend of hers, Billy, who died at the Battle of the Somme in 1916. They had grown up together, and Billy joined up when the war came. One evening, the informant saw a young man in a uniform coming across the pasture outside. She knew Billy at once and was surprised to see him, as she hadn't even heard that he'd returned home. When she opened the door, however, no one was there. She went around the house, inside and out, but could not find him, soon realizing this was likely some kind of omen. She relayed to St. Clair that the apparition had mud on his uniform. A few days later, news came that Billy had been killed while digging a trench, which collapsed, and the informant noted, "I dare say that's why the mud was on him, for he was always neat and tidy."

While St. Clair's elderly Ulster informant had noted this incidentally, she too was speaking to a phenomenon which, in its age and ubiquity, is anything but. Early Islamic convert Salma Umm al-Khayr recorded that the sixth wife of the Islamic prophet Muhammad, Umm Salima, had seen the "apostle of God in a dream with dust on his head and beard."[54] This man told her in her dream that he had just witnessed the murder of Al Husay, one of Muhammad's grandsons. "They computed the day and found that he was slain on that day," during the Battle of Karbala; he had died in the sand.

Apparitions related to deaths which occurred much longer ago may also display similarly. While these could easily take up their own volumes, one such encounter was reported to have happened to a 23-year-old English miner named Stephen Dimbleby in 1982.[55] During his night shift, Stephen saw a figure wearing an old-fashioned helmet but with no eyes, nose, or mouth. Later he found that a miner had been killed in the same tunnel fourteen years earlier, having been trapped in a coal-cutting machine that presumably had removed his face.

◆

Scholars theorizing upon the literary or otherwise suitably dramatic use of these apparition types generally fail to note they are describing an actual and long-established phenomenon. The fact that the apparitions of the dead and the dying demonstrate the manner of their passing in their appearance is widely attested. In legend, lyric, and lore, this has been a particularly convincingly veridical element and lends another unique kind of credence to the experience itself, both in the eyes of the beholder and in the minds of those who might later be told. There may, however, be no more convincing kind of account, either for those undergoing them or others attending, than those which occur during near-death and related experiences. These fascinating variants will be the subject of our next and final chapter.

TEN

Revelations Near Death and Journeys to Heaven and Hell

Experiences which men have had or which they have only thought they have had, accounts which are set down in good faith or consciously as fiction or as forgeries, and narratives written in the mood of burlesque or satire, are all grist to our mill. They all offer elements that show the tradition of Otherworld motifs, and nearly always they may have served to make a contribution in this way to literary works of a wholly different type. Moreover, they may also contain details that come ultimately from ancient sources.

HOWARD ROLLIN PATCH

The discovery of another person's death has sometimes occurred during a near-death experience or otherwise visionary visits to paradisical and purgatorial realms. It is common that during such out-of-body journeys the souls of deceased persons are encountered. Sometimes the intrepid traveler might be surprised, however, to find someone there whom they thought was alive and well at the time, later discovering that person had really died while they were away. These account types have more recently been filed under the term "Peak in Darien" experience.*

From the myths and legends of antiquity to the poems and prose of the Middle Ages, from the lives of the mystics and shamans to those tales told later by psychonauts or to physicians in emergency rooms, the otherworld has been and remains a very much attainable destination. While that "undiscovered country" has been the subject of much waxing and waning scholarly attention, very little has been written regarding these "Peak in Darien" and related experiences. The celebrated medieval visionary literature contains a number of particularly striking encounters in which both vague references are made to dead persons encountered in the otherworld and far more specific and veridical observations are made of persons unknown to have been dead at the time of the experience, the death then later being confirmed to have taken place during the experience. Indeed, in the greatly influential *Visio Pauli*, the foremost source of otherworld imagery from the Middle Ages, Paul, while out of the body, specifically asks of his guide that he might be brought to see people's souls leave their bodies just as they die. In this way, the notion of discovering a death by such non-ordinary means, so marveled at later by researchers and clinicians, may be said to lie somewhere near the very roots of medieval visionary literature, though as will become apparent, the notion is far older.

Otherworld journeys and near-death accounts, in which accurate information regarding the circumstances of a distant death is acquired and later confirmed, were considered by their protagonists and some of their authors and recorders as being especially worthy of lending legitimacy to the broader experiences themselves, and of course, in turn, any edifying elements later added also benefit. After all, the message that one must make their prayers for the burning sinner in purgatory or conduct themselves in a certain pious or socially acceptable manner is, of course, made far more substantial when the worlds of the ordinary and the extraordinary are seen to connect in this impressive way. The sign,

*See Greyson, *Seeing Dead People Not Known to Have Died*, 159–71, for by far the most comprehensive recent attempt to deal with the topic.

or *apport*, has always been a means by which the visionary confirms his visionary voyage to others. The silver bridle famously returned from the otherworld with St. Brendan in his voyage,* or the types of stigmata visible on the bodies of celebrated saints like Furseus upon their own worldly returns, were held up as proof of their experiences in other worlds.[†]

The famed Carthaginian martyr Perpetua, having drunk milk in paradise, awoke still with the "taste of something sweet" in her mouth.[1] Much further afield, in China, the remaining scents, odors, or tears of the deities they interacted with at night were frequently used to prove their existence,[‡] and in the Pacific, a man from Nganiu, Alofi, went into a trance and was transported aboard a spirit boat, where the spirits gave him a root of kava which he still had in his hand when he returned home.[2] These are common tales on all continents.

While Christian noted that most late medieval apparitions are confirmed by comparable "signs," the particular "Peak in Darien" encounters with which we are concerned have rarely been attended, either in numbers or comparatively, regarding their historical role as something of an "apport" in their own right.[3] This is especially true of the otherworldly journey, as we'll see, but they nevertheless were both (a) a powerful literary tool at the disposal of the monastic and (b) representative of an actual and still ongoing phenomenon.

While attention and the assignment of worth has varied, some scholars are nonetheless aware of the impact of these events historically. Regarding the 824 CE Latin vision of Wetti, for example, historian

---

*See Gardiner, *Visions of Heaven and Hell Before Dante*, 72–103, for the entire story. More specifically, the bridle was seen by Brendan in the otherworld as a possession of the devil, which he is said to have literally woken up in possession of. That the man awakens from a dream with something of the otherworld is a common motif.

† In Furseus's well-known vision as described in Gardiner, *Visions of Heaven and Hell before Dante*, 56, "when he was restored to his body, and throughout his whole life, on his shoulder and jaw he bore the mark of the fire that he had felt in his soul, visible to all men. In an amazing way his flesh publicly showed what the soul had suffered in private."

‡See, for instance, Owen, *The End of the Chinese "Middle Ages,"* 161, 197. Such apports and signs are incredibly common in otherworldly and related narratives across the entirety of Asia.

Eileen Gardiner noted that a particularly interesting aspect of the journey was the author's attempts to verify its truth by "mentioning facts that would not have been known to Wetti but were revealed to him in his vision and then confirmed independently."[4]

This is also apparent in the texts themselves. Gregory the Great noted that it was the fact that a certain man's distant death was discovered by another, Stephen, during his own near-death journey (during which time the body was being prepared for embalment) that proved that the sights and sounds he reported of the other world upon his return were "most true."[5]

Similarly, referring to the otherworld journey of the Monk of Wenlock as recorded by Benedictine monk Boniface, in which King Ceolrod of Mercia was seen there by another, Boniface makes a particular point in demonstrating that multiple pieces of information imparted to the monk while in the otherworld, including a certain woman's location, her sins, the location of another man, and the later actual death of Ceolred, "proved" that what the angels told him was true.[6] This veridical element has long been known.

While Gardiner, with reference to such accounts, referred to literary devices of the kind later "used to excellent dramatic effect by Dante," others such as scholar of religion Carol Zaleski or folklorist Gillian Bennet noted more directly the connection between the "Peak in Darien" experiences recorded by Gregory the Great and those reported to parapsychologists more than a millennium later.[7] The former, in fact, noted that both Gregory and others such as the authors of the vision of Wetti cite the very same kind of evidence pertaining to crisis apparitions as did then modern psychical researchers, although this connection had previously been noted at least as early as 1879.[*]

When the events following provide confirmation regarding the real-world death of a person encountered during our "Peak in Darien"

---

[*]See Lee, *More Glimpses of the World Unseen*, 87, where the author speaks about crisis apparitions appearing in Gregory's Dialogues. A number of other scholars picked up on this connection too, including classicist Lacy Collison-Morley in *Greek and Roman Ghost Stories*, who noted that the accounts recorded by Gregory in his Fouth Dialogues were "curiously like some of those collected by the Society of Psychical Research."

experiences, the potential impact upon the individual and the group is patently clear.

STRANGERS ON THE PEAK

Before exploring some of the more veridically impressive accounts, we should first investigate and establish, particularly for the reader new to literature pertaining to otherworlds, the possibility of encountering strangers and, therefore, persons often previously unknown to have been deceased during such journeys in a more general sense. In this way, we can also get a feel for the otherworld journey as a more general historical entity.

Spanning the chasm of time between those old encounters in the dim lands of Hades and Sheol and other more recent journeys reported and somewhat popularized by near-death experiencers, these accounts are part of an ancient and ongoing legacy of otherworldly and out-of-body journeys in which strangers and shades, sinners and saints, have all been mysteriously encountered. In the ancient Mesopotamian poem *The Epic of Gilgamesh*, the warrior Enkidu, while fading away upon his deathbed, claimed to have just been to the underworld, where he bore witness to the fates of kings, priests, and sages past. This includes, as the reference suggests, some past rulers previously unknown to Enkidu, who so famously said that he "heard about crowned kings who ruled the land from days of old."[8]

In the ancient Indian epic Mahabharata, Kundadhara gives a certain poor Brahmin a vision in which he also sees unnamed kings in hell.[9]

The Zohar Chadash relates the near-death experience of one Rabbi Cruspedai, who, while in another world, similarly reported seeing "departed sages."[10]

The devout Zoroastrian Arda Viraf, while being conducted through otherworlds, saw the souls of certain "pious rulers, and monarchs."[11]

On the rocky and frozen Plains of Hela too, the Teutons would meet lost friends and "ancestors from the earliest years of the world."[12]

In the Icelandic *Viga-Glúms Saga*, the hero has a significant dream in which he sees the god Freyr in company with dead members of his family.[13] Freyr was sitting in a chair beside the river, which ran through Glumr's land, and there was a crowd of people around him. Glumr saw many men on the gravel bank beside the river, and when he asked who they were, the reply came, "We are thy departed kindred."

In an old Hungarian tale, protagonist Mustapha is brought by a guide to a most indescribably pleasant and delightful place where he is shown two great old rulers undergoing punishment, and it is deemed that he should know that they were "old princes, kings, and emperors."[14]

At other times, the forms of both known and unknown deceased are encountered at once. In a Jewish story, for example, the founder of Hasidic Judaism, Rabbi Baal Shem Tov, has a visionary experience of paradise where he meets many souls, "some known to him and some unknown."[15]

In the *Tzava'at Harivash*, an anthology of writings attributed to the Baal Shem Tov and his successor, we learn of a visionary's journey to heaven, in which again it is specified that he saw "many souls of the living and the dead, known and unknown to me, without number, back and forth, to rise from world to world.[16]"

When a Hawaiian woman died and likewise visited the other world, she specified that while she met many dead people she knew, "nearly all were strangers."[17]

During a much more recently described near-death experience too, Deborah King perceived many moving lights, which she soon realized were souls, and specifically noted that "some of them I recognized, some of them I didn't."[18]

There are many more of these more general references to unknown deceased persons encountered while out of the body or in other worlds, some more widely known than others. The Greek Thespesius of Soli, in one of the earliest recorded NDEs, literary or otherwise, also recounts that upon ascending into the heavenly regions, he, similar to Paul in his Apocalypse, watched the souls of those who had just died rising up from the Earth.[19]

Returning to the monk of Wenlock, he too, having been taken aloft, saw from on high "a multitude of souls ascending, with both angels and demons trying to take hold of them."[20]

The prophet Zephaniah, in his non-canonical Apocalypse, comparably "sees the terrifying angels who bring up the souls of ungodly men to their justly deserved eternal punishment."[21]

Though the account lacks detail, there is mention of a man named Maldolus who met with St. Romuald in tenth century Italy and apparently had a vision of monks in white robes ascending to heaven.[22] The description of the monks bringing both men to God and God to men is highly suggestive that the vision was of deaths in real time.

During Cistercian novice Gunthelm's twelfth century otherworld journey, he saw a man riding a burning horse and carrying a burning shield. An angel told the Frenchman that he was a soldier who had "sustained his life through pillaging."[23]

In the history of Danish historian, theologian, and author Saxo Grammaticus, while off in another world, the hero Hading watched a battle between two armies, said to comprise men who had died in warfare.[24]

This kind of visionary scene is incredibly common. Arjuna, one of the chief protagonists of the Mahabharata, while away in the celestial city of Mount Meru, meets with "battle-slain warriors."[25]

Rodulfus Glaber, an eleventh century Benedictine monk, wrote of a man who had a vision while praying in church.[26] He saw a company of solemn men wearing white robes led by a bishop with a cross in his hands. He explained to the monk that there were monks who had been killed in battles with the Saracens and that they were on their way to the land of the blessed, that is, paradise.

The voluminously recorded lives of saints and monastics who lived during the relevant timeframe are brimming with visions of purgatory, and in many of those cases souls are encountered; in some, however, souls who have indeed "just died" in the world above are encountered while the visionary is there. Italian Catholic mystic Frances of Rome was herself "favoured" with a related tour of purgatory, accompanied by a celestial guide.[27] Seeing many regions and suffering souls, she soon saw descend the soul of a priest she knew but wouldn't name, remarking that his face was covered with a veil that concealed a stain.

While as geographically and culturally separated as one might imagine, this is conceptually similar in its fundamental aspects to an Arikara Indian account from their lands in North Dakota.[28] When a man died and entered the "dead man's country," he described having seen a special lodge where he too saw people who had just died. They arrived at that lodge and took a seat among others who had also just arrived.

In a Lipan Apache Indian underworld journey, for example, the traveler comes to a place where men are sitting, smoking, and praying; they are unnamed people who are dead and have relatives above, or in Haiti, where when a Voudou priest returned from the underworld, he reported that "everyone who was ever here before us was there."[29]

The discoveries and references in many of these cases are relatively vague: sinners are seen momentarily suffering en masse, the souls of strangers are observed at a distance but not specifically interacted with, general identities are offered by guides, and so on. While this does not necessarily speak to their impact upon the individual or their historical value, in other cases, and of greater interest here, the language is more particular still, and the timing of death or the persons involved are specifically noted either by the traveler or, more usually, upon their questioning of the guide they find themselves with while out of the body.

QUESTIONS AND ANSWERS IN THE OTHERWORLD

While there are many impressive cases we have yet to discuss in which the identity and death of the souls encountered in these otherworldly realms are later confirmed, there are also many interesting examples in which the traveler asks after a specific person or persons. The belief that this information was taken as veridical by the visionary or later by the reader of their tales seems more than strongly implied and warrants a number of examples.

One early encounter is found in the description of the biblical patriarch Enoch's descent to Sheol. We recall that one of our first visions from the Life of Adam and Eve involved Eve's dream revealing the slaying of her son. According to the book of Enoch, he himself witnessed the movement of Cain's soul while away in Sheol and discovered his death in this way. In this vision, accompanied by the angels Uriel and Raphael, Enoch "saw the spirit of a dead man making a suit."[30] Unlike the previous visions, here he then asked Raphael who it was, and the angel replied, "This is the spirit which went forth from Abel whom his brother Cain slew."

We can also turn to the experience of the Abbasid prince and military leader Al ibn al-Muwaffaq, who was transported to paradise in a dream and who also asks the identity of a soul met in the otherworld.[31] He saw a man there gazing at God and asked him his name; the reply came that he was "Macruf al-Karkhl," before he shared further elaboration upon his life and fate.

Castilian Catholic priest, mystic, and founder of the Dominican Order St. Dominicus, too, during his own celebrated visit to the otherworld, asked a devil about a spirit whom he had seen being tormented, and was told that it was one of the nobles of the kingdom of England who had just died the preceding night.[32]

Returning to the 824 CE vision of Wetti, an angel similarly told the traveler of a bishop who had "recently died" and was now suffering punishment.[33]

Gerard, a canon of the Cathedral of Florence, told this tale to Benedictine monk Peter Damian, who later included it in a letter to an unnamed bishop.[3] The letter relates how a certain priest heard a voice call him to a promontory that was hard to reach. When the man arrived, St. Benedict appeared and told him, upon further questioning, that the mystic Hildebrand had "just recently died." Soon the man was led to the depths of a valley, where he found a foul and pitch-black river. Hearing a voice, he asked who it was and received the reply, "I am that most unhappy count, Hildebrand."

Influential Italian Renaissance humanist Giovanni Boccaccio depicts one of his characters similarly discovering a death in purgatory.[35] In *The Resurrection of Ferondo*, Ferondo finds himself in purgatory, and when he asks a monk about his identity, the monk replied, "I am also dead. I lived in Sardinia, and because I lauded my master to the skies for his jealousy."

Similarly, in a gypsy folktale recorded first in 1878, the wind itself, in the form of a young boy, informed a man who had left his home and is unaware of just how much time had passed due to his forays into supernatural realms that his father and brothers had long since died during his time in the otherworld.[36] He returned home and discovered this to be true.

The Zoroastrian Arda Viraf asks a great many souls what their sins were when he sees them being punished; these are generally anonymous souls.[37] At one point, however, Viraf is told by an angel of a certain man that "this is the soul of the lazy Davanos who, when he was in the world, never did any good work but with this right foot, a bundle of grass was cast before a ploughing ox."

A similar tale is recounted in Muhammad Aufi's famous collection of Persian anecdotes, *Jawami ul-Hikayat*, written in the early thirteenth century. Wahid Ibn Zayd, one protagonist of the Persian epic *The Manju*, sees in a dream two people in Paradise and asks an "enlightened old man" who they are, receiving the reply that this is a certain dead king.[38]

During his own journey, the mythological Vedic king Nimi similarly asks the identities of certain people whom he sees suffering in a river of fire, a place he himself had asked to see, and is told the particulars regarding their deeds, including a specific reference to one named "Sonadinna."[39]

From the Sahidic fragment of the Apocalypse of Zephaniah, Zephaniah saw a soul being punished by angels.[40] Fearful, he asked, "Who is this whom they are punishing?" The reply came that this was a certain soul that was found in its lawlessness and taken out of his body in order to repent.

From one of the three surviving immrama, or ancient Irish voyage tales, we read in *The Celtic Voyage of the Húi Corra* that a certain son of the church appeared to the Húi Corra while those warriors were at sea in another world.[41] The Húi Corra specifically asked the particulars of that cleric, who replied that he was "Daga, a disciple of Andrew the Apostle," before further explaining in detail how he had died. This man, Daga, was a historical Irish bishop who is commemorated in the martyrology of the County Donegal.

In the 1666 Japanese stories, *The Otogiboko*, a man named Asahara Shinnojo visited hell, where he saw a man and a woman staked on two copper poles, their bodies being cut open and filled with boiling water.[42] Having asked his guides why they deserved this, they told him that the man was a doctor who treated the woman's husband. Later again, Asahara is told specifically and by name of some others he sees being punished, before being given details regarding where they are from and how they died.

In *Guingamor*, an anonymous twelfth century medieval lai (a lyrical poem) set in Brittany and often attributed to Marie of France, the so-named knight rode through an otherworldly forest that was "all so ill-looking and overgrown" that he got lost.[43] Soon he heard the axe of a woodcutter who had made a fire and burned charcoal. Just as the Irish hero Fionn learned in the otherworld of the long-since passed deaths of the brothers he had left in the waking world, the charcoal burner informed Guingamor that the king for whom he was searching, his own uncle, was over three hundred years dead and that "all his folk, and the castles of which thous askest have long been in ruins."

Finally, during a Hopi NDE, a woman is told of certain deaths by her guide while in the otherworld.[44] "Look closely," the guide said of a group of people before further explaining exactly who they were and their crimes.

ASCENDING THE PEAK IN DARIEN

It is, of course, clear that one may encounter the forms of deceased people while traveling in other worlds. As an extension of this, we have seen that more specific details about the identities of those encountered in the beyond can be gleaned either from the souls themselves or, more commonly from the guide upon questioning. Their identities, deeds, and the manner of their deaths may come to be known in greater or lesser detail. The veridical value of these accounts might not be greatly moving for some readers though, again, we should not speak for the experiencers themselves in this regard. Far more interesting, however, are those cases we now come to in which the information regarding these deaths is later confirmed or said to have been confirmed upon the traveler's return to the world—those "Peak in Darien" experiences proper.

Here then, we arrive at the early near-death experience of Corfidius the Elder in 77 CE, during which he discovers the death of his younger brother. This particular story had been cited by Greyson as one of the earliest examples of a "Peak in Darien" experience.[45] The account in Book 7 of Pliny the Elder's *Natural History* finds one of two brothers, both named Corfidius, appearing to have died.[46] While funeral arrangements were being made, the ostensibly deceased older brother suddenly awoke and announced that he had just come from the house of his younger brother and that funeral arrangements should be made for him instead. At that moment, a servant burst in with news that the other Corfidius had just unexpectedly died.

It is fitting that Dr. Bruce Greyson, Professor Emeritus of Psychiatry and Neurobehavioral Sciences at the University of Virginia, was one of the first to present this early account as a "Peak in Darien" experience that was analogous in important ways to experiences then and now still being recorded, as he himself has been a witness to and been moved by the same kinds of accounts among his own patients. Greyson recounted a comparable incident which occurred to a South African patient of his named Jack Bybee at a time when he was clinically dead.[47] Jack, during his NDE, met his nurse in a vividly green valley in another world. She told him to apologize to her parents, saying that she wrecked the red MGB and that she loves them. She told him that it wasn't his time yet before disappearing into the distance. When Jack finally awoke, he discovered, to his great astonishment, that Anita had died in this exact manner.

Just as had those scribes of the Middle Ages recognized the unique power of these accounts, Greyson wrote of them that they provide "some of the most persuasive evidence for the survival of consciousness after bodily death," a contrast to their less appreciated historical impact.[48] Greyson has by no means been alone in singling out these kinds of experiences for their unique persuasiveness. Van Bronkhorst noted, in fact, that "the glimmering possibility of an afterlife shines brightest when dying people are visited by close family members they hadn't yet heard were dead."[49] Much earlier too, after compiling and presenting numerous related cases, Irish professor William Barrett wrote that "the evidence of visions of the dying, when they appear to see and recognize some of their relatives, whose decease they were unaware of, affords perhaps one of the strongest arguments in favour of survival."[50]

While these statements might be greatly multiplied, what becomes clear is that these kinds of experiences have both historically been marveled at by those who have had them and their witnesses. It is with a certain irony, then, that long after Pliny, the satirist Lucian, in his dialogue *Philopseudes*, wrote of something similar. The tale seems to have been mostly missed in recent times, though Calmet had brought attention to it in the eighteenth century.[51] A man named Eucrates was taken to the underworld and presented to Pluto.[52] He was told this was a mistake and that "his thread is not yet fully spun, so let him be off, and bring me the blacksmith Demylus, for he is living beyond the spindle." Coming around and being healed of his illness, as are many modern NDE-ers, he told everybody that Demylus was "as good as dead." He lived close by, and it was not long before they "heard the wailing of his mourners."

Both Pliny and Lucian were unanimous on one thing regarding these tales, which may speak to their rather conspicuous dearth in antiquity: they did not take these stories very seriously. Of great interest, however, is that Pliny nevertheless wrote, "We are perpetually hearing of such predictions as these."[53] Importantly too, one of Lucian's characters, Cleodemus, had observed regarding the above-mentioned tale that "these sights that you saw are not novel and unseen by anyone else," while Antigonous remarked, "What is there surprising in that?"[54] Their words were to hold true even millennia later.

Strongly recalling the *Visio Pauli* was the account of St. John the Silent, the fourth and fifth century Greek saint who prayed to God specifically to reveal to him how the soul separates from the body at death.[55] He was taken outside of himself and saw a man die in front of a church in Bethlehem. He saw how angels took the man's soul and carried it to heaven. Coming back to himself from his ecstasy, John immediately set out on the road from the Monastery of St. Sava the

Sanctified to Bethlehem and found the dead body of the man exactly as he had seen it in his vision.

In a related vision which came to Pope Alexander as he was sleeping one night, he seemed to be taken to a large palace where sat a man of imposing authority, with numerous attendants at his sides.[56] A kind of bier bearing a corpse was brought before them. The pope inquired specifically as to this man's identity, to which he was told that it was the recently deceased Pope Innocent, formerly called Sinebald. Interestingly, it was said that after this vision, the pope ordered alms to be given and masses to be celebrated on behalf of the deceased and considered the vision a revelation from God.

The fifth century Georgian prince, theologian, and philosopher Peter the Iberian, while alone and paying devotions, had a related spontaneous vision, learning of further veridical details of both the kinds reported by the monk of Wenlock and near-death experiencers today.[57] He saw city authorities surrounding an Alexandrian theater and people being slaughtered. According to the account, "In an ecstasy he saw many souls being carried up by the angels into heaven. When people came from the city and told him what had occurred, it transpired that the number of those who had perished by violence in the crush and confusion was the same as that of the blessed souls that he had seen in his vision."

During her research on near-death experiences in India, author Satwant Pasricha writes of Srinivasa Reddy, who told what he saw during a period of unconsciousness brought on by illness in 1935.[58] He came to a city with two guides and saw a man with a big book who told him that he was not required there and that another was to come. Reddy's wife told Pasricha that this other person had died that very same day and that her husband was unaware of his death.

The stability of the essential experience across long spans of time and culture is impressive. In a more modern example, a Hindu man, during his NDE, was taken to a beautiful place by guides in white.[59] He too came to a man who had a book and who told him that he was the wrong person. In this case, the nurse told the researchers that another man of the same name died in that hospital just as the patient regained consciousness.

Returning to Homer, in Book XI of *The Odyssey* we meet again with Odysseus making his famous trip to the underworld in order to consult with the ghost of the dead Theban prophet Tiresias.[60] Odysseus encounters many shades here, including former and recently deceased comrades. Perhaps most notably, though, he also encounters the ghost of his mother, Anticlea, who, little to our hero's knowledge, had been recently deceased at the time of the encounter. In an account to which surprisingly little attention has been drawn in this "Peak in Darien" context, especially considering its renown, Odysseus very specifically notes that he had left his mother alive when he'd set out for Troy and that he was "moved to tears" when he'd seen her here and realized her fate.

While the vast majority of those Odysseus encountered in the underworld were known to have died, there was another notable exception. Odysseus also met his comrade Agamemnon, whom he had left alive.[61] Odysseus inquired whether it was at sea or on land that the former king of Mycenae had died. Agamemnon then explained the macabre turn of events after the fall of Troy that led to his death.

In what was reported as a first-hand account of a near-death experience, recorded by his brother in 1196, monk Edmund of Eynsham, during a visionary visit to a purgatorial otherworld, met with a cleric he had not known to have been dead at the time and very clearly and rather beautifully expressed the mystery of the "Peak in Darien" phenomenon.[62] "I had no idea that this cleric, whom I had known during my childhood, was dead, for he had moved away from the district," as Edmund told it. "But in all that vast place of torment and pain, I found him and marveled, for I believed him still to be alive and living honestly."

Similar awe was expressed in the twentieth century in an account given by John Myers.[63] He related the case of a woman who, during an NDE, perceived herself leaving her body and, viewing the hospital room, saw her distraught husband and the doctor shaking his head. She reported that she went to heaven and saw an angel and a familiar young man. She exclaimed, "Why, Tom, I didn't know you were up here," to which Tom responded that he had just arrived. The angel then went on to tell the woman that she would be returning to Earth, and she found herself back in the hospital bed. Later that night, her husband got a phone call informing him that their friend Tom had died in an auto accident.

The following account, which Dutch historian Jan Bremmer referred to as "the first Christian NDE," was recorded by Augustine of Hippo.[64] Augustine himself initially considered the experience to be something of a relatively trivial dream, for his own philosophies regarded it as impossible that the dead might have dealings with the living (with the exceedingly important exception of martyrs). This, as we have seen, is in direct contrast to Gregory the Great, who recorded numerous "Peak in Darien" experiences in his dialogues and clearly accepted the more literal presence of actual spirits. A man named Curma from the town of Tullium, being ill and having all his senses taken, lay all but dead for several days.[65] When, after a great many days, Curma awoke, he told all that he had seen. When he first opened his eyes, he demanded that someone go to the home of another Curma, a smith, and investigate what had occurred there. When someone did go, they discovered that the smith had died around the time our first Curma had come to his senses.

In 594 CE, Gregory the Great similarly wrote of a man named Stephen, whose journey we had briefly touched upon and whom he heard had once fallen ill and died in Constantinople.[66] During this time, his soul was carried to hell, where he met a judge who told him, as was also the case in Curma's account, that he was the wrong Stephen and that Stephen the Smith should have been brought, at which point he was returned to life, while Stephen the Smith departed this life at that very hour.

We now read of yet another occurrence in which the visionary themselves or someone attendant went to the distant place in order to confirm whether or not the vision had any objective reality, this time from Ancient China. In Yighzhou (modern Anhui), there was a man named Yu who died and was revived a day later.[67] After his rather detailed otherworldly journey, as he was about to depart the heavenly realm, he noticed that outside the gate there was a very beautiful girl who told him he was lucky to be able to return. When Yu asked her name, she replied that her surname was Zhang and that her home was in Maozhu, and that she had died just the previous day. When Yu was revived, he went to Maozhu, where his inquiries confirmed that there was indeed a Zhang family that had recently been bereaved of a young girl.

In another Chinese tale, published in 1740, which shares a number of fascinating resemblances to the experiences of Curma and Stephen, a man named Sung Tao was a first-degree graduate and holder of an annual government stipend.[68] This man, after lying ill in bed, finds himself in another world, being interviewed for a certain position by supernatural deities, one of whom is the "God of War." Though he wins the position after writing a short essay, Song Tao, being more concerned with his aging mother than with the growth of his career, turns down the position, allowing it to be awarded to a Mr. Chang, whom he is told about. When he awakes, Sung subsequently receives word that Mr. Chang had died the very same day that he fell into delirium. Again, in this instance, it is interesting to note that scholars reviewing this well-known tale often don't address this "Peak in Darien" element at all.

Returning to the *Otogiboko*, a man named Magohei who had fallen ill and appeared to die, revived and claimed that he went to the land of death.[69] Asahara disbelieved him until one night he was seized by two demons and brought to a "palace of justice" in another world. There, Asahara spoke with its king, Hyojobu, and debated with him on matters of life and death, belief and disbelief. After witnessing the fates of sinners, he sees the King ordering Magohei to be brought back to the otherworld, and Asahara sees him being escorted to hell. Of greatest interest in this tale, however, is that when Asahara revived, he asked his family immediately, "How is Magohei, our neighbor?" He learned that the man had actually died again around the same time he had seen him in the other world.

In another old Japanese tale, a monk from Miidera came to Mount Taishaku, where the underworld demons were said to gather.[70] While walking, the monk met a young woman, whom he assumed to be a demon. She told him that her home was in Gamo County, Omi Province, where her parents still lived, and that after their deaths, she fell into a hell from which she was still suffering. She begged that he tell her parents what had happened to her. The monk went straight to Omi to find out if all of this was true. He located her parents, and they "wept to hear the news he brought them."

Caesarius also recorded such accounts and, as previously demonstrated, noted the "Peak in Darien" element specifically.[71] In one of his records, a certain pilgrim drank so much that he lost his wits and was presumed dead. That same hour, his spirit was "conducted to the place of punishment," where he saw the devil. While the pilgrim, was there, the soul of the abbot of Corvey, among others, was brought there, and the devil, after giving him a hearty greeting, offered him a sulfurous draught from a fiery cup. When the abbot had gotten drunk, he was put into the pit. As that pilgrim stood before the door of hell nearby and trembled at seeing those things, the devil cried out: "Bring also the gentleman standing outside, who lately pledged his cloak for wine and became drunken." Hearing this, the pilgrim looked at the angel who had brought him and promised he would never get drunk again if only he would just deliver him in that hour from his imminent peril. Having eventually recovered his senses, the pilgrim noted the day and hour and, returning to his own land, learned that the very abbot he had seen in that other world had actually died.

In the anonymously produced *Awesome and Edifying Vision of the Monk Cosmas*, alleged to have taken place in Byzantium in 933, Cosmas, chamberlain to the Emperor Alexander, had become insensibly ill and visited another world.[72] While in its dazzling celestial city, two residents eventually order Cosmas to be taken back, saying that he was missed in his world and should leave along another path, while instead of him, the monk Athanasios from the monastery at Traianos should be received. After recovering his senses and telling his brothers of this, one of them was sent to Traianos and found that Athanasious had died at the exact time of Cosmas's vision.

In the twentieth century now, physician K. M. Dale related the case of nine year old Eddie Cuomo, who, having awoken from an ongoing illness, like Curma and Yu of Yighzhou, urgently told his parents that he had been to heaven, where he saw his deceased grandpa, auntie Rosa, and uncle Lorenzo.[73] While his father disregarded this, Eddie added that he also saw his nineteen year old sister, Teresa, who told him he had to go back. Later that morning, Eddie's parents learned that Teresa had been killed in an automobile accident just after midnight.

Similarly, physicians Melvin Morse and Paul Perry described the case of a seven-year-old boy dying of leukemia who told his mother that he had traveled up a beam of light to heaven, where he visited a "crystal castle" and talked with God.[74] The boy said that a man there approached him and introduced himself as an old high school boyfriend of the boy's mother, saying that he had been crippled in the accident, but in the crystal castle, he had regained his ability to walk. The boy's mother had never mentioned this old boyfriend to her son, but after hearing of this vision, she called some friends and confirmed that her former boyfriend had died the very day of the vision.

Reported to Dr. Jeffrey Long was the case of a five-year-old girl named Sandy who, during her NDE, having traveled through darkness, met a girl that looked a little like her and later her next-door neighbor Glen.[75] He soon started to shout at Sandy that she should "go home now." When Sandy woke up, she found out that Glen had died the day after she went into the hospital suddenly from a heart attack and that she had a sister who died of accidental poisoning a year before she was born.

In the case of a child named Thomas, as reported by American physician Allan Hamilton, the very first words out of his mouth after having survived a near-fatal fall onto a live power line were, "What happened to my father?"[76] Hamilton lied and told him everything was fine, though Thomas noted that his father, who had died while he was unconscious, was just standing at the end of his bed. Hamilton, a young man at the time, referred to this as a "hammer blow." Perhaps most powerfully, he called this experience his own "fragile moment of awakening."

While not neccesarily common, children reporting these kinds of encounters during a life-threatening situation is nothing new. The similar near-death experience of another child was long ago recorded among the acts of the saints.[77] The young boy in question died at Cascia, in

Naples, at the age of eleven. The day after his death, while being carried to the grave, the boy awoke and told of his near-death experience. It's worth noting that, while the boy claims he was led by a guide through various regions and saw many souls, it was specifically stated that he witnessed the arrival of two who "had just died," named Buccerelli and Frascha.

An interesting early modern account involved the 1796 experience of American entomologist, conchologist, and herpetologist Thomas Say.[78] At about the age of sixteen, Say became very ill and described leaving his body on the ninth day of his illness. He described, among other things, seeing his parents shake his body and check for his pulse. When he returned to his body and told them what he had seen and asked why they had thought him dead, they were "much surprised." Having been asked, Say told them he thought he had gone to heaven after he left his body. He heard wonderful laments and described the green as like nothing seen on this Earth, as do those who recount having traveled to other worlds today. Interestingly, as Say passed along towards a "higher state of bliss," and in a manner which again recalls Paul looking down from above and seeing souls leaving their bodies in the *Visio Pauli*, he wrote that he "cast his eyes upon the Earth," which he "saw plainly," and beheld three men he knew die. He saw a gate opening. When he was about to step in with one of them, he returned to his body. Say noted that "after I told them of the death of the three men, they sent to see if it was so, and when the messenger returned, he told them they were all dead and died in the rooms, etc., as I told them. These men, upon inquiry, were found to have died at the very time I saw them, and all the circumstances of their deaths were found to be as I related them."

Almost a century earlier still, according to the record book of the Frankfurt Burial Society a certain Jewish man died in 1718 and his burial was delayed for some hours.[79] As they were preparing for the burial, the man recovered. He soon related that on this very day, a man named Haham Zvi, who had died in Poland, was invited to "sit on the Heavenly Court." According to the journal, it was later verified that Haham Zvi had indeed died on that very same day in 1718.

While Thomas Say, like Odysseus, learned of multiple deaths, in another account from antiquity, two people undergo a near-death experience around the same time and discover the very *same* death. According to the *Gospel of Nicodemus*, another non-canonical text in which Christ descends to the underworld, two others who happened to be undergoing near-death experiences themselves saw him while he was there. According to Shushan, the account is "ostensibly testimony to three separate NDEs—their own and that of Jesus."[80] The men themselves noted that "these are the divine and holy mysteries which we, Kariaskednus, and Leucius, saw and heard."

Still in antiquity, although returning to China, we read that during the Chien-an reign (196–220), a sixty-year-old Chinese woman, Li O, had been buried outside the city for fourteen days. Having been told she had been summoned by mistake (something common to, although not exclusive to, Far Eastern accounts), she revived and told what she had seen.[81] "As I passed out of the western gates (while still in the other-world)," she noted, "I happened to see my cousin Liu Po-wen. We were both startled and asked about each other's situation." Po-wen said he too had been mistakenly summoned. When Li O asked him for help returning, he asked the "Chancellor of the Bureau of Households," who told her he would help and that yet another was being sent back at that time. All three near-death experiences were confirmed by a messenger to have occurred during the cited time periods.

In a 161 BC Jewish account, Rabbi Yose ben Yoezer of the early Maccabean period was condemned to death and led to be hanged.[82] His sister's son became fearful after speaking to him, for if this was the fate of a man who led such an exemplary life, what should be his own? The rabbi's nephew Yakim ben Zeroroth went away and hanged himself. While this was happening, the soon-to-be-killed Rabbi fell into a trance, felt his soul leave his body, and saw the gates of paradise open. As he reached them, he saw an illuminated soul entering and soon heard the singing of angelic choirs: "Open wide the gates for Yakim ben Zeroroth!" When he awoke, he looked around and said, "Know, O my sons, that in my dream it was revealed to me that the penitent Yakim ben Zeroroth entered Paradise one hour before me!"

The near-death experience of the young English girl Anne Atherton in 1669, perhaps the best-known example given of an early "Peak in Darien" account, is notably similar.[83] At fourteen, Anne became very ill and lay like this for a week. She told her mother that during this period she had been accompanied to heaven by an angel. Anne saw many glorious and hard-to-explain things and was told that it wasn't her time and that she must return. Disappointed that her mother wouldn't believe her, Anne told her that while standing at heaven's gate, she saw several people enter and, most interestingly, named several people she knew who had died during the time she was ill. While this appears to be a real account, even assuming it was contrived, the narrative speaks greatly to how much the author, just as had those medieval scribes, valued the "Peak in Darien" aspect specifically as bolstering proof of the broader experience.

In 1887, Episcopal Missionary John Chapman told the story of an Alaskan girl of the Deg Hit'an people who went missing while hunting with her family.[84] During a period of unconsciousness, she found herself in front of a house and soon heard voices discussing why she was there. An old woman appeared and illuminated the room with a wand. The girl was told to look over a vast village outside, which was filled with people. Back on Earth, her family thought she was dead and eventually made funerary offerings on her behalf. Some time later in this other world, while walking along a riverbank, she saw her father floating in the direction from which she had come, although he didn't notice her. When this girl returned to life and told of her experiences, her mother revealed that her father had died in her absence.

While not necessarily regarding an otherworld journey, an account told to the informant's daughter "before the prophecy came to pass" by the wife of a Lutheran minister shares some strikingly similar imagery.[85] One night, this woman dreamed she was standing on a riverbank among a group that seemed to have their eyes fixed on some object upstream. She noticed a barge with a motionless figure covered in flowers, which she soon realized was her sister-in-law, and that she was clearly dead, as her hair was lying in two strands over her breast and fresh flowers were massed around her face. That very morning, soon after she woke up, she wrote a letter to her sister-in-law. That same afternoon, she received a telephone call from Chicago bringing news of her sister-in-law's death.

Anthropologist Dorothy Counts recorded the following experience in the small hamlet of Vuvu, Melanesia.[86] During his otherworldly sojourn, having been apparently dead for several hours, Andrew met a woman, who had died just a short while before. Shortly thereafter Andrew came to a lush field of flowers, and after being led to a house, he was told that it wasn't his time to come. He saw this woman on the road again, but she wouldn't answer him. The voice told him that it was not his time but that the woman he saw must stay, as it was hers. All of this happened before he returned to his body on a beam of light to discover she had died while he was still unconscious.

A highly related, if not entirely comparable, curiosity is an NDE recorded in the *Tales of the Heavenly Court*, a collection of stories gathered from the Talmud Bavli and Yerushalmi, Midrashim, and Hassidic sources.[87] Jose of Pike'in died and visited the Heavenly Academy. Jose's son had fainted during the ordeal and said that when his own soul was on its way up, he had met his father there.

That the otherworld has inspired art is patently clear in the works of Bosch, the prose and poetry of Chaucer, or the incredibly beautiful combinations of both, such as the Middle English poem *Pearl*, in which a father laments the death of his daughter before later meeting her in an otherworldly dream vision. Such visionary visits beyond Earth, however, still hold the power to bring themselves to our attention and imagination in these forms.

Author Marisa St. Clair reported on the case of Durdanda Khan, a Pakistani woman.[88] At age two and a half, she died for around fifteen minutes, and when she came to she said that she had been to the stars, where she saw a beautiful tree-filled garden and met her dead grandpa and his mother. Several months later, Durdanda and her family were visiting some other relatives, and she correctly identified a person in a photo as her grandpa's mother. Durdanda later painted a picture of the garden she was in during her NDE.

Humanistic psychologist and founder of the International Association for Near-Death Studies Margot Grey gave us a case from

England in which an NDEer was also in a bright and beautiful garden filled with pomegranate trees.[89] There the informant met not only her grandfather but also her mother, whom she had never known. Grey noted that sometime after the NDE, when visiting a relative's house, the informant's parents were amazed when she recognized a photograph of her great-grandmother. She pointed it out and said, "That's the lady I saw and that's my grandfather." Both had died long before she was born, and she had never seen either of them.

American cardiologist Maurice Rawlings similarly described the case of a forty-eight-year-old man who had a cardiac arrest.[90] During his near-death stay in another world full of lush light and beautiful flora, he met his stepmother as well as his biological mother, who had died when he was only fifteen months old. A few weeks after this episode, his aunt, having heard about this vision, visited and brought a picture of his mother posing with a number of other people. The man had no difficulty picking out his mother, of whom he had never seen a picture, much to the astonishment of his father.

In a tale told in Mexico, we read of a pagan officer named Placido who sets out from his home in Egypt to be baptized.[91] On the way there, Placido and his children become separated from his wife as they stay on a certain island. While Placido sleeps, an angel escorts him briefly to heaven, where he sees his wife. Although not impressively eventful, special mention is made of the fact that he thus "learns of the death of his wife" in this way, making it clear she had died in the interim.

Psychiatrist Elisabeth Kübler-Ross described a Native American woman who was struck by a hit-and-run driver on a highway and, before dying, was comforted by a stranger who stopped to help her.[92] When he asked her if there was anything he could do for her, she told him to tell her mother not to worry, as she was already with her father. She died a few minutes later. The stranger was so moved that he drove far out of his way to the Indian reservation to find her mother, where he learned that her father had died of a coronary seven hundred miles away, just one hour before the car accident had occurred.

A tale involving an Inuit woman named Nivikgana was told to Knudd Rasmussen.[93] Having traveled "below the Earth" to save the life of a fellow sick villager, she saw her deceased brother in the under-world but also saw two others: one man she knew well, though it's not revealed if she knew that he was dead, and the other being Alqatsiaq, a person she did not know as he was apparently from another village and whose death she could not have been aware of by ordinary channels.

WE'VE BEEN EXPECTING YOU

Just as Sulpicius Severus had written in his letters of his crisis appari-tion involving Martin of Tours, so too had the early Christian Bishop of Antioch Evodius written to Augustine in 414 CE of an experience regarding a widow from the village of Figentes. In his letters, Evodius writes of this woman who had a "vision in a dream" in which she saw a deacon preparing a palace made entirely of silver. This woman asked the deacon for whom the palace was being prepared and received the reply that it was for a young man who had died less than a day before. This young man was known to Evodius, as he had attended him at his end; however, this is something she could not have known. Word came to her from the man's village with news of his death. The experience had a tangible impact on Evodius, which is apparent in the letters. To read of Evodius so openly questioning the influential Augustine on these mat-ters, on the heels of this "Peak in Darien" experience, is particularly fascinating.[94]

A more recent account of some striking similarity was reported to Margot Grey in her somewhat underappreciated work on British near-death experiences, *Return from Death*, and involved an elderly woman undergoing cardiac arrest.[95] Having flatlined, this woman saw her mother at the end of a beautiful path and her uncle Alf, a man she did not particularly care for, inside what looked like a World War I prefab, and she noticed that they both seemed to be preparing the place for a visitor. When she asked to come in, her mother told her somewhat firmly that it was not her time to stay and that she must return. Having asked whom they were waiting for, she learned that they were prepar-ing for her aunt Ethel, who would apparently be arriving shortly. After pleading to enter that "warm and sunny" place, this woman found herself back in her hospital bed and was told that her aunt Ethel had died of a sudden heart attack. In her own words, this elderly woman replied, "I thought, well I could have told them that, as I already knew."

It is said that one Brother Pacificus, on a certain morning, found St. Francis of Assisi in prayer.[96] Waiting for him outside, he suddenly found himself in heaven, where he saw many thrones. One was more exalted and glorious than the others, adorned and glowing with precious stones. When he wondered who it was for, a voice told him this seat was being prepared for the time of Francis's death.

Around the time that the Venerable Thais, who was Egyptian by birth, died in 340 CE, Paul the Simple saw a vision of the "most beautiful habitation in paradise, prepared by God for St. Thais."[97]

In an account from as recently as 2022, in which a kind of welcoming party is again referenced, bereavement therapist William Peters tells us of a Floridian named Gail whose father was in the hospital.[98] While in the waiting room, she felt as if she were in "two places at once." Having also found herself in a beautiful garden, she heard a voice saying that Walter, her father, was coming and that he was almost there. Gail looked towards what seemed to be a mansion and noted that people there seemed to be, bringing flowers, setting tables and preparing for something important. Then she felt the presence of her father pass through the gate, although she wasn't allowed to pass with him. The very next minute, a doctor came in and told her he was sorry and that her father had gone. Gail responded as if in continuity with the seeming reality of the vision: "It's okay. He went to the party!" The doctor gave her a funny look and walked out, but she "knew" what had happened.

Similarly, although from late antiquity, we read that on the night in 470 CE when Theodora of Alexandria died in her cell, the abbot of that monastery saw in a vision certain preparations being made for a great wedding, to which came angels, prophets, and martyrs alike.[99] In their midst, he saw Theodora walking in shining glory. A voice announced that this was her. The abbot awoke, rushed to her cell with the monks, and discovered that she had died.

Many related examples are scattered widely through the ages. Physician Joseph Ennemoser documented some in his own time.[100] One evening, after a conversation with his professor about natural philosophy, a certain man dreamed that he had ascended to the summit of a mountain where a temple stood: "As I entered it I perceived a company of Freemasons sitting in a room which was hung with black. I heard a glorious inspiring funeral chant. To my inquiry for whom these ceremonies were being held, they replied, for brother Sachs. Three months afterwards I received the intelligence of Sachs' death, which had resulted from a dangerous illness produced by the ascent of a steep mountain."

In the near-death vision of Barontus from the end of the seventh century, he too saw mansions being "prepared for others yet to come."[101]

Many ages later came a Kongo (in what is now Angola) NDE in which a woman told of a room that she was apparently meant to get the key to but that it was "reserved for another newcomer" other than herself.[102]

Interestingly, the prophets of the Tanzanian, Kenyan, and other Makonde people are said to see dreams in which the house of the chief to die is being built for him in the spirit world, awaiting his arrival.[103] They know that when it is finished, the person for whom it is intended must soon go.

More recently an account with multiple witnesses that centered on a series of dreams regarding the death of a woman the author calls Hilda was given to Canadian philosopher Phillip Wiebe.[104] In one dream, Hilda's grandparents were seen in heaven with their arms outstretched, welcoming someone whose identity the dreamer didn't know. A telephone call came from a family friend in Wales, where someone had had an identical dream. Finally, a chaplain who knew Hilda called her parents, saying that he had dreamed that he met her in heaven. He did not know, of course, that Hilda had in fact just died.

FUTURE SIGHT

While the previous types of vision, in which one sees a welcoming party waiting to usher the unknown deceased into the otherworld, frequently appear and often speak to deaths that occurred concurrently with the vision, others are more concerned with the future. An account found in the letters of an eleventh century Italian Benedictine monk, Peter Damian, also features a welcoming party of sorts, although of a far less agreeable kind than those we have seen.[105] During a vision experienced by an unnamed priest, while he was in another world, he saw a terrible and dreadful house with many servants, all of whom were fierce and savage, rushing about in a great hurry as if to prepare for "some great and distinguished guest." When this priest inquired, he was told that count Guido II of the Guidi family was due to die the following Wednesday and that this location was being prepared for him. The prediction was exactly fulfilled.

Regarding the Byzantine saint Eupraxia, daughter of the Constantinople dignitary Antigonos (379–395), a sister of hers, Theodula, was taken to paradise in a dream. There she saw palaces and chambers of "incomparable glory."[106] She saw Eupraxia there, being allowed to pass through to the chamber, though Theodula herself was not. She saw too that this place had been prepared for Eupraxia, and she heard a voice tell that woman that she would die in nine days, which proved true after she developed a fever.

In an ancient Roman account, after his plague-related near-death experience, a young Livonian shepherd regained consciousness and explained that he had been taken to heaven and learned there the names of certain persons who were to die of the plague.[107] All of this came to pass exactly as he had laid it out.

In 1997 a Thai man had a related near-death experience. He found himself in front of Yama, the lord of the underworld, who was holding a book.[108] Yama said that he was the wrong person and had to be taken back. The patient "sneaked" a look into the book and saw the name of a person he knew from his village, with the date of his death written as three days in the future. The man named in Yama's book did, in fact, die on the date named.

While India, Thailand, Japan, and China are usually noted for NDE's in which the mistaken identity occurs, a far more obscure account from Kenya contained similar elements. A woman who had recently become a mother was out collecting firewood when she was seized by a spirit and taken to his hut.[109] An old man there said he had taken the wrong woman and was meant to retrieve someone else. He ordered the spirit to return the woman at once. During the conversation between these men, she noticed spirits passing by and carrying a long-haired warrior in their arms, followed by hyenas and chanting. The woman recognized the warrior as a neighbor of hers. When she returned to the land of the living, she found that the warriors, including the one she had seen there, had been searching for her. She related what she had seen, and two days later, the warrior was killed by a buffalo in the valley.

Something alike also came from among the Eskimo of the Bering Strait, in a tale related to their fundamental notions of the next world and its inhabitants.[110] The morning after a young woman in the lower Yukon became ill, died, and traveled to the Otherworld alongside her guides before returning safely, a mistake had seemingly been made. As Nelson writes, "Early the next morning her namesake, a woman in the same village, died, and her shade went away to the land of the dead in the girl's place."

There is an interesting parallel, of at least passing poetic interest, that we might note.[111] In the Eddic poem *Balder's Dream*, Odin, having risen a seeress from the ground while traveling in Niffel, asks her, "Why are gold rings strewn along the benches in Hel's hall and why is the whole place decorated with gold? Who are you expecting?" To which the seeress replied that the place was being prepared for Balder.

Of still more ancillary but noteworthy interest are cases such as the following, in which the visionary witnesses preparations not for another's death but for their own. These are incredibly common among the mystics and saints and deserve their own extended treatment. For one single example, in a 250 CE vision experienced by early Italian martyr St. Vitalis as he neared his end, an angel is said to have shown him "the crown which was being prepared for him in heaven," before he expired there and then.[112]

The seers of the Konyaks, a major Northeastern Indian ethnic group, claim that they can enter the world of the dead in their dreams.[113] Of great interest here is that if they encountered someone there whom they knew to be alive on Earth, they knew that person was soon to die.

Comparably we read of a Taos Indian example from the Caribbean in which a man named Magpie Tail attempted to bring his wife back from the land of the dead.[114] At one point, this man heard people singing and saw a light on a hillside. This was the home of the dead, and he heard some of them talking, saying to hurry and take their tools and axes to cut timber and carry it to the river so they might build a bridge, as some new people were coming to the world of the dead. As it turned out, the preparations they were making were for him and his wife.

PARADISE FOUND

The fact that people are "seen entering paradise" or generally visualized there is a common reference; it was in a number of previous accounts in which the soul is apparently seen ascending skyward, though unlike the final account of the last section, which was rather clear, it can sometimes be difficult to say whether or not the visionary actually proceeded to or visualized the otherworld itself. Nevertheless, the suggestion alone gives us license to include a few examples in rounding out our final chapter.

From an anonymous tale recorded in the *Catalogue of Romances in the Department of Manuscripts in the British Museum*, we read that the abbots of St. Saturninus at Toulouse and St. Antoninus at Pamiers went to Bome, fleeing from persecution by their lords, the Counts of Toulouse and Foix, and the Vicomte de Limoges.[115] On the way back, the abbot of St. Saturninus has a vision of SS. Saturninus, Martial, and Antoninus appealing to the Supreme Judge and being promised redress. Shortly afterwards, word arrives of the three persecutors' untimely deaths.

Returning to St. Anthony, also known as Ferdinand, we read that while he was taking mass at his monastery in Portugal, he had a vision of a certain well-regarded friar passing through purgatory and "gloriously entering into heaven."[116] St. Anthony's vision turned out to have occurred at the very moment the friar died.

In 615 CE, Gallus, a kinsman and follower of St. Columbus, called his deacon Magnus and told him, "During the watches of the night I have learned through a dream that my lord and father Columbanus has this day passed from the troubles of this life to the joys of Paradise."[117]

Much later, martyrologist Bede Camm relayed that at the very moment a Father John Morris was suddenly killed, a holy nun in America saw him being escorted to paradise by a great company of martyrs.[118] She didn't know his name; she only knew that he was an English Jesuit, and the inquiries later sent to England found that he had died at the same time as this vision. Of interest too, Camm noted that this fact should not be surprising, "for God's saints have ever had grateful hearts."

From 589 CE, it is also said of the Welsh missionary Kentigern, of the Brittonic Kingdom of Strathclyde, that he was praying at the time of his friend the Welsh bishop David's death and had a vision in which he saw David being led to heaven with heavenly music and later being "crowned with glory and honor," suggesting a visualization in that otherworld itself.[119]

In a legend from what is now Germany, it is said that when the Huns took the provinces there one by one, a maiden named Corbula escaped during the massacre of her village.[120] That night, she saw in a dream that all her companions whom she had left were enjoying "everlasting happiness in heaven." And so, she gave herself up to the barbarians.

The biographer of the Frankish Benedictine Abbess Aldegund wrote that, while in her monastery of Maubeuge around 679 AD, the Abbess had a vision which revealed to her the death of Amand, Bishop of Tongres, someone she was very close to.[121] The imagery strongly suggests a visualization of paradise itself. She saw him "crowned by the Lord and a great troop of souls with him."

Likewise, in 1426, at the moment a devout hermit from Cologne named Gerard died, his death was revealed in a vision to the Dutch mystic Lydwina, who apparently saw his soul borne into Paradise at the very hour of his passing.[122]

Meeting one final time with Belgian mystic Lutgarde, we read that when she announced that one Father Baldwin had died, another astonished priest who was himself aware of Baldwin's death asked how she could have known.[123] She related that she was told in a vision that he was "appearing before the judgment seat of God to give an account of all his omissions" at the time of his death.

It is said that on the day Sister Mary of St. Joseph died, Italian religious sister Mother Isabella, while hearing mass and praying, had a vision of her crowned in glory.[124]

There are other similar references scattered throughout the lives of the mystics and saints which may or may not be related, including, for example, a spontaneous out-of-body journey in which Mary Magdalen De Pazzi saw the soul of another man "at the moment he passed from his deathbed to the eternal torments."[125] It is again unclear whether or not she actually saw him in these agonies or simply assumed his destination for some other reason.

In other cases, it is even difficult to determine if the visionary knew if those he or she visualized were dead at all, and thus whether or not seeing them was a surprise or if the visionary was long aware of their passing. St. Christine, during her own near-death experience, for instance, recognized among the souls she encountered some whom she had "formerly known."[126]

In a similarly inconclusive but interesting tale from northeastern Wisconsin, a Fox Indian named Painter fell from a tree and visited the otherworld during a near-death experience.[127] He saw many people enjoying themselves, including his previously dead family members, and soon met a woman, one he "used to woo while he was yet a youth." The text states she had long been dead, but does not state if this was specifically known to Painter. This does seem highly likely, however.

During an Ojibwa near-death experience, a woman, while in the otherworld, specifically approaches a group of people she meets there to "try to see if we know anybody."[128] She eventually does see, as she notes, "a woman I used to know." This is of course inconclusive but suggestive nonetheless.

We read too that during a Lipan Apache near-death experience from the Southern Plains, a little girl is guided around by her deceased father.[129] After being told it wasn't her time and that she must return, the girl noticed that there were other children around her. She only heard their voices, but she recognized them as children who had died. She remembered them; she had played with them when they were alive.

In a Jewish folktale, a man visited hell in a dream.[130] At one point, he met a Jewish man wearing a prayer shawl and phylacteries. This man asked him where he was from, and he gave the name of a town, though for certain reasons, not actually his own town. At this, the man told him that he should take a look at the other side of a pile of bodies and that he would see someone from that town here. He was surprised to see that man in hell, as he apparently had a fine reputation in the world of the living.

Finally, similarly and worlds apart, in my own country, in 1902 an old army man from Galway, Ireland, had seen a vision of purgatory.[131] It was a bright, blazing place with souls suffering apparently nearly as much as they do in hell. This man then heard a call to him from the flames: "Help me to come out o' this!" As the man then explained, "When I looked it was a man I used to know in the army, an Irishman, and from this country." He tried, but could not help him.

◆

It is unusually rare that these travelers, upon their return from these strange realms, find what they have seen unconvincing. They make as much of an impression as, and often more than, the waking world they left behind. With that said, for the rest of us, it is the apport that has long been held up as our own way of making this corroboration and of bridging this gap. By some means as yet undefined, while near death or while away in worlds other than what they consider their own, people have conclusively attained accurate information regarding the passing of another. This is our apport of sorts, our "Peak in Darien" experience, and it is expressed widely according to both historical and literary sources.

At times, these experiences have been reported in earnest; at others, they have been used toward didactic ends. There is nothing new in the co-opting of the sacred for profane ends; nevertheless, the extent to which this "Peak in Darien" aspect has been singled out speaks strongly to its very particular novelty and impact. While these tales and accounts often make a profound and powerful impression, and the cross-cultural similarities between them lend evidence to their importance and potentially their ontological status, relatively little has been written of them. Clearly, however, something akin to a "motif" is far too restrictive a classification under which we might file away these personally and otherwise vast experiences.

Scholars have long marveled at and puzzled over the idiosyncratic similarities and motifs between near-death and otherworld journeys across continents, cultures, and time periods. The persistent incredulity with which they are often regarded, however, may simply be because they have so often failed to consider that all have entered and will continue to enter broadly the same space, that same undiscovered country, whatever or wherever its nature may be.

Conclusion

Now that we have reached the end of our journey, one which could easily be extended well beyond the allotted page count, what can be said in summary of these visions? Apart from the more scientific surveys that have gone before, here we have documented something closer to the true depth and breadth of the phenomenon in almost all of its forms and from as wide a variety of sources as could be found. From history's most renowned epics and romances to the most obscure legends and lore of everyday folks, perhaps we can say at least that if ever there was any doubt as to the universality of the crisis apparition and its visionary relatives, it can surely now be disregarded. Of course, much further work can still be done. A similar survey of solely poetical sources would bear great fruit; so too would a deep dive into still untranslated, non-European medieval, and especially Latin literature. The lives of the saints have only been touched upon in terms of the number of relevant visions therein, despite the many pages we've devoted here. Much more scholarly work might be done to sift through those accounts so as to firmly establish which were ascribed by the hagiographer and which were recorded in earnest. Work could begin in establishing links between particular accounts and biblical or pre-biblical motifs, although caution is advised, as of course, we have established the experience very clearly does not have literary origin. Statistical analysis could be applied. There are many potential avenues here and it is hoped that at least some of them will soon be tread. Folklorists have perhaps collected many more of these visions, if not at least as many as have the parapsychologists, a fact which underlines the unfortunate lack of historical dialogue. Surveys confined to some of the regions only mentioned here once or twice would also be a helpful exercise.

As for the book, for some readers, these pages may suggest to them that the world is a little stranger and a little more magical, perhaps even imbued with a little more meaning than they might have imagined; for others, it may confirm what they had already suspected about these long-established experiences or of the metaphysical workings and ways of things in general. In either case, I hope that at the very least, the reader has at some point felt a little of the mystery, the strangeness, and indeed, the humanity that we have seen expressed by those who have experienced a strange yet undeniable form of communication which has brought them hope and expanded their horizons, even in the most dire of moments.

For many reasons, the idea that we "die alone" may be one of the strangest and most criminally unsubstantiated of all our platitudes. Even the briefest survey of the literature revolving around deathbed phenomena is enough to dispel this unhelpful notion. We cannot be said to come into the world alone; we are entirely harbored and guided by strange, still poorly understood and dauntingly complex biological processes from the moment of our conception until the moment of our death. Neither should we expect nature to only allow us a solitary passage out of this world. Death, then, is no cold and unfeeling "worm at the core," as nineteenth century psychologist William James had referred to our knowledge of our mortality. And while those legitimate and painful emotions of loss are there to be honored and felt at its arrival, death nevertheless very often extends a hand not only to the dying with their mirthful visions of those gone before but also to their most loved significant others. Why to some and not to others is something for those strange and perhaps unknowable forces which magically mediate these exchanges to know and for us yet to discover. For those who have been allowed that final goodbye, however, they have been a witness to a quirk of the cosmos which, in a moment, might change them for the better, and forever. We, in turn, would do well to lend them our ear.

Acknowledgments

I am grateful to Patricia Pearson for her wonderful foreword, which adds some much-needed context to the work. My thanks also go to Gregory Shushan for sending some accounts my way! A huge thanks to my editors, both Albo Sudekum and Sharon Reed, for their careful critiques and corrections. This would be no book without them. I am grateful to Richard Grossinger, Jon Graham, and Ehud Sperling for believing in the project. Sincere thanks also to one of my old tutors, Martin, for the slap on the wrist those years ago; it was very much needed! To those friends and flames too, who returned my love, I am grateful; to those who did not, I am perhaps more grateful still.

No long or drawn-out words could ever do justice to those most important to me, so I will simply dedicate this work to them. To those who gave me life, my mother and father, and to those who give me life, my two brothers. With love forever.

Oh, and to an old friend: You were right; I had a book in me after all!

◆

A promise kept

Notes

FOREWORD

1. Piccinini and Rinaldi, *Fantasmi die Morenti*.
2. Cohn, "A Questionnaire Study on Second Sight Experiences," 129–157.
3. Schmied-Knittel and Schetsche, "Everyday Miracles: Results of a Representative Survey in Germany," 11.
4. Elsaesser et al., "The Phenomenology and Impact of Hallucinations Concerning the Deceased," 148.
5. Hardy, *The Spiritual Nature of Man*, 124.
6. Hardy, *The Spiritual Nature of Man*, 21.
7. Beitman, *Meaningful Coincidences*.

INTRODUCTION

1. Pearson, Mossbridge, and Beischel, *Crisis Impressions*, 9.
2. Schouten, "Analysing Spontaneous Cases," 9–48.
3. Lavater, *Of Ghostes and Spirites, Walking by Night*, 72.
4. Prince, *Noted Witnesses For Psychic Occurrences*, 150–51.
5. Lang, *Cock Lane and Common Sense*, 63.
6. Lang, *Book of Dreams and Ghosts*, 116.
7. Blum, *Ghost Hunters*, 124–5.
8. Pearson, Mossbridge, and Beischel, *Crisis Impressions*, 4.
9. Prince, Walter Franklin. *Noted Witnesses for Psychic Occurrences*, 151.
10. Hosmer, *Harriet Hosmer Letters and Memories*, 128–9.
11. Von Bronkhorst. *Dreams at the Threshold*, 14.

I. APPARITIONS, GHOSTS, DEATH, AND HOPE

1. Foster, *Echoes of Egyptian Voices*, 36–9.

2. Foster, *Echoes of Egyptian Voices*, 36–9.

3. Finucane, *Appearances of the Dead*, 2–3.

4. Finkel, *The First Ghosts*, 95–6.

5. Felton, *Haunted Greece and Rome*, 28.

6. Falconer, *Cicero*, 521.

7. Falconer, *Cicero*, 287.

8. Morton, *Ghosts: A Haunted History*, 17–18.

9. Felton, *Haunted Greece and Rome*, 30.

10. Collison-Morley, *Greek and Roman Ghost Stories*, 18.

11. Collison-Morley, *Greek and Roman Ghost Stories*, 62.

12. Sels, "Ambiguity and Mythic Imagery in Homer: Rhesus' Lethal Nightmare," 555–70.13.

13. Plutarch, *De Genio Socratis*. XVI.

14. Harrison, *Prolegomena to the Study of Greek Religion*, 598.

15. Euripedes, *The Plays of Euripides Vol. II*, 133–51.

16. Obeyesekere, *The Awakened Ones*, 104.

17. Jayantakumar and Singh, *Folktales of Manipur*, 16–18.

18. Jayantakumar and Singh, *Folktales of Manipur*, 179.

19. Smith, *Ancient Tales and Folklore of Japan*, 29–35.

20. Iwasaka, *Ghosts and the Japanese*, 92–3.

21. Kim, *The Story Bag*, 208.

22. McClenon, *Wondrous Events*, 152–3.

23. Groot, *The Religious System of China*, vol. V, book II, 638–9.

24. Dennys, *The Folk-Lore of China*, 42–3.

25. Dennys, *The Folk-Lore of China*, 75–6.

26. Hunt, *Popular Romances of the West of England*, 374–6.

27. Rogers, "A Deathbed Vision," 186.

28. Craigie, *Scandinavian Folk-Lore*, 291.

29. Davies, *Balm from Beyond*, 56–8.

30. St. Clair, *Unexplained Encounter*, 28.

31. Jaffe, *Apparitions and Precognition*, 80.

32. Pearson, *Opening Heaven's Door*, 47–8.

33. Flammarion, *Death and its Mystery*, 287.

34. Dance, *Shuckin' and Jivin'*, 32.

35. Hopkins, *Chuj (Mayan) Narratives*, 66.
36. Kracke, "To Dream, Perchance to Cure," 109.
37. Cluness, *Told Round the Peat Fire*, 226–8.
38. Long, *The Secret Science Behind Miracle*, 128.
39. Landtman, *The Kiwai Papuans of British New Guinea*, 278.
40. Landtman, *The Kiwai Papuans of British New Guinea*, 291–2.
41. Malinowski, *Magic, Science and Religion and Other Essays*, 165.
42. Malinowski, *Magic, Science and Religion and Other Essays*, 166.
43. Oliver, *A Solomon Island Society*, 74.
44. Hughes, *New Guinea Folk-Tales*, 72–4.
45. Lohman, *Dream*, 78.
46. Handy, *Marquesan Legends*, 32–4.
47. Terada, *The Magic Crocodile*, 95–6.
48. Cole, *Philippine Folk Tales*, 79–91.
49. Cole, *Philippine Folk Tales*, 47.
50. Burrows, *An Atoll Culture*, 19–10.
51. Firth, "Tikopia Dreams," 17.
52. Baldick, *Imaginary Muslims*, 137–9.
53. Baldick, *Imaginary Muslims*, 210.
54. Văcărescu, *Songs of the Valiant Voivode*, 51–61.
55. Coxwell, *Siberian and Other Folk-Tales*, 395.
56. Parrinder, *African Traditional Religion*, 137.
57. Hayashida, *Dreams in the African Literature*, 227.
58. Flammarion, *Death and its Mystery*, 286.
59. Little, *The Mende of Sierra Leone*, 138.
60. Malcolm, "Notes on the Religious Beliefs of the Eghap, Central Cameroon," 358.
61. Sartori, *The Wisdom of Near-Death Experiences*, 107.
62. Knappert, *The Aquarian Guide to African Mythology*, 21.
63. Htin Aung, *Folk Elements in Burmese Buddhism*, 67–73.
64. Olson, *Social Structure and Social Life of the Tlingit in Alaska*, 72.
65. Converse, *Myths and Legends of the New York State Iroquois*, 43–4.
66. Talayesva, *Sun Chief: The Autobiography of a Hopi Indian*, 253.
67. Westervelt, *Hawaiian Legends of Ghosts and Ghost-Gods*, 7–10.
68. Thrum, *Hawaiian Folk Tales*, 143.
69. Bourne, *Dancing With Witches*, 177.
70. Gusinde, *Folk Literature of the Yamana Indians*, 142–6.

71. Hansen, *The Types of the Folktale in Cuba, Puerto Rico, the Dominican Republic, and Spanish South America*, 92.

72. Reichel-Dolmatoff, *The People of Aritama*, 433.

73. Zur, *Violent Memories: Mayan War Widows*, 207–208.

74. Jagendorf and Boggs, *The King of the Mountains*, 227–8.

75. Jenness, *The Northern D'Entrecasteaux*, 89.

76. Landtman, *The Kiwai Papuans of British New Guinea*, 87.

77. Crawford, *The Wildest Rivers, The Oldest Hills*, 115.

78. Allen, *Korean Tales*, 86.

79. Rahner, *Visions and Prophecies*, 37; Harrison, *Spirits Before Our Eyes*, 140; White, "An Analysis of ESP Phenomena in the Saints," 15–18.

80. Moreira, *Dreams, Visions, and Spiritual Authority in Merovingian Gaul*, 55.

81. "Genuine Letters Sulpitius Severus."

82. Consitt, *Life of Saint Cuthbert*, 3–5.

83. Budge, *The Book of the Saints of the Ethiopian Church*, 426.

84. Florentius, *The Church Historians of England, Vol II: Part I*, 316.

85. McNamara, Halborg, and Whatley, *Sainted Women of the Dark Ages*, 229–30.

86. Rose, *St. Ignatius Loyola and the Early Jesuits*, 235.

87. O'Hanlon, *Lives of the Irish Saints*, 172.

88. De Vitry, *The Exempla*, 1890: 166.

89. Roberts, *Ghosts of the Southern Mountains and Appalachia*, 135.

90. Roberts, *Ghosts of the Southern Mountains and Appalachia*, 135.

91. Merton, *What are These Wounds?*, 55.

92. Johnson, *Purgatory Prov'd by Miracles*, 3–4.

93. Seuse, *The Life of Blessed Henry Suso*, 236–7.

94. Merton, *What are These Wounds?*, 56–7.

95. Lockhart, *Bonaventura*, 135.

96. Bradbury, *The Life of St. Juliana of Cornillon*, 141–2.

97. Stokes, *Lives of Saints, from the Book of Lismore*, 146.

98. Gregory, *The Dialogues of Saint Gregory*, 187

99. Bede, *The Age of Bede*, 88.

100. Ligouri, *Victories of the Martyrs*, 177.

101. Capes, *St. Catherine De' Ricci*, 264.

102. Reeves, 1874, 99.

103. Virtanen, *That Must Have Been ESP!*, 43.

104. Virtanen, *That Must Have Been ESP!*, 45.
105. Bell, *Lives and Legends of the English Bishops and Kings, Mediaeval Monks, and Other Later Saints*, 58.
106. Fenwick, *The Art of Dying*, 155.
107. Rhine, *Hidden Channels of the Mind*, 156.
108. Ligouri, *Victories of the Martyrs*, 237–8.
109. Forbes, *Life of Saint Elizabeth*, 397.
110. Felton, *Haunted Greece and Rome*, 30.
111. Segal, *Life after Death*, 242.
112. O'Hanlon, *Lives of the Irish Saints*, 33.
113. Fielde, *Pagoda Shadows*, 102–3.
114. Kellner, "Token Stories of Indiana," 224–5.
115. Hoffman, *After the Death of a Loved One*, 90.
116. Callanan and Kelley, *Final Gifts*, 84–5.
117. Hitschmann, "Telepathy and Psychoanalysis," 118.
118. Mackenzie, *Apparitions and Ghosts*, 116–7.
119. Morse, *Parting Visions*, 30–1.
120. Fenwick, *The Art of Dying*, 130.
121. Harrison, *Spirits Before Our Eyes*, 113.
122. Lu, *Encounters with the World of Spirits*, 82.
123. Petit, *The Spirituality of the Premonstratensians in the Twelfth and Thirteenth Centuries*, 138–9.
124. Fabrini, *The Life of St. Mary Magdalen De-Pazzi*, 111.
125. All About Heaven, "Dream Meeting with his Dead Friend."
126. Seibold, *Shipwrecks Near Barnegat Inlet*, 92.
127. Lee, *More Glimpses of the World Unseen*, 35.

2. VISIONS, DREAMS AND MEN OF HIGH ESTEEM

1. Kenner and Miller, *Strange but True*, 117.
2. Walker, Jr., *Witchcraft and Sorcery of the American Native Peoples*, 45.
3. Lang, *Book of Dreams*, 93.
4. Charles, *The Apocrypha and Pseudepigrapha of the Old Testament in English*, 138–9.
5. Musick, *The Telltale Lilac Bush and Other West Virginia Ghost Tales*.
6. Owen, *Footfalls on the Boundary of Another World*, 173–8.
7. Garnett, *The Women of Turkey and Their Folk-Lore*, 161–62.

8. Ross and Walker, *On Another Day*, 253–4.

9. Dennett, *Notes of the Folklore of the Fjort (French Congo)*, 33–4.

10. Doke, *The Lambas of Northern Rhodesia*, 217.

11. Doke, *The Lambas of Northern Rhodesia*, 218.

12. Adamson, *Folk-Tales of the Coast Salish*, 155.

13. Skinner, *Myths & Legends of Our Own Land*, 322.

14. *Chippewa Customs*, 78.

15. Luthin, *Surviving Through the Days*, 291–3.

16. St. Clair, "Traditions of the Coos Indians of Oregon," 34–5.

17. Elwin, *Baiga*, 152.

18. Keene, *The Manyoshu*, 224.

19. Guerber, *Legends of The Middle Ages*, 233.

20. Evans-Wentz, *Tibet's Great Yogi Milarepa*, 158–176.

21. Kelley, "Reflections on the Dream Traditions of Islam," 11.

22. Calofonos, "Dream Narratives in Historical Writing," 133–144.

23. Michael the Syrian, *Michael Rabo's Chronicle*, 477.

24. Ibn Khallikan, *Biographical Dictionary*, 124.

25. Bowles and Nichols, *Annals and Antiquities of Lacock Abbey, in the County of Wilts*, 254–6.

26. Mac Firbisigh, *Annals of Ireland*, 159–61.

27. Proctor, *Short Lives of the Dominican Saints*, 48.

28. Sels, *Ambiguity and Mythic Imagery in Homer*, 555–70.

29. Spinka and Downey, *The Chronicle of John Malalas Books VIII-XVIII*, 76.

30. Aeschylus, *Persians*, 15.

31. Skylitzes, *The Chronicle of John Skylitzes*, 228.

32. Dodds, "Telepathy and Clairvoyance in Classical Antiquity," 34.

33. Appianus. *Appian's Roman History*, 403.

34. Tabor, *The Saints in Art: With Their Attributes and Symbols Alphabetically Arranged*, 7–8.

35. Walsh, *New Dictionary of Saints: East and West*, 594.

36. Paterson, *Curiosities of Christian History Prior to the Reformation*, 175–6.

37. Josephus, *The Genuine Works*, 328.

38. Boys, *The Suppressed Evidence*, 305.

39. Wilbert and Simoneau 1988: 253–4.

40. David-Neel, *Magic and Mystery in Tibet*, 143–5.

41. Sinel, "To Dream, Perchance to Cure," 11.

42. Sinel, "To Dream, Perchance to Cure," 83–4.

43. Kerr, *Teresa Helena Higginson*, 356.
44. Kerr, *Teresa Helena Higginson*, 85.
45. Hill, *Keepers of the Sacred Chants*, 208–9.
46. Ferreira, *Mapping Time, Space and the Body: Indigenous Knowledge and Mathematical Thinking in Brazil*, 201–2.
47. Rasmussen, *Across Arctic America*, 12–17.
48. London Dialectical Society, *Report on Spiritualism of the Committee of the London Dialectical Society*, 216.
49. Bierhorst, *The Mythology of South America*, 73.
50. Skeat, *Malay Magic*, 285.
51. Davies, *Folklore of West and Mid-Wales*, 278.
52. Brittan, *Man and His Relations*, 336–7.
53. Schouppe, *Purgatory*, 296–7.
54. Peters, *At Heaven's Door*, 76–94.
55. Boas, *Tsimshian Mythology*, 9–11.
56. Boas, *Tsimshian Mythology*, 18.
57. Turner, *Revelation and Divination in Ndembu Ritual*, 247–8.
58. Landtman, *The Kiwai Papuans of British New Guinea*, 278.
59. Steward, *Northern and Gosiute Shoshone*, 286.
60. Kroeber, *Walapai Ethnography*, 70.
61. Lawrie, *Myths and Legends of the Torres Strait*, 224.
62. Elwin, *Bondo Highlander*, 156.
63. Schwab, "Bulu Folk-Tales," 273.
64. Moss, *The Secret History of Dreaming*, 6.
65. Head, *Hagiography and the Cult of Saints*, 146–7.
66. Gusinde, *Folk Literature of the Yamana Indians*, 195–6.
67. Barbeau, *Haida Myths Illustrated in Argillite Carvings*, 332–3.
68. Downing, *Russian Tales and Legends*, 135–7.
69. Ury, *Tales of Times Now Past Collection*, 71–3.
70. Dykstra, *The Otogiboko*, 169–172.
71. Robe, *Hispanic Legends from New Mexico*, 66–7.
72. Virtanen, *That Must Have Been ESP!*, 126.
73. Kalweit, *Shamans, Healers and Medicine Men*, 66; Gaddis, *American Indian Myths and Mysteries*, 135.
74. Frazer, *Lectures on the Early History of the Kingship*, 57.
75. Long, *The Secret Science Behind Miracles*, 128.
76. Gurney, Myers, and Podmore, *Phantasms of the Living*, 300–301.

77. Jenness, *The Life of the Copper Eskimos*, 200.

78. Codrington, *The Melanesians: Studies in their Anthropology and Folklore*, 209.

79. Boas, "Traditions of the Tillamook Indians," 27.

80. Velimirovic, *Stories of Saints from the Prologue*, 64.

81. Schwartz, *Lilith's Cave: Jewish Tales of the Supernatural*, 28.

82. Dodds, *The Ancient Concept of Progress*, 175.

83. Carey, *Maryland Folklore*, 43.

84. Laubscher, *Sex Custom and Psychopathology*, 41.

85. Shirokogorov, *Pyschomental Complex of the Tungus*, 117–8; Berndt and Berndt, *The World of the First Australians*, 458.

86. Casagrande, "The Ojibwa's Psychic Universe," 33–40.

87. Creighton, *Folklore of Lunenburg County, Nova Scotia*, 29.

88. El Eflaki, *Legends of the Sufis*, 99.

89. Dodds, *The Ancient Concept of Progress and Other Essays on Greek Literature and Belief*, 169.

90. Craigie, *Scandinavian Folk-Lore*, 291–2.

91. Lang, *Cock Lane and Common Sense*, 43.

92. Maori, *Old New Zealand*, 164.

93. Kennedy, "Psychic Phenomena in the Orkney Islands," 129.

94. Rogers, *Dreams and Premonitions*, 49–50.

95. Buck, *Vikings of the Pacific*, 225–6.

96. Attwater, *Martyrs: from St. Stephen to John Tung*, 78.

97. Mayer, *Extraordinary Knowing: Science, Skepticism, and the Inexplicable Powers of the Human Mind*, 1–10.

98. Wimberly, *Death and Burial Lore in the English and Scottish Popular Ballads*, 68.

99. van der Post, *The Lost World of the Kalahari*, 236–7.

100. Hedin, *Sven Hedin: A Conquest of Tibet*, 71–4.

101. Green, *These Wonders to Behold*, 44–5.

102. Green, *These Wonders to Behold*, 48–9.

103. McClenon, *Wondrous Events*, 47.

104. Shirokogorov, *Pyschomental Complex of the Tungus*, 118–9.

105. Kidd, *The Essential Kaffir*, 344–5.

106. Gaddis, *American Indian Myths and Mysteries*, 168.

107. Long, *The Secret Science Behind Miracles*, 154.

108. Bound, *Falkland Islanders at War*, 18.

109. Matthews, *The Two Worlds of Jimmie Barker*, 70.
110. Matthews, *The Two Worlds of Jimmie Barker*, 70.
111. Routledge, *The Mystery of Easter Island*, 142.
112. Creighton, *Bluenose Ghosts*, 26.
113. Godsell, "Moccasin Telegraph," 95–9.
114. Codrington, *The Melanesians*, 207–8.
115. Toelken, "The Moccasin Telegraph," 46–7.
116. Toelken, "The Moccasin Telegraph," 48.
117. Kidd, *The Essential Kaffir*, 340.
118. Schwab, *Tribes of the Liberian Hinterland*, 232, 241.
119. Maori, *Old New Zealand*, 166–7.
120. Britten, *Nineteenth Century Miracles*, 264.
121. Redesdale, *Tales of Old Japan*, 103.
122. Russell, *The Lives of the Desert Fathers*, 97.
123. John of Ephesus, *Lives of the Eastern Saints I*, 297.
124. Davies, *Supernatural Vanishings*, 59–60.
125. Tyler, *Japanese Tales*, 129.
126. Aries, *The Hour of Our Death*, 7.
127. Bell, *Lives and Legends*, 193.
128. Elkin, *Australian Aborigines*, 211–2.
129. McGovern, *Jungle Paths and Inca Ruins*, 197.
130. Kensinger, "Banisteriopsis Usage Among the Peruvian Cashinahua," 9.
131. Homan, "Charlatans, Seekers, and Shamans," 57.
132. Ayahuasca Timeline, "1905—'Telepathine' is Suggested as a Name for the Active Ingredient in the Ayahuasca Vine."
133. Grof, *Human Encounter with Death*, 111.
134. Schouppe, *Purgatory: Illustrated by the Lives and Legends of the Saints*, 16–7.
135. Caesarius, *The Dialogue on Miracles vols 1–2*, 264.
136. Hamilton, "God Wills It: Signs of Divine Approval in the Crusade Movement," 113.
137. Leslie, *Among the Zulus and Amatongas*, 56.
138. Leslie, *Among the Zulus and Amatongas*, 57.
139. Powers, *Tribes of California*, 91.
140. Morrison and Russell, *Streams in the Desert*, 28.
141. Jockle, *Encyclopedia of Saints*, 172–3.
142. Poignant, *Oceanic Mythology*, 84.

143. Scott, *The Minstrelsy of the Scottish Border*, 78–9.

144. Sinel, "To Dream, Perchance to Cure," 468.

145. Rose, *Living Magic*, 146.

146. Rose, *Living Magic*, 18–9.

147. Rose, *Living Magic*, 155.

148. Malinowski, *Sexual Life of Savages in North-Western Melanesia*, 388.

149. Shirokogorov, *Psychomental Complex of the Tungus*, 118.

150. Rhine, *New Fronters of the Mind*, 2–3.

151. Laskow, "The Role of the Supernatural in the Discovery of EEGs."

3. THOSE WHO SEE, THOSE WHO DON'T

1. Numbers 12:6.

2. Samuel 28:3–25.

3. Finkel, *The First Ghosts*, 69.

4. Emerson, *Unwritten Literature of Hawaii*, 212.

5. Bäckman, *Studies in Lapp Shamanism*, 95.

6. Beckwith, *Black Roadways*, 88.

7. Eliade, *Man and the Sacred*, 30.

8. Talbot, *In the Shadows of the Bush*, 230.

9. Parker, *The Euahlayi Tribe*, 30.

10. Kroeber, *Ethnology of the Gros Ventre*, 233.

11. Karsten, *The Civilization of the South American Indians*, 118.

12. Hanauer, *Tales Told in Palestine*, 139.

13. Caesarius, *The Dialogue on Miracles vols 1–2*, 493.

14. Gregory I, *The Dialogues of Saint Gregory*, 187.

15. Howells, *Cambrian Superstitions*, 13.

16. Tylor, *Primitive Culture*, 449.

17. Oberg, *Indian Tribes of the Northern Mato Grosso*, 60.

18. Kennedy, "Psychic Phenomena in the Orkney Islands," 134–5.

19. Podmore, *Apparitions and Thought-Transference*, 258.

20. Mason Neale, *The Unseen World*, 168–9.

21. Gurney, Myers, and Podmore, *Phantasms of the Living*, 357.

22. Harrisson, "Cultural Memory and Imagination," 197.

23. Devereux, *Dreams in Greek Tragedy*, 28.

24. Teeter, *Religion and Ritual in Ancient Egypt*, 102.

25. Hornung, *Conceptions of God in Ancient Egypt*, 130.

26. Finkel, *The First Ghosts*, 70.

27. Taillepied, *A Treatise of Ghosts*, 97–8.

28. Wade, *Select Proverbs of all Nations*, 180.

29. Finucane, *Appearances of the Dead*, 39.

30. Friedman, *The Penguin Book of Folk Ballads of the English-Speaking World*, 34.

31. Belsey, *Tales of the Troubled Dead*, 15.

32. Cartlidge and Dungan, *Documents for the Study of the Gospels*, 240.

33. Dodds, "Telepathy and Clairvoyance in Classical Antiquity," 34.

34. White, *Life of Emanuel Swedenborg*, 141.

35. Mason, *The Historic Martyrs of the Primitive Church*, 119–20.

36. Virtanen, *That Must Have Been ESP!*, 35.

37. Spence, *Legends and Romances of Spain*, 335–8.

38. Gurney, Myers, and Podmore, *Phantasms of the Living*, 557.

39. Connor, *Shamans of the World*, 171–2.

40. Gregory I, *The Dialogues of Saint Gregory*, 188.

41. Kenney, *The Sources for the Early History of Ireland*, 611.

42. Adamnan, *Life of Saint Columba, Founder of Hy*, 21.

43. Adamnan, *Life of Saint Columba, Founder of Hy*, 83.

44. Keenan, "Life of St. Anthony," 187–8.

45. Fabrini, *The Life of St. Mary Magdalen De-Pazzi*, 118.

46. Fabrini, *The Life of St. Mary Magdalen De-Pazzi*, 119.

47. Bede, *The Age of Bede*, 79–81.

48. Bede, *The Age of Bede*, 87–8.

49. Rolfe, *The Attic Nights of Aulus Gellius vol. 3*, 103.

50. Calmet, *The Phantom World*, 210.

51. Spence, *Legends and Romances of Spain*, 339–40.

52. Calmet, *The Phantom World*, 187.

53. Velimirovich, "Reflection," under December 24 in *The Prologue from Ohrid*.

54. Inglis, *The Paranormal*, 50.

55. Betzinez, *I Fought with Gerolimo*, 115.

56. Mackenzie, *The Spirit-Ridden Konde*, 168–9.

57. Summers, *The Physical Phenomena of Mysticism*, 66.

58. Vyasa, *The Mahābhārata*, 588.

59. Mackenzie, *Indian Myth and Legend*, 287.

60. Bhatt, *Yogic Powers and God Realization*, 198–9.

61. al-Suyuti, *History of the Caliphs*, 478.

62. Moosa, *Crusades*, 250.

63. Kieckefer, *Unquiet Souls*, 162.

64. Wodrow, *Analecta*, 64.

65. Dalyell, *The Darker Superstitions of Scotland*, 515.

66. Owen, *The Legend of Roland: A Pageant of the Middle Ages*, 182.

67. Jirasek, *Legends of Old Bohemia*, 136–7.

4. ALLEGORICAL VISIONS
AND SYMBOLIC APPARITIONS

1. Zupitza, *The Romance of Guy of Warwick*, 231–2.

2. Rickert, *Early English Romances in Verse*, 19–21.

3. Loomis, *Three Middle English Romances*, 46–7.

4. Loomis, *Three Middle English Romances*, 46–7.

5. Halliwell, *Morte Arthure*, 14–5.

6. Bedier, *The Romance of Tristan and Iseult*, 149.

7. Jung, *Memories, Dreams, Reflections*, 303.

8. Smartt, *Words at the Threshold*, 47.

9. Callanan and Kelley, *Final Gifts*, 72.

10. Fenwick, *The Art of Dying*, 62.

11. Pearson, *Opening Heaven's Door*, 22.

12. Virtanen *That Must Have Been ESP!*, 41.

13. Gregory, *Visions and Beliefs in the West of Ireland*, 92.

14. Davies, *Folklore of West and Mid-Wales*, 277.

15. Wodrow, *Analecta*, 45–6.

16. Morgan, *Talking to the Dead*, 27–8.

17. Asai, *The Otogiboko: A Collection of Ghost Stories of Old Japan*, 83.

18. Asai, *The Otogiboko*, 86.

19. Kao, *Classical Chinese Tales of the Supernatural and the Fantastic*, 78.

20. Ritter, *The Ocean of the Soul*, 196.

21. Ritter, *The Ocean of the Soul*, 648–9.

22. Gregg, *Devils, Women, and Jews*, 116.

23. Caesarius, *The Dialogue on Miracles vols 1–2*, 273.

24. O'Grady, *Silva Gadelica*, 182–3.

25. Jakobsen, *Slavic Epic Studies*, 329.

26. Guerber, *Legends of The Middle Ages*, 149–50.

27. Macpherson, *The Poems of Ossian Volume I*, 234.

28. Simpson, *The Northmen Talk*, 72.

29. Fraser, "The First Battle of Moytura," 1–63.

30. Curtin, *Myths of the Modocs*, 153–8.

31. Curtin, *Myths of the Modocs*, 159–67.

32. Fowke, *Folktales of French Canada*, 106–7.

33. Dasent, *The Story of Gisli the Outlaw*, 42–48.

34. Schwartz, *Lilith's Cave*, 160–5.

35. Anonymous, "The Saga of Viga-Glum," 31.

36. Adams, *Ghost Stories of the Lehigh Valley*, 87.

37. Crum, "Another Fragment of the Story of Alexander," 475–7.

38. Klotsche, *The Supernatural in the Tragedies of Euripides*, 48–9.

39. Klotsche, *The Supernatural in the Tragedies of Euripides*, 24.

40. Watson, "Hiding from Pandemics, and from Ourselves: The Case of Ben Jonson."

41. van Diemerbroeck, *Tractatus de Peste*, 262–3.

42. Gregory I, *The Dialogues of Saint Gregory*, 96.

43. Caesarius, *The Dialogue on Miracles vols 1–2*, 449.

44. Pinch, *Magic in Ancient Egypt*, 35.

45. Tabor, *The Saints in Art*, 42.

46. Halpert, "Death Beliefs from Indiana," 208.

47. Børtnes, *Visions of Glory*, 75.

48. Curtin, *A Journey in Southern Siberia*, 114.

49. Rink, *Tales and Traditions of the Eskimo*, 43.

50. Jockle, *Encyclopedia of Saints*, 172–3.

51. Iwasaka, *Ghosts and the Japanese*, 93.

52. Windham, *Sixty Saints for Girls*, 195–6.

53. Bradbury, *The Life of St. Juliana of Cornillon*, 58.

54. Gurney, Myers, and Podmore, *Phantasms of the Living*, 187.

55. Sacheverell, *An Account of the Isle of Man*, 20.

56. Kennedy, "Psychic Phenomena in the Orkney Islands," 129.

57. Algarin, *Japanese Folk Literature*, 136.

58. Henderson, *Notes on the Folklore of the Northern Counties of England and the Borders*, 339–40.

59. Pearson, *Opening Heaven's Door*, 6.

60. Wanley, *The Wonders of the Little World*, 291.

61. Trevelyan, *Garibaldi and the Thousand*, 17–18.

62. Pearson, *Opening Heaven's Door*, 7.

63. Ennemoser, *The History of Magic Volume I*, 68.

64. Vitalis, Ordericus. *The Ecclesiastical History of England and Normandy Vol. II*, 511–20.

65. Gurney, Myers, and Podmore, *Phantasms of the Living*, 366–7.

66. Allingham, "The Dream," 23–4.

67. Gregory, *Poets and Dreamers*, 25–6.

68. Dale, *Footfalls on the Boundary of Another World*, 178.

69. Iwasaka, *Ghosts and the Japanese*, 100.

70. Robe, *Hispanic Legends from New Mexico*, 67–8.

71. Crawford, *The Wildest Rivers, The Oldest Hills*, 116.

72. Carey, *A Faraway Time and Place*, 193.

73. Leeson, "Certain Canadian Superstitions," 76.

74. Jenness, *The Life of the Copper Eskimos*, 200.

75. Gregory, *Visions and Beliefs in the West of Ireland*, 59.

76. Deitz, *The Greenbriar Ghost and Other Strange Stories*, 58.

77. Watkins, "Ghosts and Visions that People have Seen," 6.

78. Terkel, *Will the Circle Be Unbroken*, 174–5.

79. Melland, *In Witch-Bound Africa*, 246.

80. Tremearne, *The Ban of the Bori*, 144.

81. Jaffe, *Apparitions and Precognition*, 20.

82. Schwarz, *Beyond the Gates of Death*, 61.

83. Proctor, *Short Lives Of The Dominican Saints*, 247–8.

84. Velimirovich, "Hymn of Praise," under February 14 in the *Prologue from Ohrid*.

5. MAGIC, THINGS BROKEN, AND THE LEGENDS OF THE LIFE TOKEN

1. Rink, *Tales and Traditions of the Eskimo*, 44.

2. Bellows, *The Poetic Edda*, 463.

3. Latham, *The Folklore Record Part I*, 58.

4. Elwin, *The Religion of an Indian Tribe*, 501.

5. Steel, *Tales of the Punjab Told by the People*, 71–9.

6. Knappert, *Pacific Mythology*, 305.

7. Moldenke, *The Tale of the Two Brothers*, 62.

8. Talbot, *Tribes of the Niger Delta*, 121.

9. Harrison, *Themis*, 103.

10. Doran, *The Lives of Simeon Stylites*, 172.

11. Sturluson, *Heimskringla*, 75.

12. Meltzer, *Birth*, 205.

13. Cole, *Philippine Folk Tales*, 27–8.

14. Neusner, *The Tosefta: An Introduction*, 259.

15. Strauss, "The Death of Meleager in the Mid-Sixteenth Century," 32.

16. Hanauer, *Tales Told in Palestine*, 163.

17. Winters, "The Saga of Norna-Gest: Does Man Control His Destiny?"

18. Bournoutian, *The Travel Accounts of Siméon of Poland*, 88.

19. Davidson, *Myths and Symbols in Pagan Europe*, 140.

20. Malory, *Le Morte d'Arthur*, 65.

21. Grose, *A Provincial Glossary*, 120.

22. Robe, *Hispanic Legends from New Mexico*, 60.

23. Erben and Strickland, *Russian and Bulgarian Folklore Stories*, 62.

24. Calvino, *Italian Folk Tales*, 98–9.

25. Pedroso and Monteiro, *Portuguese Folktales*, 50–1.

26. Christiansen, *Folktales of Norway*, 177.

27. Stroebe, *The Swedish Fairy Book*, 43–51.

28. Bain, *Cossack Fairy Tales and Folk Tales*, 211.

29. Kriza et al., *The Folktales of the Magyars*, 111–2.

30. Wardrop, *Georgian Folk Tales*, 53.

31. Afanas'ev, *Russian Fairy Tales*, 186.

32. Villa, *100 Armenian Tales*, 280–1.

33. St. Lys, *From a Vanished German Colony*, 108.

34. Hooper, *The Cahuilla Indians*, 135.

35. Kincaid, *The Indian Heroes*, 135.

36. Rafy, *Folk-Tales of the Khasis*, 26–35.

37. Steel, *Tales of the Punjab Told by the People*, 71–9.

38. Theal, *The Yellow and Dark-Skinned People of Africa South of the Zambesi*, 296.

39. Doke, *The Lambas of Northern Rhodesia*, 19.

40. Larson, *Opaque Shadows and Other Stories from Contemporary Africa*, 31.

41. Vigil, *The Eagle on the Cactus*, 142.

42. Parker, *The Euahlayi Tribe*, 47.

43. Parker, *The Euahlayi Tribe*, 49.

44. Kroeber, *More Mohave Myths*, 105–6.

45. Senungetuk, *Wise Words of Paul Tiulana*, 49.

46. Reichard, *An Analysis of Coeur d'Alene Indian Myths*, 69.

47. Kelly, *The End of Empire*, 265.

48. Warner, *Heroes, Monsters and Other Worlds from Russian Mythology*, 20.

49. MacManus, *Donegal Fairy Stories*, 49–50.

50. Oakley and Gairola, *Himalayan Folklore*, 45.

51. Fenwick, *The Art of Dying*, 134–5.

52. Fenwick, *The Art of Dying*, 136.

53. Creighton, *Folklore of Lunenburg County, Nova Scotia*, 29.

54. Carey, *A Faraway Time and Place*, 193.

55. Truss, "The Psychic Story of a Parson," 62.

56. Creighton, *Folklore of Lunenburg County, Nova Scotia*, 24.

57. Creighton, *Folklore of Lunenburg County, Nova Scotia*, 25.

58. Wimberly, *Death and Burial Lore*, 43.

59. Wimberly, 42.

60. Wimberly, 72.

61. Wimberly, 73.

62. Wimberly, 8, 71.

63. Work, *Songs of Henry Clay Work*, 178–80.

6. MESSENGERS, TOTEMS, ANGELS, AND TOKENS

1. Bassett, *Sea Phantoms*, 293.

2. Calmet, *The Phantom World*, 280.

3. Perera, *Sinhalese Folklore Notes: Ceylon*, 11.

4. FitzRoy, *Surveying Voyages of His Majesty's Ships*, 181, 204.

5. Virtue, *Angel Visions*, 65–6.

6. Morgan, *Talking to the Dead*, 142.

7. Aubrey, *Miscellanies upon Various Subjects*, 62–3.

8. Rhine, *Hidden Channels of the Mind*, 82.

9. Chadwick, *Anglo-Saxon and Norse Poems*, 118.

10. Snorrason, *The Sagas of Olaf Tryggvason and of Harald the Tyrant*, 60.

11. Percy, *Reliques of Ancient English Poetry Vol. III*, 223.

12. Lichtenstadter, *Introduction to Classical Arabic Literature*, 206.

13. Green, *Words and Ways*, 128–9.

14. Lysaght, *Banshee*, 66.

15. Lysaght, *Banshee*, 238–9.

16. Jaffe, *Apparitions and Precognition*, 20.

17. Flammarion, *Death and its Mystery*, 285–286.

18. Leloudis, "Tokens of Death: Tales from Perquimans County," 49.

19. Gregory, *Visions and Beliefs in the West of Ireland*, 49.

20. Espinosa, "New-Mexican Spanish Folk-Lore," 395–418.

21. Elwin, *Bondo Highlander*, 202.

22. Wanley, *The Wonders of the Little World*, 290–1.

23. Heathcote-James, *After-Death Communication*, 44–5.

24. Chamberlain, *Things Japanese*, 29.

25. Thrum, *Hawaiian Folk Tales*, 215–220.

26. Westervelt, *Hawaiian Legends of Ghosts and Ghost-Gods*, 14–5.

27. Skeat, *Malay Magic*, 70.

28. Curtin, *A Journey in Southern Siberia*, 114–15.

29. Teit, *Traditions of the Thompson River Indians of British Columbia*, 84–5.

30. von Haxthausen, *Transcaucasia*, 272.

31. Wells, *Untold Stories and Unknown Saints*, 153.

32. Peebles, "Sulpicius Severus Writings," 132.

33. Goldman, *The Cubeo: Indians of the Northwest Amazon*, 148.

34. Blacker, *The Catalpa Bow*, 177.

35. Walsh, "Rendering 20th Century Peruvian Folklore," 46–7.

36. Sturluson, *The Elder Edda*, 206.

37. Minov, *The Marvels Found in the Great Cities Vol. 6*, 65.

38. Bierhorst, *The Mythology of Mexico and Central America*, 102–10.

39. Bierhorst, *The Mythology of Mexico and Central America*, 38–42.

40. Talayesva, *Sun Chief*, 300–01.

41. Steele, *The Russian Garland*, 5.

42. Dolch and Dolch, *Stories from Italy*, 13–31.

43. Hunt, *Popular Romances of the West of England*, 372–3.

44. Webster, *Basque Legends*, 73–5.

45. Robe, *Hispanic Legends from New Mexico*, 73.

46. Theal, *Kaffir Folk-Lore*, 54–63.

47. Bierhorst, *The Mythology of South America*, 132–3.

48. Gaster, *The Exempla of the Rabbis*, 125–6.

49. Elliot, *The Apocryphal New Testament*, 369.

50. Moosa, *Ghulat Beliefs*, 68.

51. Barbeau, *Huron and Wyandot Mythology*, 142–4.

52. Wheeler, *Albanian Wonder Tales*, 99–125.

53. Kinberg, "The Individual's Experience as it Applies to the Community," 429–30.

54. Sayers, "Gunnarr, his Irish Wolfhound Sámr, and the Passing of the Old Heroic Order in Njáls saga," 51.

55. Bourns, "Between Nature and Culture," 65.

56. Haggard, *The Days of My Life, Vol. 2*, 159–161.

57. Rose, *Living Magic*, 148–9.

58. Latham, *The Folklore Record Part I*, 52.

59. Ruby and Brown, *Dreamer-Prophets of the Columbia Plateau*, 20.

60. Garfield and Forrest, *The Wolf and the Raven*, 83.

61. Shirokogorov, *Psychomental Complex of the Tungus*, 117–8.

62. Gaddis, *American Indian Myths and Mysteries*, 173.

63. Spier, *The Sinkaietk or Southern Okanagon*, 212.

64. Wallace, *The Comanches*, 172–3.

65. Rose, *Living Magic*, 146.

66. Parker, *The Euahlayi Tribe*, 28.

67. Giles, *William of Malmesbury's Chronicle of The Kings of England*, 230.

68. Courlander, *People of the Short Blue Corn*, 47.

69. Schwarz, *Tales from the Smokehouse*, 37–41.

70. Spier, *The Sinkaietk or Southern Okanagon*, 171.

71. Armstrong, *Rossel Island*, 118.

72. O'Donnel, *The Meaning of Dreams*, 10.

73. Virtanen, *That Must Have Been ESP!*, 127.

74. Rose, *Living Magic*, 152.

75. Herbermann, *The Catholic Encyclopedia. Vols. 1–16*, 507.

76. Bäckman, *Studies in Lapp Shamanism*, 96.

77. Fraser, *Folklore of Nova Scotia*, 45.

78. Barbeau, *Totem Poles of the Gitksan*, 11–12.

79. Karsten, *The Civilization of the South American Indians*, 275.

80. Carey, *A Faraway Time and Place*, 176.

81. Smith, *Life is Forever*, 74–76.

82. Hogg, *The Tales of James Hogg*, 272–75.

83. Walton, *The Lives of Dr. John Donne*, 46–7.

84. Henderson, *Notes on the Folklore of the Northern Counties of England and the Borders*, 341.

85. Parrinder, *West African Psychology*, 92–3.

86. Guggenheim and Guggenheim, *Hello from Heaven*, 226–7.

87. Kellner, "Token Stories of Indiana," 225.

88. Heathcote-James, *After-Death Communication*, 50–2.

89. Stevenson, *Telepathic Impressions*, 1–2.

90. Fabrini, *The Life of St. Mary Magdalen De-Pazzi*, 110.

91. Pearson, *Opening Heaven's Door*, 6.

92. Virtue, *Angel Visions*, 103.

93. Green and Kiddell-Monroe, *A Book of Myths*, 18.

94. Rhine, *Hidden Channels of the Mind*, 70.

95. Grattan, *Considerations on the Human Mind*, 103–4.

96. Kepelino, *Kepelino's Traditions of Hawaii*, 122.

97. Reed, *Papua New Guinea's Last Place*, 12–13.

98. Reed, *Papua New Guinea's Last Place*, 14.

99. Kroeber, *Indian Myths of South Central California*, 242.

7. VERIDICAL VOICES AND SUPERNATURAL NOISES

1. Pearson, *Opening Heaven's Door*, 7.

2. Livo, *Story Medicine*, 78.

3. Herbermann, *The Catholic Encyclopedia. Vols. 1–16*, 515.

4. The William Davidson Talmud, Sotah 33a.

5. The William Davidson Talmud, Taanit 29a, Avodah Zarah 18a:13.

6. Alexander and Donaldson, *Ante-Nicene Christian Library, Vol. 16*, 14.

7. Elliot, *The Apocryphal New Testament*, 282.

8. Elliot, *The Apocryphal New Testament*, 699.

9. Attar, *Muslim Saints and Mystics*, 51.

10. Ginzberg, *The Legends of the Jews*, 473.

11. Plutarch, *Plutarch's Morals*, 23.

12. Britannica, "Pan."

13. Maclagan, "Ghost Lights of the West Highlands," 235.

14. Caesarius, *The Dialogue on Miracles vols 1–2*, 298.

15. Caesarius, *The Dialogue on Miracles vols 1–2*, 299.

16. Morse, *Parting Visions*, 30.

17. Günther, *Tale and Legends of the Tyrol*, 1–8.

18. Asbjørnsen, *Norske Huldreeventyr og Folkesagn*, 15.

19. Adamson, *Folk-Tales of the Coast Salish*, 124–6.

20. Bateman, *Zanzibar Tales Told by Natives of the East Coast of Africa*, 208.

21. Schwab, *Tribes of the Liberian Hinterland*, 241.

22. Bromhall, *An History of Apparitions*, 231–2.

23. Child, *Isaac T. Hopper: A True Life*, 262–3.

24. Child, *Isaac T. Hopper*, 263.

25. Haraldsson, *The Departed Among the Living*, 98.

26. Virtanen *That Must Have Been ESP!*, 90.

27. Grayson, *Myths and Legends from Korea*, 238–9.

28. Boys, *The Suppressed Evidence*, 306–7.

29. Flammarion, *Death and its Mystery*, 298.

30. Merton, *What are These Wounds?*, 55.

31. Schouppe, *Purgatory*, 179–80.

32. Nicholson, *Studies in Islamic Mysticism*, 164–5.

33. Keenan, *Early Christian Biographies Vol. 15*, 188–9.

34. Clarke, *The Lausiac History of Palladius*, 59.

35. Lang, *The Arabian Nights Entertainment*, 216–45.

36. Podmore, *Apparitions and Thought-Transference*, 181.

37. Pedroso and Monteiro, *Portuguese Folktales*, 41–4.

38. Pearson, Mossbridge, and Beischel, *Crisis Impressions*, 20.

39. Inglis, *The Paranormal*, 177.

40. Radcliffe, *Fiends, Ghosts, and Spirits*, 241–2.

41. Coffin, *Death in Early America*, 64–5.

42. Denham and Hardy, *The Denham Tracts*, 272–3.

43. Boswell, *Everybody's Boswell*, 404–5.

44. MacLean, *The Indians of Canada*, 179.

45. Jones, *Fox Texts*, 337–9.

46. Welsch, *A Treasury of Nebraska Pioneer Folklore*, 223.

47. Olson, *The Quinault Indians*, 168–9.

48. Courlander, *Tales of Yoruba Gods and Heroes*, 101–9.

49. Inglis, *The Paranormal*, 52.

50. Courlander, *Tales of Yoruba Gods and Heroes*, 153–4.

51. Savage, *Life Beyond Death*, 31.

52. Britten, *Nineteenth Century Miracles*, 136.

53. Lysaght, *Banshee*, 45, 47.

54. Lysaght, *Banshee*, 51; Camerarius, *The Living Librarie*, 284.

55. Thompson, *The Mystery and Lore of Apparitions*, 26–7.

56. Felton, *Haunted Greece and Rome*, 60.

57. Flammarion, *Death and its Mystery*, 262.

58. Lavater, *Of Ghostes and Spirites*, 77.

59. Creighton, *Folklore of Lunenburg County, Nova Scotia*, 26.

60. Creighton, *Folklore of Lunenburg County, Nova Scotia*, 26.

61. Robe, *Hispanic Legends from New Mexico*, 72.

62. Virtanen, *That Must Have Been ESP!*, 33.

63. Normann, "Norwegian Folktales," 64.

64. Summers, *The Vampire in Europe*, 177.

65. Newell, "Current Superstitions," 20.

66. Senungetuk, *Wise Words of Paul Tiulana*, 49.

67. Halpert, "Death Beliefs from Indiana," 213.

68. Baker, *Hoosier Folk Legends*, 43.

69. Matthews, *The Two Worlds of Jimmie Barker*, 72.

70. Johnson, *What they Say in New England*, 112.

71. Rose, *Living Magic*, 151.

72. Lavater, *Of Ghostes and Spirites*, 78–9.

73. McClintock, *Old Indian Trails*, 135.

74. Grinnell, *The Cheyenne Indians*, 99.

75. Grinnell, *The Cheyenne Indians*, 109.

76. Kroeber, *Ethnology of the Gros Ventre*, 233.

77. Vickers, "Cultural Adaptation to Amazonian Habitats," 236.

78. Faron, *Hawks of the Sun*, 58.

79. Jackson, *The Fish People*, 113–4.

80. Calmet, *The Phantom World*, 284.

81. Beckwith, *Black Roadways*, 90.

82. Hobley, *Ethnology of A-Kamba and other East African Tribes*, 86.

83. Burton, *Sindh and the Races That Inhabit the Valley of the Indus*, 354.

84. Rogers, *New Guinea: Big Man Island*, 56.

85. Landtman, *The Kiwai Papuans of British New Guinea*, 278; Newton, *In Far New Guinea*, 227.

86. Hyatt, *Folk-Lore from Adams County Illinois*, 602.

87. Malinowski, *Magic, Science and Religion and Other Essays*, 151.

88. Parker, *Australian Legendary Tales*, 82.

89. Tabor, *The Saints in Art*, 45.

90. Le Braz, *La Légende de la Mort*, 273.

91. Hauteville, *Histoire de la Tres Ancienne et Illustre Maison de Saint Francois de Sale*, 318–9.

92. Paris, *Matthew Paris's English History Vol III*, 50–1.

93. Temperley, *Tales of Galloway*, 238–241.

94. Iwasaka, *Ghosts and the Japanese*, 92–3.
95. Randolph, *Ozark Superstitions*, 302.
96. Flammarion, *Death and its Mystery*, 301.
97. Flammarion, *Death and its Mystery*, 261–2.
98. Hight, *The Saga of Grettir the Strong*, 96.
99. Masters, *The Natural History of the Vampire*, 145.
100. Hobley, *Ethnology of A-Kamba and other East African Tribes*, 88.
101. Rose, *Living Magic*, 20.
102. Seymour and Neligan, *True Irish Ghost Stories*, 149–151.
103. Hooper, *The Cahuilla Indians*, 340.

8. MAKING THE ROUNDS
AND COLLECTIVE ACCOUNTS

1. Guggenheim and Guggenheim, *Hello from Heaven*, 221.
2. Mesegeuer, *The Secret of Dreams*, 130.
3. Zerffi, *Spiritualism and Animal Magnetism*, 111.
4. Martin, *A Description of the Western Islands of Scotland*, 301.
5. Clarke, *The Lausiac History Of Palladius*, 52.
6. Sozomen, *The Ecclesiastical History of Sozomen*, 246.
7. Southwell, *A Short Rule of Good*, 4.
8. Keenan, *Early Christian Biographies Vol. 15*, 390.
9. Attar, *Muslim Saints and Mystics*, 98.
10. Jockle, *Encyclopedia of Saints*, 231–2.
11. Sevcenko, "Canon and Calendar," 103.
12. Baring-Gould, *The Lives of the British Saints* (1907), 298–9.
13. Maclagan, "Ghost Lights of the West Highlands," 252.
14. Morgan, *Talking to the Dead*, 150.
15. Peers, *The Early Northern Painters*, 128.
16. Capes, *St. Rose of Lima: The Flower of the New World*, 181.
17. Baring-Gould, *The Lives of the British Saints* (1911), 313.
18. Adamnan, *Life of Saint Columba, Founder of Hy*, 98–9.
19. Verrier, *Myths of Middle India*, 441.
20. Caesarius, *The Dialogue on Miracles vols 1–2*, 15.
21. Jones and Kropf, *The Folktales of the Magyars*, 34–5.
22. Kroeber, *Seven Mohave Myths*, 4.
23. Calmet, *The Phantom World*, 188.

24. Connor, *Shamans of the World*, 31.

25. Buzand, *History of the Armenians*, 98.

26. Masoneale, *The Unseen World*, 164–5.

27. Elliot, *The Apocryphal New Testament*, 702.

28. Merton, *What are These Wounds?*, 2–4.

29. Schouppe, *Purgatory*, 94.

30. Schouppe, *Purgatory*, 9–10.

31. Hansen, *The Types of the Folktale*, 91.

32. Yanagita, *The Legends of Tono*, 60.

33. Hong, *Record of the Listener*, 186–7.

34. Wanley, *The Wonders of the Little World*, 290–1.

35. Budge, *The Book of the Saints of the Ethiopian Church*, 126.

36. Capes, *St. Catherine De' Ricci*, 264.

37. Garcez, *Adobe Angels*, 92–9.

38. Bede, *Bede's Ecclesiastical History of England*, 215–6.

39. al-Suyuti, *History of the Caliphs*, 369.

40. Anonymous, "The Saga of Gunnlaug the Worm-Tongue and Rafn the Skald," 65–6.

41. Zerffi, *Spiritualism and Animal Magnetism*, 112.

42. Tyrrell, *Science and Psychical Phenomena*, 32.

43. Windham, *Sixty Saints for Girls*, 58.

44. Harrison, *Spirits Before Our Eyes*, 113.

45. Pu, *Strange Stories from a Chinese Studio*, 1–3.

46. Johnson and Treharne, *Readings in Medieval Texts*, 139.

47. Keenan, *Early Christian Biographies Vol. 15*, 194–5.

48. Caesarius, *The Dialogue on Miracles vols 1–2*, 448–9.

49. Gregory I, *The Dialogues of Saint Gregory*, 188–9.

50. Peters, *Monks, Bishops, and Pagans*, 70.

51. Shortland, *Traditions and Superstitions of the New Zealanders*, 140.

52. Mukerji, *Mr. Mukerji's Ghosts*, 123.

53. Seymour and Neligan, *True Irish Ghost Stories*, 155–6.

54. Dasent, *The Story of Burnt Njal*, 29.

55. Haraldsson, *The Departed Among the Living*, 202–3.

56. Westwood, *The Penguin Book of Ghosts*, 63.

57. Roy and Roy, *Kharias Vol 2*, 429.

58. Ramsay, *Folklore, Prince Edward Island*, 9–10.

59. d'Assier, *Posthumous Humanity: A Study of Phantoms*, 24–5.

60. Westwood, *The Penguin Book of Ghosts*, 63.

61. Marwick, *The Folklore of Orkney and Shetland*, 93.

62. Mackenzie, "The Prophecies of the Brahan Seer, Coinneach Odhar Fiosaiche," 304.

63. Bennet, *Traditions of Belief*, 55.

64. Ralph, *The Folklore of Wiltshire*, 120.

65. Coffin, *Death in Early America*, 62.

66. Hyatt, *Folk-Lore from Adams County Illinois*, 547.

67. Funk, *Widow's Mite and Other Psychic Phenomena*, 28.

68. Musick, *The Telltale Lilac Bush*, 264–5.

69. Musick, *The Telltale Lilac Bush*, 267.

70. Allred, "Notes on the Appearance of a Spectral Death Messenger," 197–9.

71. Feather, *The Gift*, 254.

72. Moncrieff, *Old Booty! A Serio-Comic Sailor's Tale*, 4–6.

73. Aubrey, *Miscellanies Upon Various*, 77.

9. ALCYONE'S TRADITION AND THE VERIDICAL APPEARANCE OF APPARITIONS

1. Ogden, *Greek and Roman Necromancy*, 221.

2. Apuleius. *The Golden Ass*, 225.

3. Felton, *Haunted Greece and Rome*, 17.

4. Palmer, *Heretics, Saints and Martyrs*, 193–4.

5. Homer, *Odyssey* (Fitzgerald), 186.

6. Shakespeare, *Macbeth*, 242.

7. Mackenzie, *Teutonic Myth and Legend*, 302–3.

8. Ong, "The Interpretation of Dreams in Ancient China," 124.

9. Jackson, *The Fish People*, 200–01; Beckwith, *Black Roadways*, 89.

10. Lawrence, *Gods, Ghosts, and Men in Melanesia*, 86.

11. Iwasaka, *Ghosts and the Japanese*, 92–3.

12. Gurney, Myers, and Podmore, *Phantasms of the Living*, vol. 1, 332–33.

13. Campbell, *Witchcraft and Second Sight in the Highlands and Islands of Scotland*, 127.

14. Macrae, *Highland Second-Sight*, 43.

15. Gregor, *Notes on the Folk-Lore of the North-East of Scotland Vol 7*, 29.

16. Apuleius, *The Golden Ass*, 265.

17. Virtanen, *That Must Have Been ESP!*, 42.

18. Landtman, *The Kiwai Papuans of British New Guinea*, 284.

19. Walker, "A Sampling of Folklore from Rutherford County," 14–15.

20. Beaumont, *An Historical, Physiological and Theological Treatise of Spirits, Apparitions, Witchcrafts, and Other Magical Practices*, 245.

21. Daniels, *Encyclopaedia of Superstitions, Folklore, and the Occult Sciences of the World*, 1208.

22. Ovid, *Metamorphosis*, 11.

23. Fantham, "Ovid's Ceyx and Alcyone," 330–45.

24. Fantham, "Ovid's Ceyx and Alcyone," 330–45.

25. Felton, *Haunted Greece and Rome*, 17.

26. Dennys, *The Folk-Lore of China*, 73–4.

27. Bennett, *The Sky-Sifter*, 11–13.

28. Terry, *The Shanty Book: Sailor Shanties*, xiii.

29. Ferriar, *An Essay Towards a Theory of Apparitions*, 66–7.

30. Ottway, *News from the Invisible World*, 246.

31. Almqvist, "The Dead from the Sea in Old Icelandic Tradition," 11.

32. Árnason, *Icelandic Legends*, 268–9.

33. Inglis, *The Paranormal*, 175.

34. Giraldus, *The Journey Through Wales, and, The Description of Wales*, 163.

35. Scott, *Tales From French History*, 144–5.

36. Gregory, *Letters to a Candid Inquirer on Animal Magnetism*, 356–7.

37. Sacheverell, *An Account of the Isle of Man*, 20–1.

38. D'Aguilers, *Historia Francorum qui ceperunt Iherusalem*, 99.

39. Craigie, *Scandinavian Folk-Lore*, 283–4.

40. Anonymous, "The Saga of Gunnlaug the Worm-Tongue and Rafn the Skald," 65–6.

41. Arnason, *Icelandic Legends*, liii.

42. Virtanen, *That Must Have Been ESP!*, 89.

43. Parrinder, *West African Psychology*, 93.

44. Inglis, *The Paranormal*, 174.

45. Bennett, *Traditions of Belief*, 133.

46. Haraldsson, *The Departed Among the Living*, 69, 134.

47. Haraldsson, *The Departed Among the Living*, 91–2.

48. Thompson, *The Mystery and Lore of Apparitions*, 48.

49. Lu, *Encounters with the World of Spirits*, 182.

50. Child, *Isaac T. Hopper*, 262–3.

51. Glanvill, *Daducismus Triumphatus*, 349–51.

52. Almqvist, "The Dead from the Sea in Old Icelandic Tradition," 8.

53. St. Clair, *Unexplained*, 28–9.

54. Jalal al-Din al-Suyuti. *History of the Caliphs*, 212.

55. Davies, *Balm from Beyond*, 35–6.

10. REVELATIONS NEAR DEATH AND JOURNEYS TO HEAVEN AND HELL

1. Musorillo, *The Acts of the Christian Martyrs*, 113.

2. Lester, *Kava Drinking in Vitilevu, Fiji*, 97–121.

3. Christian, *Apparitions in Late Medieval and Renaissance Spain*, 8.

4. Gardiner, *Visions of Heaven & Hell before Dante*, 181.

5. Gregory I, *The Dialogues of Saint Gregory*, 224.

6. Boniface, *The Letters of Saint Boniface*, 31.

7. Gardiner, *Visions of Heaven & Hell before Dante*, 181; Zaleski, *Otherworld Journeys*, 84;, Bennett, *Traditions of Belief*, 61.

8. Moreman, *Beyond the Threshold*, 13.

9. Vyasa, *The Mahābhārata*, 646–7.

10. Neumann, "Near-Death Experiences in Judaic Literature," 225–36.

11. Haug and West, *The Book of Arda Viraf*, xiii.

12. Mackenzie, *Teutonic Myth and Legend*, 18.

13. Anonymous, "The Saga of Viga-Glum," 105.

14. Fumée, *The Historie of the Troubles of Hungarie*, 268.

15. Schwartz, *Tree of Souls: The Mythology of Judaism*, 209.

16. Elior, *The Mystical Origins of Hasidism*, 50.

17. Haley, "A Visit to the Spirit Land," 60.

18. Anthony Chene production, "The Near Death Experience of Deborah King."

19. Plutarch, *Plutarch's Morals*, 357–8.

20. Bremmer, *The Rise and Fall of the Afterlife*, 98.

21. Charlesworth, *The Old Testament Pseudepigrapha*, 502.

22. Herbermann, *The Catholic Encyclopedia Vols. 1–16*, 179.

23. Wilson, "The Dissemination of Visions of the Otherworld in England and Northern France c.1150–c.1321," 157–8.

24. Davidson, *Myths and Symbols in Pagan Europe*, 184.

25. Mackenzie, *Indian Myth and Legend*, 17.

26. Aries, *The Hour of Our Death*, 7.

27. Schouppe, *Purgatory*, 12.

28. Dorsey, *Traditions of the Arikara*, 152.

29. Courlander, *The Piece of Fire, and other Haitian Tales*, 74.

30. Charles, *The Book of Enoch*, 48.

31. Ritter, *The Ocean of the Soul*, 588–9.

32. Gardiner, *Visions of Heaven & Hell before Dante*, 168.

33. Gardiner, *Visions of Heaven & Hell before Dante*, 65.

34. Damian, *Letters*, 136.

35. Boccaccio, *The Decameron*, 241.

36. Tong, *Gypsy Folk Tales*, 152–6.

37. Haug and West, *The Book of Arda Viraf*, 175.

38. Seyed-Gohrab, *Layli and Majnun*, 123–4.

39. Ancient Buddhist Texts, "Ja 541 Nimijātaka: The Story about (King) Nimi (Mahānipāta)."

40. Charlesworth, *The Old Testament Pseudepigrapha*, 502.

41. Stokes, "The Voyage of the Hui Corra," 22–69.

42. Asai, *The Otogiboko*, 69.

43. Anonymous, *Guingamor*, 23.

44. Talayesva, *Sun Chief: The Autobiography of a Hopi Indian*, 132.

45. Greyson, "Seeing Dead People Not Known to Have Died: 'Peak in Darien' Experience," 165.

46. Pliny, *Natural History, Vol. 2, books 3–7*, 624–5.

47. Greyson, *After*, 132–3.

48. Greyson, "Seeing Dead People Not Known to Have Died," 169.

49. Van Bronkhorst, *Dreams at the Threshold*, 89.

50. Barrett, *Deathbed Visions*, 10.

51. Calmet, *The Phantom World*, 352.

52. Lucian, *Lucian III*, 359.

53. Pliny, *The Natural History Vol, 2*, 213.

54. Lucian, *Lucian III*, 359, 361.

55. Velimirovic, *Stories of Saints from the Prologue*, 41.

56. Paris, *Matthew Paris's English History Vol III*, 117–8.

57. Lang, *Lives and Legends of the Georgian Saints*, 71.

58. Pasricha, "Near-Death Experiences in India," 272–3.

59. Osis and Haraldsson, *At the Hour of Death*, 154–5.

60. Homer, *Odyssey* (Butler), 134–6.

61. Homer, *Odyssey* (Butler), 140.

62. Adam of Eynsham, *The Revelation of the Monk of Eynsham*, 22.

63. Myers, *Voices From the Edge of Eternity*, 55–6.

64. Bremmer, *The Rise and Fall of the Afterlife*, 95.

65. Gregory I, *The Dialogues of Saint Gregory*, 224.

66. Gregory I, *The Dialogues of Saint Gregory*, 224.

67. Campany, "Return-From-Death-Narratives in Early Medieval China," 91–125.

68. Pu, *Strange Stories from a Chinese Studio*, 1–3.

69. Asai, *The Otogiboko*, 69–71.

70. Tyler, *Japanese Tales*, 209.

71. Caesarius, *The Dialogue on Miracles vols 1–2*, 329.

72. Mango, *Byzantium: The Empire of New Rome*, 151–3.

73. Steiger and Steiger, *Children of the Light*, 42–46.

74. Morse and Perry, *Closer to the Light*, 53.

75. Long, *God and the Afterlife*, 121–3.

76. Hamilton, *The Scalpel and the Soul*, 74–6.

77. Schouppe, *Purgatorys*, 66.

78. Say, *Short Compilation of the Extraordinary Life and Writings of Thomas Say*, 87–90.

79. Neumann, "Near-Death Experiences in Judaic Literature," 232.

80. Shushan,"The Harrowing of Hell: Did Jesus Have a Near-Death Experience?"

81. Kao, *Classical Chinese Tales*, 87–9.

82. Ausubel, *A Treasury of Jewish Folklore*, 112–4.

83. Atherton, *A Treasury of Jewish Folklore*, 2.

84. John Chapman, "The Happy Hunting-Ground of the Ten'a," 66–7.

85. Oliver, *The Mystery of Dreams*, 173–4.

86. Counts, "Near-Death and Out-of-Body Experiences in Melanesian Society," 118–9.

87. Neumann, "Near-Death Experiences in Judaic Literature," 229.

88. Punzak, A *Spiritual Hypothesis*, 102.

89. Grey, *Return from Death*, 80–81.

90. Rawlings, *Beyond Death's Door*, 17–22.

91. Robe, *Index of Mexican Folktales*, 150.

92. Kübler-Ross, *Index of Mexican Folktales*, 208–9.

93. Rasmussen, *The People of the Polar North*, 110–11.

94. Knight, "Letter 158 (A.D. 414)."

95. Grey, *Return from Death*, 54–55.

96. Leo, *St. Francis of Assisi*, 60–1.

97. Velimirovich, "The Venerable Thais," under October 8 in *The Prologue from Ohrid*.

98. Peters, *At Heaven's Door*, 4–5.

99. De Voragine, *The Golden Legend: Readings on the Saints*, 368.

100. Ennemoser, *The History of Magic Volume I*, 50.

101. Patch, *The Other World*, 98.

102. McClenon, "Kongo Near-Death Experiences: Cross-Cultural Patterns," 21–34.

103. Mackenzie, *The Spirit-Ridden Konde*, 219–20.

104. Wiebe, *God and other Spirits*, 66–7.

105. Damian, *Letters*, 138.

106. Madigan and Osiek, *Ordained Women in the Early Church: A Documentary History*, 59.

107. Calmet, *The Phantom World*, 353.

108. Murphy, "Near-Death Experiences in Thailand," 161–78.

109. Massam, *The Cliff Dwellers of Kenya*, 197–8.

110. Nelson, *The Eskimo about Bering Strait*, 488–90.

111. Norman, "Balder's Dream."

112. Ligouri, *Victories of the Martyrs*, 63.

113. von Furer-Haimendorf, *The Konyak Nagas*, 89–90.

114. Parsons, *Taos Tales*, 24.

115. Herbert, *Catalogue of Romances Vol. III*, 625.

116. Rieti, *Life of St. Anthony of Padau*, 29–30.

117. Stokes, *Six Months in the Apennines*, 146.

118. Camm, *Tyburn and the English Martyrs*, 128.

119. Baring-Gould, *The Lives of the British Saints* (1908), 305.

120. Bennett, *Rhineland and Its Legends*, 51–2.

121. McNamara, Halborg, and Whatley, *Sainted Women of the Dark Ages*, 247.

122. Kempis, *Lydwine of Schiedam, Virgin*, 152.

123. Merton, *What are These Wounds?*, 58.

124. Schouppe, *Purgatory: Illustrated by the Lives and Legends of the Saints*, 311.

125. Fabrini, *The Life of St. Mary Magdalen De-Pazzi*, 111.

126. Schouppe, *Purgatory*, 35.

127. Jones, *Fox Texts*, 209.

128. Knight, "Ojibwa tales from Sault Ste. Marie, Mich.," 91–6.

129. Opier, *Myths and Legends of the Apache Indians*, 98–101.

130. Schwartz, *Lilith's Cave*, 256.

131. Glassie, *Irish Folktales*, 78.

Bibliography

Adamnan. *Life of Saint Columba, Founder of Hy.* Edited by William Reeves. Edinburgh: Edmonston & Douglas, 1874.

Adam of Eynsham. *The Revelation of the Monk of Eynsham.* Translated by Richard Scott-Robinson. Self-published, 2017.

Adams, Charles. *Ghost Stories of the Lehigh Valley.* Reading, PA: Exeter House Books, 1993.

Adamson, Thelma. *Folk-Tales of the Coast Salish.* New York: The American Folk-Lore Society, G.E. Stechert & Co., Agents, Kraus Reprint, 1934.

Aeschylus. *Persians.* Translated by Janet Lembke and C. J. Herington. New York: Oxford University Press, 1981.

Afanas'ev, Aleksandr. *Russian Fairy Tales.* Translated by Norbert Guterman. New York: Pantheon Books, 1975.

Alexander, Roberts, and James Donaldson, eds. *Ante-Nicene Christian Library, Vol. 16: Apocryphal Gospels, Acts, And Revelations.* Translated by Alexander Walker. Edinburgh: T&T Clark, 1870.

Algarin, Joanne. *Japanese Folk Literature: A Core Collection and Reference Guide.* New York: R.R. Bowker, 1982.

Allen, Horace. *Korean Tales: Being a Collection of Stories Translated from the Korean Folk Lore.* New York: G. P. Putnam's Sons, 1889.

Allingham, William. *Poems.* London: Macmillan and Co., Ltd., 1912.

Allred, Grover. "Notes on the Appearance of a Spectral Death Messenger." *Western Folklore* 19/3 (1960): 197–9.

Almqvist, Bo. "The Dead from the Sea in Old Icelandic Tradition." In *Islanders and Water-Dwellers,* edited by Patricia Lysaght, Séamas Ó Catháin, and Dáithí Ó hÓgáin, 1–18. Dublin: DBA Publications Ltd., 1999.

Ancient Buddhist Texts. "Ja 541 Nimijātaka The Story about (King) Nimi (Mahānipāta)." Ancient Buddhist Texts website, November 2021.

Anonymous. *Guingamor*. London: D. Nutt, 1900.

Anonymous. *The Saga of Gunnlaug the Worm-Tongue and Rafn the Skald*. Translated by William Morris & Eirikr Magnusson. Icelandic Saga Database, Sveinbjorn Thordarson (ed.), 1901.

Anonymous. *The Saga of the Ere-Dwellers*. Translated by William Morris & Eirikr Magnusson. Icelandic Saga Database, Sveinbjorn Thordarson (ed.), 1892.

Anonymous, *The Saga of Viga-Glum*. Translated by Edmund Head. Icelandic Saga Database, Sveinbjorn Thordarson (ed.), 1866.

Anthony Chene Production. "The Near Death Experience of Deborah King." Youtube, Uploaded by Nov 16, 2022.

Appianus. *Appian's Roman History I*. Translated by Horace White. Cambridge, MA: Harvard University Press, 1912.

Apuleius. *The Golden Ass*. Translated by E. J. Kennedy. London: Penguin Books Ltd., 1998. Kindle.

Aries, Philippe. *The Hour of Our Death*. New York: Knopf: Distributed by Random House, 1981.

Armstrong, Edwin. *Rossel Island*. New York: Cambridge: At the University Press, 1978.

Árnason, Jón. *Icelandic Legends*. Translated by George Powell and Eirikr Magnusson. London: Bentley, 1864.

———. *Icelandic Legends: Second Series*. Translated by George Powell and Eirikr Magnusson. London: Longman, Green & Co., 1866.

Asai, Ryoi. *The Otogiboko: A Collection of Ghost Stories of Old Japan*. Translated by Yoshiko Dykstra. Honolulu: Kanji Press, 2014.

Asbjørnsen, Peter. *Norske Huldreeventyr og Folkesagn*. Christiania, PT: Steensballe, 1870.

Atherton, Henry. *The Resurrection Proved; Or, the Life to Come Demonstrated*. London: T. Dawks, 1680.

Attar, Farid al-Din. *Muslim Saints and Mystics: Episodes from the Tadhkirat al-Auliya*. Translated by Arthur John Arberry. London: Routledge & K. Paul, 1966.

Attwater, Donald. *Martyrs: from St. Stephen to John Tung*. New York: Sheed Ward, 1957.

Aubrey, John. *Miscellanies Upon Various Subjects 5th ed., to which is added*

Hydiotaphia, or Urn Burial by Sir Thomas Browne. London: Reeves & Turner, 1890.

Ausubel, Nathan. *A Treasury of Jewish Folklore: Stories, Tradition, Legends, Humour, Wisdom and Folk Songs of the Jewish People*. New York: Crown, 1972.

Ayahuasca Timeline. "1905—'Telepathine' is Suggested as a Name for the Active Ingredient in the Ayahuasca Vine," Ayahuasca Timeline website.

Bäckman, Louise. *Studies in Lapp Shamanism*. Stockholm: Almqvist & Wiksell International, 1978.

Bain, Nisbet, ed. *Cossack Fairy Tales and Folk Tales*. London: G. G. Harrap & Co., 1916.

Baker, Ronald. *Hoosier Folk Legends*. Bloomington: Indiana University Press, 1982.

Baldick, Julian. *Imaginary Muslims: The Uwaysi Sufis of Central Asia*. Washington Square, NY: New York University Press, 1993.

Barbeau, Marius. *Haida Myths Illustrated in Argillite Carvings*. Ottawa: National Museum of Canada, 1953.

———. *Huron and Wyandot Mythology: With an Appendix Containing Earlier Published Records*. Ottawa: Government Printing Bureau, 1915.

———. *Totem Poles of the Gitksan, Upper Skeena River, British Columbia*. Ottawa: F. A. Acland, 1929.

Baring-Gould, Sabine. *The Lives of the British Saints: The Saints of Wales and Cornwall and Such Irish Saints as have Dedications in Britain Vols. 1–4*. London: For the Honourable Society of Cymmrodorion by C.J. Clark, 1907–11.

Barrett, William. *Deathbed Visions*. London: Methuen & Co. Ltd., 1926.

Bassett, Fletcher. *Sea Phantoms; or, Legends and Superstitions of the Sea and of Sailors in All Lands and at All Times*. Chicago: Morrill, Higgins & Co, 1892.

Bateman, George. *Zanzibar Tales Told by Natives of the East Coast of Africa*. A. C. McClurg, 1910.

Beaumont, John. *An Historical, Physiological and Theological Treatise of Spirits, Apparitions, Witchcrafts, and Other Magical Practices*. London: Printed for D. Browne, etc., 1705.

Beckwith, Martha. *Black Roadways: A Study of Jamaican Folk Life*. Chapel Hill: The University of North Carolina Press, 1929.

Bede. *The Age of Bede*. Edited by D. H. Farmer. Translated by J. F. Webb. Edited by D. H. Farmer. Hammondsworth, London: Penguin Classics, 1998.

———. *Bede's Ecclesiastical History of England*. Edited by J. A. Giles. London: George Bell & Sons, 1903.

Bédier, Joseph. *The Romance of Tristan and Iseult as Retold by Joseph Bedier*. Translated by Hilaire Belloc and Completed by Paul Rosenfeld. New York: Vintage Books, 1945.

Beitman, Bernard. *Meaningful Coincidences*. Rochester, VT: Park Street Press, 2002.

Belasco, David. *The Return of Peter Grimm*. Project Gutenberg website, 2020.

Bell, Arthur. *Lives and Legends of the English Bishops and Kings, Mediaeval Monks, and Other Later Saints*. London: George Bell & Sons, 1904.

Bellows, Henry Adams, trans. *The Poetic Edda*. New York: The American-Scandinavian Foundation, 1923.

Belsey, Catherine. *Tales of the Troubled Dead. Ghost Stories in Cultural History*. Edinburgh: Edinburgh University Press, 2019.

Bennett, Gillian. *Traditions of Belief: Women and the Supernatural*. London: Penguin Books, 1987.

Bennett, William, trans. *Rhineland and Its Legends*. London: J. T. Hayes, 1868.

Bennett, William. *The Sky-Sifter*. Oakland, CA: Pacific Press Publishing Company, 1892.

Berndt, Ronald and Catherine Berndt. *The World of the First Australians*. Sydney: Ure Smith, 1977.

Betzinez, Jason. *I Fought with Geronimo*. New York: Bonanza Books, 1959.

Bhatt, Vishna. *Yogic Powers and God Realization*. Chaupatty, Bombay: Bhartya Vidya Bhavan, 1960.

Bierhorst, John. *The Mythology of Mexico and Central America*. New York: William Morrow, 1990.

———. *The Mythology of South America*. New York: Quill/W. Morrow, 1988.

Blacker, Carmen. *The Catalpa Bow: A Study of Shamanistic Practice in Japan*. London: Allen & Unwin, 1975.

Blum, Deborah. *Ghost Hunters: William James and the Search for Scientific Proof of Life after Death*. New York: Penguin Press, 2006.

Boas, Franz, "Traditions of the Tillamook Indians." *Journal of American Folklore* 11/40 (1898): 23–38.

Boas, Franz and Henry Tate. *Tsimshian Mythology*. Washington: Government Printing Office, 1916.

Boccaccio, Giovanni. *The Decameron*. Translated by G. H. McWilliam. Franklin Centre, PA: Franklin Library, 1981.

Bonaventure. *The Life of St. Francis of Assisi: from the "Legenda Santa Francisci" of St. Bonaventura*. Edited by Miss Lockhart. London: R. & T. Washbourne, 1915.

Boniface. *The Letters of Saint Boniface*. Translated by Ephraim Emerton. Edited by Austin P. Evans. New York: Colombia University Press, 1940.

Børtnes, Jostein. *Visions of Glory: Studies in Early Russian Hagiography*. Oslo: Solum Forlag A/S, 1988.

Boswell, James. *Everybody's Boswell; Being the Life of Samuel Johnson Abridged from James Boswell's Complete Text*. New York: Harcourt, Brace & Co., 1930.

Bound, Graham. *Falkland Islanders at War*. Barnsley: Pen & Sword, 2006.

Bourne, Lois. *Dancing With Witches*. London: Robert Hale, 1988.

Bournoutian, George, trans. *The Travel Accounts of Siméon of Poland*. Costa Mesa, CA: Mazda Publishers Inc., 2007.

Bourns, Timothy. "Between Nature and Culture: Animals and Humans in Old Norse Literature." PhD diss., St. John's College, University of Oxford, 2017.

Bowles, William, and John Nichols. *Annals and Antiquities of Lacock Abbey, in the County of Wilts*. London: Nichols & Sons, 1835.

Boys, Thomas. *The Suppressed Evidence*. London: Hamilton, Adams, 1832.

Bradbury, George. *The Life of St. Juliana of Cornillon*. London: Thomas Richardson, 1873.

Bremmer, Jan. *The Rise and Fall of the Afterlife*. London: Routledge, 2002.

Brittan, Samuel Byron. *Man and His Relations*. New York: Cotton W. Bean, 1865.

Britten, Emma Hardinge. *Nineteenth Century Miracles*. New York: Lovell & Co., 1884.

Bromhall, Thomas. *An History of Apparitions*. London: Streater, 1658.

Buck, Peter Henry. *Vikings of the Pacific*. Chicago: University of Chicago Press, 1959.

Budge, E. A. Wallis. *The Book of the Saints of the Ethiopian Church Vol. III*. Cambridge: At The University Press, 1928.

Bulkeley, Kelly. "Reflections on the Dream Traditions of Islam." *Sleep and Hypnosis* 4/1 (2002): 1–11.

Burrows, Edwin. *An Atoll Culture: Ethnography of Ifaluk in the Central Carolines*. Westport, CT: Greenwood Press, 1970.

Burton, Richard Francis. *Sindh and the Races that Inhabit the Valley of the Indus.* New Delhi: Asian Educational Services, 1992.

Busk, Rachel. *Patranas, or Spanish Stories, Legendary and Traditional.* London: Griffith & Farran, 1870.

Caesarius. *The Dialogue on Miracles vols 1–2.* Translated by H. Von, E. Scott, and C. C. Swinton Bland. Edited by G. G. Coulton and Eileen Power. New York: Harcourt, Brace & Company, 1929.

Callanan, Maggie, and Patricia Kelley. *Final Gifts: Understanding the Special Awareness, Needs, and Communications of the Dying.* New York: Bantam Books, 1997.

Calmet, Augustin. *Dissertations sur les Apparitions.* Paris: De Bure l'aine, 1746.

———. *The Phantom World.* Translated by Henry Christmas. Philadelphia: A. Hart, Late Carey & Hart, 1850.

Calofonos, George. "Dream Narratives in Historical Writing. Making Sense of History in Theophanes' Chronographia." In *History as Literature in Byzantium Papers from the Fortieth Spring Symposium of Byzantine Studies,* edited by Ruth Macrides, 133–144. London: Routledge, 2007.

Calvino, Italo. *Italian Folk Tales.* London: Dent, 1975.

Camerarius, Phillip. *The Living Librarie.* London: Adam Islip, 1621.

Camm, Dom Bede. *Tyburn and the English Martyrs.* New York: Benziger, 1924.

Campany, Robert. "Return-From-Death-Narratives in Early Medieval China." *Journal of Chinese Religions* 18/1 (1990): 91–125.

Campbell, John. *Witchcraft and Second Sight in the Highlands and Islands of Scotland.* Glasgow: James Maclehose & Sons, 1902.

Capes, Florence. *St. Rose of Lima: The Flower of the New World.* London: Washbourne, NY: Benziger Brothers, 1913.

———. *St. Catherine De' Ricci: Her Life, Her Letters, Her Community.* London: Burns & Oats, 1905.

———. *St. Rose of Lima: The Flower of the New World.* London: Washbourne, NY: Benziger Brothers, 1913.

Carey, George. *A Faraway Time and Place.* New York: Arno Press, 1977.

———. *Maryland Folklore.* Centreville, MD: Tidewater Publishers, 1989.

Cartlidge, David, and David Dungan. *Documents for the Study of the Gospels.* Philadelphia: Fortress Press, 1980.

Casagrande, Joseph B. "The Ojibwa's Psychic Universe." *Tomorrow* 4 (1956): 33–40.

Chadwick, Nora. *Anglo-Saxon and Norse Poems.* Cambridge: At The University Press, 1922.

———. *Poetry and Letters in Early Christian Gaul*. London: Bowes & Bowes, 1955.

Chamberlain, Basil. *Things Japanese*. London: J. Murray, 1905.

Chapman, John. "The Happy Hunting-Ground of the Ten'a." *The Journal of American Folklore* 25 (1912): 6–1.

Charles, Robert. *The Apocrypha and Pseudepigrapha of the Old Testament in English vol.2*. Oxford: Clarendon Press, 1913.

———. *The Book of Enoch*. Oxford: Clarendon Press, 1912.

Charlesworth, James. *The Old Testament Pseudepigrapha*. Garden City, NY: Doubleday & Co. Inc., 1983.

Child, Lydia. *Isaac T. Hopper: A True Life*. Boston: J.P. Jewett, 1853.

Christian, William. *Apparitions in Late Medieval and Renaissance Spain*. Princeton, NJ: Princeton University Press, 1981.

Christiansen, Reidar. *Folktales of Norway*. Chicago: University Press, 1964.

Cicero. *De Senectute, De Amicitia, De Divinatione*. London: Harvard University Press, 1964.

Clarke, William. *The Lausiac History of Palladius*. London: The Macmillan Company, 1918.

Cluness, Andrew. *Told Round the Peat Fire*. London: Robert Hale Ltd., 1955.

Codrington, Robert. *The Melanesians: Studies in their Anthropology and Folklore*. Oxford: Clarendon Press, 1891.

Coffin, Margaret. *Death in Early America*. Nashville: Neslon, 1976.

Cohn, S. A. "A Questionnaire Study on Second Sight Experiences." *Journal of the Society for Psychical Research* 63 (1999): 129–157.

Cohoe, Caleb. "Alexander of Aphrodisias on the Soul, Part I: Soul as Form of the Body, Parts of the Soul, Nourishment, and Perception translated by Victor Caston (review)." *Journal of the History of Philosophy* 52/1 (2014): 163–164.

Cole, Mabel. *Philippine Folk Tales*. A. C. McClurg & Co., 1916.

Collison-Morley, Lacy. *Greek and Roman Ghost Stories*. London: Simpkin, Marshall & Co. Ltd., 1912.

Connor, Nancy. *Shamans of the World: Extraordinary First-Person Accounts of Healings, Mysteries, and Miracles*. Boulder, CO: Sounds True, 2008.

Consitt, Edward. *Life of Saint Cuthbert*. London: Burns & Oates, 1904.

Converse, Harriet. *Myths and Legends of the New York State Iroquois*. Albany: University of the State of New York, 1908.

Counts, Dorothy. "Near-Death and Out-of-Body Experiences in Melanesian Society," *Anabiosis: The Journal for Near-Death Studies* 3/2 (1983): 115–135.

Courlander, Harold. *People of the Short Blue Corn: Tales and Legends of the Hopi Indians*. New York: H. Holt, 1996.

———. *Tales of Yoruba Gods and Heroes*. Greenwich, CT: Fawcett Publications, 1973.

———. *The Piece of Fire, and other Haitian Tales*. New York: Harcourt, Brace & World, 1964.

Coxwell, Fillingham. *Siberian and Other Folk-Tales*. London: The C. W. Daniel Company, 1935.

Craigie, William. *Scandinavian Folk-Lore: Illustrations of the Traditional Beliefs of the Northern Peoples*. London: A. Gardner, 1896.

Crawford, Venetia. *The Wildest Rivers, The Oldest Hills: Tales of the Gatineau and Pontiac*. Maitland, OT: Voyageur Publishing/Voyageur North America, 1996.

Creighton, Helen. *Bluenose Ghosts*. Halifax, NS: Nimbus, 1994.

———. *Folklore of Lunenburg County, Nova Scotia*. Ottawa: E. Cloutier, 1950.

Crum, Walter. "Another Fragment of the Story of Alexander." *Proceedings of the Society of Biblical Archeology* 14 (1892): 473–482.

Curtin, Jeremiah. *A Journey in Southern Siberia, the Mongols, Their Religion and Their Myths*. Boston: Little, Brown & Company, 1909.

———. *Myths of the Modocs*. Boston: Little, Brown & Company, 1912.

D'Aguilers, Raymond. *Historia Francorum qui ceperunt Iherusalem*. Translated by John Hugh. Independence Square, PA: The American Philosophical Society, 1968.

Dale Owen, Robert. *Footfalls on the Boundary of Another World*. Philadelphia: J. B. Lippincott & Co., 1868.

Dalyell, John. *The Darker Superstitions of Scotland*. Edinburgh: Waugh & Innes, 1834.

Damian, Peter. *Letters*. Translated by Owen Blum. Washington, D.C.: Catholic University of America Press, 1989.

Dance, Daryl. *Shuckin' and Jivin': Folklore from Contemporary Black Americans*. Bloomington: Indiana University Press, 1978.

Daniels, Linn. *Encyclopaedia of Superstitions, Folklore, and the Occult Sciences of the World*. Detroit: Gale Research Co., 1971.

Danziger, Edmund. *The Chippewas of Lake Superior*. Norman: University of Oklahoma Press, 1978.

Dasent, George. *The Story of Burnt Njal*. London: Grant Richards, 1900.

———. *The Story of Gisli the Outlaw*. Edinburgh: Edmonston & Douglas, 1866.

D'assier, Adolphe. *Posthumous Humanity: A Study of Phantoms.* Translated by Henry Steel. London: George Redway, 1887.

David-Neel, Alexandra. *Magic and Mystery in Tibet.* New York: Dover Publications, 1971.

Davidson, Hilda. *Myths and Symbols in Pagan Europe: Early Scandinavian and Celtic Religions.* Manchester: Manchester University Press, 1988.

Davies, Jonathon. *Folklore of West and Mid-Wales.* Aberystwyth: Printed at the "Welsh Gazette" Offices, 1911.

Davies, Rodney. *Balm from Beyond: How the Departed Can Help Us.* London: Robert Hale, 2010.

———. *Supernatural Vanishings: Otherworldly Disappearances.* New York: Sterling Pub., 1996.

Deferrari, Roy. *Early Christian Biographies Vol. 15.* Translated by Deferrari et al. New York: Fathers of the Church, Inc., 1952.

de Hauteville, Nicolas. *Histoire de la Tres Ancienne et Illustre Maison de Saint Francois de Sale.* Paris: Chez George Iosse, 1669.

Deitz, Dennis. *The Greenbriar Ghost and Other Strange Stories.* South Charlestown, WV: Mountain Memories Books, 1990.

Dendy, Walter. *The Philosophy of Mystery.* New York: Harper & Brothers, 1845.

Denham, Michael, and James Hardy. *The Denham Tracts.* London: D. Nutt, 1892.

Dennett, Richard. *Notes of the Folklore of the Fjort (French Congo).* London: D. Nutt, 1898.

Dennys, Nicholas. *The Folk-Lore of China and its Affinities with that of the Aryan and Semitic Races.* London: Trübner & Co., 1876.

Densmore, Francis. *Chippewa Customs.* New York: Johnson Reprint, 1970.

Devereux, George. *Dreams in Greek Tragedy: An Ethnopsychoanalytical Study.* Berkeley: University of California Press, 1976.

De Vitry, Jacques. *The Exempla or Illustrative Stories from the Sermones Vulgares of Jacques de Vitry.* Edited by Thomas Frederick Crane. London: D. Nutt, 1890.

De Voragine, Jacobus. *The Golden Legend: Readings on the Saints,* Volume I. Translated by William Granger Ryan. Princeton, NJ: Princeton University Press, 1993.

Dodds, Eric. "Telepathy and Clairvoyance in Classical Antiquity." *The Journal of Parapsychology* 10 (1946): 290–309.

———. *The Ancient Concept of Progress and Other Essays on Greek Literature and Belief.* Oxford: Clarendon Press, 1973.

———. *The Greeks and the Irrational.* Berkeley: University of California Press, 1951.

Doke, Clement. *The Lambas of Northern Rhodesia.* London: G.G. Harrap & Company, Ltd., 1931.

Dolch, Edward, and Marguerite Dolch. *Stories from Italy.* Champaigne, Ill: Garrard Publishing Company, 1962.

Doran, Robert. *The Lives of Simeon Stylites.* Kalamazoo, MI: Cistercian Publications, 1992.

Dorsey, George. *Traditions of the Arikara.* Washington, D.C.: Carnegie Institution of Washington, 1904.

Downing, Charles. *Russian Tales and Legends.* Oxford: Oxford University Press, 1989.

Durand, Maurice. *An Introduction to Vietnamese Literature.* New York: Columbia University Press, 1985.

El Eflaki, Shemsu-'d-Din Ahmed. *Legends of the Sufis.* Translated by James Redhouse. London: Theosophical Publishing House, 1976.

Eliade, Mircea. *Man and the Sacred.* New York: Harper & Row, 1974.

Elior, Rachel. *The Mystical Origins of Hasidism.* Oxford: Littman Library of Jewish Civilization, 2006.

Elkin, Adolphus. *The Australian Aborigines.* Garden City, NY: Anchor Books, 1964.

Elliot, James. *The Apocryphal New Testament: A Collection of Apocryphal Christian Literature in an English Translation.* Oxford: University Press Inc., 1993.

Elsaesser, Evelyn, Chris A Roe, Callum E. Cooper, and David Lorimer. "The Phenomenology and Impact of Hallucinations Concerning the Deceased." *BJPsych Open* 7/5 (2021): 148.

Elwin, Verrier. *Baiga.* London: Wyman & Sons, 1939.

———. *Bondo Highlander.* London: Oxford University Press, 1950.

———. *Myths of Middle India.* London: Oxford University Press, 1949.

———. *The Religion of an Indian Tribe.* London: Oxford University Press, 1955.

———. *Tribal Myths of Orissa.* London: Oxford University Press, 1954.

Emerson, Nathaniel. *Unwritten Literature of Hawaii: The Sacred Songs of the Hula.* Washington: Government Printing Office, 1909.

Ennemoser, Joseph. *The History of Magic Volume I.* Translated by William Howitt. London: H. G. Bohn, 1854.

Erben, Karel, and Walter Strickland. *Russian and Bulgarian Folklore Stories.* London: Standring, 1907.

Espinosa, Aurelio. "New-Mexican Spanish Folk-Lore." *The Journal of American Folklore* 23/90 (1910): 395–418.

Euripides. *The Plays of Euripides Vol. II*. Translated by Edward Phillip Coleridge. London: George Bell & Sons, 1891.

Evans-Wentz, Y. W. *Tibet's Great Yogi Milarepa*. New York: Oxford University Press, 1928.

Fabrini, Placido. *The Life of St. Mary Magdalen De-Pazzi: Florentine Noble, Sacred Carmelite Virgin*. Translated by Antonio Isoleri. Philadelphia: n.p., 1900.

Fantham, Elaine. "Ovid's Ceyx and Alcyone: The Metamorphosis of a Myth." *Phoenix* 33 (1979): 330–45.

Faron, Louis. *Hawks of the Sun: Mapuche Morality and its Ritual Attributes*. Pittsburgh: University of Pittsburgh Press, 1964.

Feather, Sally. *The Gift: ESP, the Extraordinary Experiences of Ordinary People*. New York: St. Martin's Press, 2005.

Felton, Debbie. *Haunted Greece and Rome*. AU: University of Texas Press, 2010. Kindle.

Fenwick, Peter. *The Art of Dying*. London: Continuum, 2008.

Ferreira, Mariana. *Mapping Time, Space and the Body: Indigenous Knowledge and Mathematical Thinking in Brazil*. Rotterdam: Sense Publishers, 2015.

Ferriar, John. *An Essay Towards a Theory of Apparitions*. London: Cadell & Davies, 1813.

Fielde, Marion. *Pagoda Shadows: Studies from Life in China*. Boston: W. G. Corthell, 1885.

Finkel, Irving. *The First Ghosts*. London: Hodder & Stoughton, 2021. Kindle.

Finucane, Ronald. *Appearances of the Dead: A Cultural History of Ghosts*. London: Junction Books, 1982.

Firth, Raymond. "Tikopia Dreams: Personal Images of Social Reality." *The Journal of the Polynesian Society* 110/1 (2001): 7–29.

FitzRoy, Robert. *Narrative of the Surveying Voyages of His Majesty's Ships Adventure and Beagle Between the Years 1826 and 1836*. London: Henry Colburn, 1839.

Flammarion, Camille. *Death and its Mystery at the Moment of Death*. London: T. Fisher Unwin, 1922.

Florentius. *The Church Historians of England. Vol II. Part I. The Anglo-Saxon Chronicle. The Chronicle of Florence of Worcester, with a Continuation and Appendix*. Translated by Rev. Joseph Stevenson. Fleet Street: Seeleys 1853.

Forbes, comte de Montalembert, Charles. *Life of Saint Elizabeth of Hungary, Duchess of Thuringia.* Translated by Francis Hoyt. London: Longmans, Green & Co., 1904.

Foster, John. *Echoes of Egyptian Voices.* Norman, OK: University of Oklahoma Press, 1992.

Fowke, Edith. *Folktales of French Canada.* Toronto: NC Press, 1981.

Fraser, John. "The First Battle of Moytura." *Ériu* 8 (1916): 1–63.

Fraser, Mary. *Folklore of Nova Scotia.* Halifax, NS: Formac Publishing, 2009.

Frazer, J. G. *Lectures on the Early History of the Kingship.* London: Macmillan & Co., Limited, 1905.

Friedman, Albert. *The Penguin Book of Folk Ballads of the English-Speaking World.* Hammondsworth, UK: Penguin, 1982.

Fumée, Martin. *The Historie of the Troubles of Hungarie.* Translated by R. C. Gentleman. London: Felix Kyngston, 1600.

Funk, Isaac. *Widow's Mite and Other Psychic Phenomena.* New York: Funk & Wagnalls Company, 1904.

Gaddis, Vincent. *American Indian Myths and Mysteries.* New York: Indian Head Books, 1992.

Garcez, Antonio. *Adobe Angels: Ghost Stories of O'Keeffe Country.* Truth or Consequences, NM: Red Rabbit Press, 1998.

Gardiner, Eileen. *Visions of Heaven & Hell before Dante.* New York: Italica Press, 2019 Kindle.

Garfield, Viola, and Linn Forrest. *The Wolf and the Raven: Totem Poles of Southeastern Alaska.* Seattle: University of Washington Press, 1984.

Garnett, Lucy. *The Women of Turkey and Their Folk-Lore.* London: D. Nutt, 1893.

Gaster, Moses. *The Exempla of the Rabbis.* London: The Asia Pub. Co., 1924.

Gellius, Aulus. *The Attic Nights of Aulus Gellius vol. 3.* Translated by John C. Rolfe. London: William Heinemann Ltd, 1927.

Giles, John. *William Of Malmesbury's Chronicle Of The Kings Of England.* London: Henry G. Bohn, 1847.

Ginzberg, Louis. *The Legends of the Jews.* Philadelphia: The Jewish Publication Society of America, 1909.

Giraldus, Cambrensis. *The Journey Through Wales* and *The Description of Wales.* Translated by Lewis Thorpe. New York: Harmondsworth, 1980.

Glanvill, Joseph. *Daducismus Triumphatus, 4ᵗʰ ed.* London: A. Bettesworth & J. Batley, etc., 1726.

Glassie, Henry. *Irish Folktales*. New York: Pantheon Books, 1985.

Godsell, Jean. "Moccasin Telegraph." *Fate Magazine* 9/54 (1954): 95–9.

Goedicke, Hans. "The Beginning of the Instruction of King Amenemhet." *Journal of the American Research Center in Egypt* 7 (1968): 15–21.

Goldman, Irving. *The Cubeo: Indians of the Northwest Amazon*. Urbana IL: University of Illinois Press, 1979.

Gordon, Richard. *Ancient Tales and Folklore of Japan*. London: A. & C. Black, 1908.

Grattan, Richard. *Considerations on the Human Mind: Its Present State, and Future Destination*. London: George Manwaring, 1861.

Grayson, James. *Myths and Legends from Korea: An Annotated Compendium of Ancient and Modern Materials*. Richmond, SY: Curzon, 2001.

Green, Lawrence. *These Wonders to Behold*. Cape Town: H. Timmins, 1959.

Green, Paul. *Words and Ways: Stories and Incidents from my Cape Fear Valley Folklore Collection*. Durham, NC: North Carolina Folklore Society, 1968.

Green, Roger, and Joan Kiddell-Monroe. *A Book of Myths*. London: J. M. Dent, 1976.

Gregg, Joan. *Devils, Women, and Jews*. Albany: State University of New York Press, 1997.

Gregor, Walter. *Notes on the Folk-Lore of the North-East of Scotland, Vol 7*. London: Pub. for the Folk-Lore Society by E. Stock, 1881.

Gregory, Lady. *Poets and Dreamers: Studies and Translations from the Irish*. Dublin: Hodges, Figgis, & Co., Ltd., 1903.

———. *Visions and Beliefs in the West of Ireland*. New York: G. P. Putman's Sons, 1920.

Gregory, Saint, Bishop of Tours. *History of the Franks*. Edited by James Shotwell. New York: Columbia University Press, 1916.

Gregory I, Pope. *The Dialogues of Saint Gregory*. Translated by Edmund Garratt Gardner. London: P.L. Warner, 1911.

Gregory of Nyassa. *St. Gregory of Nyssa: The Life of St. Macrina*. Translated by W. K. Lowther Clarke. London: Society for Promoting Christian Knowledge, 1916.

Gregory, William. *Letters to a Candid Inquirer on Animal Magnetism*. Philadelphia: Blanchard & Lea, 1851.

Grey, Margot. *Return From Death*. London: Arkana, 1985.

Greyson, Bruce. *After*. London: Transworld, 2021. Kindle.

———. "Seeing Dead People Not Known to Have Died: 'Peak in Darien'

Experiences." *Anthropology and Humanism* 35/2 (2010): 159–171.

Grinnell, George. *The Cheyenne Indians: Their History and Ways of Life.* New York: Cooper Square Publishers, 1962.

Grof, Stanislav. *The Human Encounter with Death.* New York: E. P. Dutton, 1977.

Groot, Jan. *The Religious System of China, Vol V, book II.* Leyden: Brill, 1892.

Grose, Francis. *A Provincial Glossary: With a Collection of Local Proverbs, and Popular Superstitions.* London: E. Jeffery, 1811.

Guerber, Hélène. *Legends of The Middle Ages.* New York: American Book Company, 1896.

Guggenheim, Bill and Judy Guggenheim. *Hello from Heaven.* New York: Bantam Books, 1996.

Günther, Marie. *Tales and Legends of the Tyrol.* London: Chapman & Hall, 1874.

Gurney, Edmund, Frederick Myers, and Frank Podmore. *Phantasms of the Living, Volumes 1–2.* London: Rooms of the Society for Psychical Research; Trübner & Co., 1886.

Gusinde, Martin. *Folk Literature of the Yamana Indians.* Berkeley: University of California Press, 1977.

Haggard, H. Rider. *The Days of My Life: An Autobiography Vol. 2.* Edited by Charles James Longman. London: Longmans, Green & Co. Ltd., 1923.

Haley, E. "A Visit to the Spirit Land; or, The Strange Experience of a Woman in Kona, Hawaii." In *Hawaiian Folk Tales,* edited by Thomas Thrum, 58–62. Chicago: A. C. McClurg & Co., 1907.

Halliwell, James. *Morte Arthure.* Edited by James Orchard Halliwell. Brixton Hill: For Private Circulation Only, 1847.

Halpert, Violetta. "Death Beliefs From Indiana." *Folklore Journal* 2/4 (1952): 205–219.

Hamilton, Allan. *The Scalpel and the Soul.* New York: Jeremy P. Tarcher/ Putnam, 2008.

Hamilton, Bernard. "God Wills It: Signs of Divine Approval in the Crusade Movement." In *Signs, Wonders, Miracles: Representations of Divine Power in the Life of the Church,* edited by Kate Cooper and Jeremy Gregory, 88–98. Woodbridge, Suff. Published for the Ecclesiastical History Society by the Boydell Press, 2005.

Hanauer, James Edward. *Tales Told in Palestine.* Cincinnati: Jennings & Graham, 1904.

Handy, Edward. *Marquesan Legends.* Honolulu, HI: The Museum, 1930.

Hansen, Terence. *The Types of the Folktale in Cuba, Puerto Rico, the Dominican*

Republic, and Spanish South America. Berkeley: University of California Press, 1957.

Haraldsson, Erlendur. *The Departed Among the Living: An Investigative Study of Afterlife Encounters*. Guildford, UK: White Crow Books, 2012. Kindle.

Hardy, Alister. *The Spiritual Nature of Man*. Oxford: Clarendon Press, 1979.

Harner, Michael. *Hallucinogens and Shamanism*. New York; Oxford University Press, 1973.

Harrison, Jane. *Prolegomena to the Study of Greek Religion*. New York: Meridian Books, 1959.

———. *Themis: A Study of the Social Origins of Greek Religion*. Oxford: At The University Press, 1912.

Harrison, William. *Spirits Before Our Eyes*. London: W.H. Harrison, 1879.

Harrisson, Juliette Grace. "Cultural Memory and Imagination: Dreams and Dreaming in the Roman Empire 31 BC–AD 200." PhD diss., University of Birmingham, 2010.

Hart, Hornell. "Six Theories About Apparitions." *Proceedings of the Society for Psychical Research* 50 (1956): 153–239.

Haug, Martin, and Edward William West. *The Book of Arda Viraf*. Bombay: Government Central Book Depot, 1872.

Hayashida, Nelson Osamu. *Dreams in the African Literature*. Amsterdam: Rodopi, 1999.

Head, Thomas. *Hagiography and the Cult of Saints: The Diocese of Orleans, 800–1200*. Cambridge: Cambridge University Press, 1990.

Heathcote-James, Emma. *After-Death Communication*. London: Metro, 2004.

Hedin, Sven. *Sven Hedin: A Conquest of Tibet*. New York: E.P. Dutton, 1935.

Henderson, William. *Notes on the Folklore of the Northern Counties of England and the Borders*. London: Published for the Folklore Society by W. Satchell, Peyton & Co., 1879.

Herbermann, Charles. *The Catholic Encyclopedia: An International Work of Reference on the Constitution, Doctrine, Discipline, and History of the Catholic Church. Vols. 1–16*. New York: The Encyclopedia Press, 1907–1914.

Herbert, John. *Catalogue of Romances in the Department of Manuscripts in the British Museum Vol. III*. London: Printed by Order of the Trustees, 1910.

Hight, George, trans. *The Saga of Grettir the Strong*. London: Dent, 1913.

Hill, Jonathon. *Keepers of the Sacred Chants*. Tucson: University of Arizona Press, 1993.

Hitschmann, Eduard. "Telepathy and Psychoanalysis." In *Psychoanalysis and the Occult*, edited by George Devereaux, 117–127. Madison, CT: International University Press, Inc., 1970.

Hobley, Charles. *Ethnology of A-Kamba and other East African Tribes*. London: Cass, 1971.

Hoffman, Luellen. *After the Death of a Loved One*. Montgomery, AK: E-Book Time, 2008.

Hogg, James. *The Tales of James Hogg, The Ettrick Shepherd*. London: Sands, 1900.

Holy Bible, New International Version, 2011.

Homan, Joshua. "Charlatans, Seekers, and Shamans: The Ayahuasca Boom in Western Peruvian Amazonia." Master's thesis, University of Kansas, Lawrence, 2011.

Homer. *The Odyssey*. Translated by Samuel Butler. New York: Walter J. Black, 1944.

———. *The Odyssey*. Translated by Robert Fitzgerald. New York: Farrar, Straus, & Giroux, 1998.

Hong, Mai. *Record of the Listener: Elections of Chinese Supernatural Stories*. San Francisco: Long River Press, 2012.

Hooper, Lucile. *The Cahuilla Indians*. Berkeley: University of California Press, 1920.

Hopkins, Nicholas. *Chuj (Mayan) Narratives*. Louisville: University Press of Colorado, 2021.

Hornung, Erik. *Conceptions of God in Ancient Egypt: The One and the Many*. Ithaca: Cornell University Press, 1982.

Hosmer, Harriet. *Harriet Hosmer Letters and Memories*. Edited by Cornelia Carr. New York: Moffat, Yard & Company, 1912.

Howells, William. *Cambrian Superstitions*. London: Longman & Co., 1831.

Htin Aung, Maung. *Folk Elements in Burmese Buddhism*. London: Oxford University Press. 1962.

Hughes, Brenda. *New Guinea Folk-Tales*. New York: Roy Publishers, 1959.

Hultkrantz, Åke. *The North American Indian Orpheus Tradition: Native Afterlife Myths and Their Origins*. Afterworlds Press, 2022. Kindle, 2022.

Hunt, Robert. *Popular Romances of the West of England; or, The Drolls, Traditions, and Superstitions of Old Cornwall*. London: Chatto & Windus, 1908.

Hyatt, Harry. *Folk-Lore from Adams County Illinois*. New York: Alma Egan Hyatt Foundation, 1935.

Ibn Khallikan. *Ibn Khallikan's Biographical Dictionary Vol. IV.* Translated by William McGuckin De Slane. Paris: Printed for the Oriental Translation Fund of Great Britain and Ireland, 1871.

Inglis, Brian. *The Paranormal: An Encyclopedia of Psychic Phenomena.* London: Granada, 1985.

Iwasaka, Michiko. *Ghosts and the Japanese: Cultural Experience in Japanese Death Legends.* Logan, UT: Utah State University Press, 1994.

Jackson, Jean. *The Fish People: Linguistic Exogamy and Tukanoan Identity in Northwest Amazonia.* Cambridge: Cambridge University Press, 1983.

Jaffe, Aniela. *Apparitions and Precognition.* New Hyde Park, NY: University Books, 1963.

Jagendorf, Moritz, and Ralph Boggs. *The King of the Mountains: A Treasury of Latin American Folk Stories.* New York: Vanguard Press, 1960.

Jakobsen, Roman. *Slavic Epic Studies.* The Hague, Paris: Mouton, 1966.

Jalal al-Din al-Suyuti. *History of the Caliphs.* Translated by Major Jarret. Calcutta: Printed by J.W. Thomas for The Asiatic Society, 1881.

Jenness, Diamond. *The Life of the Copper Eskimos.* Ottawa: Printer to the King's Most Excellent Majesty, 1922.

———. *The Northern D'Entrecasteaux.* Oxford: Clarendon Press, 1920.

Jirasek, Alois. *Legends of Old Bohemia.* London: P. Hamlyn, 1963.

Jockle, Clemens. *Encyclopedia of Saints.* London: Alpine Fine Arts Collection, 1995.

John of Ephesus. *Lives of the Eastern Saints I.* Translated by Ernest Brooks. Paris: Firmin-Didot, 1923.

Johnson, Clifton. *What they Say in New England.* Boston: Lee & Shepherd, 1896.

Johnson, David, and Elaine Treharne. *Readings in Medieval Texts: Interpreting Old and Middle English Literature.* Oxford, NY: Oxford University Press, 2005.

Johnson, Samuel. *Purgatory Prov'd by Miracles.* London: Printed for Richard Baldwin, 1688.

Jones, William. *Fox Texts.* Leiden, NL: E. J. Brill, 1907.

Josephus, Flavius. *The Genuine Works of Josephus.* Translated by William Whiston. Bridgeman, CT: M. Sherman, 1828.

Jung, Carl. *Memories, Dreams, Reflections.* New York: Vintage Books, 1973.

Kalweit, Holgar. *Shamans, Healers and Medicine Men.* Boston: Shambhala, 1992.

Kao, Karl. *Classical Chinese Tales of the Supernatural and the Fantastic.* Bloomington: Indiana University Press, 1985.

Karsten, Rafael. *The Civilization of the South American Indians: With Special Reference to Magic and Religion.* New York: Knopf, 1926.

Keenan, Mary Emily, trans. "Life of St. Anthony by St. Athanasius." In *Early Christian Biographies Vol. 15*, edited by John Deferrari, 125–216. n.a. Fathers of the Church Inc., 1952.

Keene, Donald. *The Manyoshu.* New York: Colombia University Press, 1940.

Kellner, Esther. "Token Stories of Indiana." *Midwest Folklore Journal* 3/4 (1953): 223–30.

Kelly, Christopher. *The End of Empire: Attila the Hun and the Fall of Rome.* New York: W. W. Norton & Company, 2009.

Kempis, Thomas. *Lydwine of Schiedam, Virgin.* Translated by Vincent Scully. London; Burns & Oates, 1912.

Kennedy, Alexander. "Psychic Phenomena in the Orkney Islands." *Occult Review* 13/3 (1911): 127–37.

Kenner, Corrine, and Craig Miller. *Strange But True.* St. Paul, MN: Llewellyn Publications, 1997.

Kenney, James. *The Sources for the Early History of Ireland: An Introduction and Guide.* New York: Columbia University Press, 1929.

Kensinger, Kenneth. "Banisteriopsis Usage Among the Peruvian Cashinahua." In *Hallucinogens and Shamanism*, edited by Michael James Harner, 1–14. New York: Oxford University Press, 1973.

Kepelino, Keauokalini. *Kepelino's Traditions of Hawaii.* Translated by Martha Warren Beckwith. New York: Kraus Reprint, 1971.

Kerr, Anne. *Teresa Helena Higginson: Servant of God, "The Spouse of the Crucified," 1844–1905.* Rockford, Ill: Tan Books & Publishers, 1978.

Kidd, Dudley. *The Essential Kaffir.* London: A. & C. Black, 1904.

Kieckefer, Richard. *Unquiet Souls: Fourteenth-Century Saints and their Religious Milieu.* Chicago: University of Chicago Press, 1984.

Kim, So-un. *The Story Bag: A Collection of Korean Folk Tales.* Translated by Setsu Higashi. Rutland, VT: Tuttle, 1955.

Kinberg, Leah. "The Individual's Experience as it Applies to the Community: An Examination of Six Dream Narrations Dealing with the Islamic Understanding of Death." *Al-Qantara* 21/1 (2000): 425–444.

Kincaid, Charles. *The Indian Heroes.* London: Humphrey Milford, 1919.

Klotsche, Ernest. *The Supernatural in the Tragedies of Euripides as Illustrated in Prayers, Curses, Oaths, Oracles, Prophecies, Dreams, and Visions*. Lancaster, PA: Press of the New Era Printing Company, 1919.

Knappert, Jan. *Pacific Mythology: An Encyclopedia of Myth and Legend*. Hammersmith, London: Aquarian/Thorsons, 1992.

———. *The Aquarian Guide to African Mythology*. Wellington, Northants: The Aquarian Press, 1990.

Knight, Julia. "Ojibwa tales from Sault Ste. Marie, Mich." *Journal of American Folklore* 26/99 (1913): 91–96.

Knight, Kevin. "Letter 158 (A.D. 414)." From the *New Advent* website, 2021.

Kracke, Waud. "To Dream, Perchance to Cure: Dreaming and Shamanism in a Brazilian Indigenous Society." *Social Analysis: The International Journal of Social and Cultural Practice* 50/2 (2006): 106–120.

Kriza et al. *The Folktales of the Magyars*. Translated and edited by Rev. W. Henry Jones and Lewis Kropf. London: Published for the Folklore Society by E. Stock, 1889.

Kroeber, Alfred. *Ethnology of the Gros Ventre*. New York: The Trustees, 1908.

———. *Indian Myths of South Central California*. Berkeley: The University Press, 1907.

———. *More Mohave Myths*. Berkeley: University of California Press, 1972.

———. *Seven Mohave Myths*. Berkeley: University of California Press, 1948.

———. *Walapai Ethnography*. New York: Kraus Reprint, 1964.

Kübler-Ross, Elisabeth. *On Children and Death*. New York: Collier Books, 1985.

Landtman, Gunnar. *The Kiwai Papuans of British New Guinea: A Nature-Born Instance of Rousseau's Ideal Community*. New York: Johnson Reprint Company, 1970.

Lang, Andrew. *The Arabian Nights Entertainment*. New York: Dover Publications, 1969.

———. *The Book of Dreams and Ghosts*. London: Longmans, Green & Co., 1897.

———. *Cock Lane and Common Sense*. London: Longmans, Green & Co., 1894.

Lang, David, trans. *Lives and Legends of the Georgian Saints*. Crestwood, NY: St. Vladimir's Seminary Press, 1976.

Larson, Charles. *Opaque Shadows and Other Stories from Contemporary Africa*. Washington: Inscape, 1976.

Laskow, Sarah. "The Role of the Supernatural in the Discovery of EEGs," *The Atlantic* website, November 23, 2014.

Latham, Charlotte. *The Folklore Record Part I*. n.p. Publications of the Folk-Lore Society, 1878.

Laubscher, Barend. *Sex Custom and Psychopathology: A Study of South African Pagan Natives*. London; George Routledge & Sons Ltd., 1937.

Lavater, Ludwig. *Of Ghostes and Spirites, Walking by Night*. London: Thomas Creede, 1596.

Lawrence, Peter. *Gods, Ghosts, and Men in Melanesia: Some Religions of Australian New Guinea and the New Hebrides*. Melbourne: Oxford University Press, 1965.

Lawrie, Margaret. *Myths and Legends of the Torres Strait*. St. Lucas, Queensland: University of Queensland Press, 1972.

Le Braz, Anatole. *La Légende de la Mort*. Paris: H. Champion, 1923.

Lecouteaux, Claude. *The Return of the Dead*. Translated by Jon E. Graham. Rocherster, VT: Inner Traditions, 2009.

Lee, Frederick. *The Other World*. London: H.S. King & Co., 1875.

———. *More Glimpses of the World Unseen*. London: Chatto & Windus, 1879.

Leeson, Alice. "Certain Canadian Superstitions." *Journal of American Folk-Lore* 10/36 (1897): 76–78.

Leloudis, James. "Tokens of Death: Tales from Perquimans County." *North Carolina Folklore Journal* 25/2 (1977): 47–59.

Leo, Sherley. *St. Francis of Assisi, His Life and Writings as Recorded by his Contemporaries*. New York: Harper & Brothers, 1960.

Leslie, David. *Among the Zulus and Amatongas*. Edinburgh: Edmonston & Douglas, 1875.

Lester, R. H. "Kava Drinking in Vitilevu, Fiji." *Oceania* 12/2 (1941): 97–121.

Lichtenstadter, Ilse. *Introduction to Classical Arabic Literature: with Selections from Representative Works in English Translation*. New York: Schocken Books, 1976.

Ligouri, Alfonso Maria de'. *Victories of the Martyrs*. Translated by Eugene Grimm. New York: Benziger Brothers, 1888.

Little, Kenneth. *The Mende of Sierra Leone*. London: Routledge & Kegan Paul, 1967.

Livo, Norma. *Story Medicine: Multicultural Tales of Healing and Transformation*. Englewood, CO: Libraries Unlimited, 2001.

Lohman, Roger. *Dream Travelers: Sleep Experiences and Culture in the Western Pacific*. New York: Palgrave Macmillan, 2003.

London Dialectical Society. *Report on Spiritualism of the Committee of the London Dialectical Society.* London: J. Burns, 1873.

Long, Jeffrey. *God and the Afterlife: The Groundbreaking New Evidence for God and Near-Death Experience.* New York: HarperOne, 2016.

Long, Max. *The Secret Science Behind Miracles: Unveiling the Huna Tradition of the Ancient Polynesians.* Marina del Ray, CA: DeVorss, 1954.

Loomis, Laura. *Three Middle English Romances.* London: D. Nutt, 1911.

Lu, Sheng-yen. *Encounters with the World of Spirits.* San Bruno, CA: Purple Lotus Society, 1995.

Lucian. *Lucian III.* Translated by Austin Harmon. London: William Heinemann, 1857.

Luke, David. "Anthropology and Parapsychology: Still Hostile Sisters in Science?" *Time and Mind* 3/3 (2010): 245–66.

Luthin, Herbert. *Surviving Through the Days: Translations of Native California Stories and Songs.* Berkeley: University of California Press, 2002.

Lysaght, Patricia. *Banshee: The Irish Death-Messenger.* Boulder, CO: Roberts Rinehart Publishers, 1997.

Mac Firbisigh, Dubhaltach. *Annals of Ireland: Three Fragments.* Translated and edited by John O'Donovan. Dublin: Irish Archaeological and Celtic Society, 1860.

Mackenzie, Alexander. "The Prophecies of the Brahan Seer, Coinneach Odhar Fiosaiche." *The Celtic Magazine* 2/20, 1877: 297–304.

MacKenzie, Andrew. *Apparitions and Ghosts.* London: Littlehampton Book Services Ltd., 1971.

Mackenzie, Donald. *Indian Myth and Legend.* London: Gresham, 1913.

———. *Teutonic Myth and Legend: An Introduction to the Eddas and Sagas Beowolf, the Nibelungenlied, etc.* London: Gresham, 1912.

Mackenzie, Duncan. *The Spirit-Ridden Konde.* Philadelphia: J. B. Lippincott, 1925.

MacLagan, Robert. "Ghost Lights of the West Highlands." *Folklore* 8 (1897): 203–56.

MacLean, John. *The Indians of Canada: Their Manners and Customs.* London: C. H. Kelly, 1892.

MacManus, Seumas. *Donegal Fairy Stories.* New York: Dover Publications, 1968.

Macpherson, James, trans. *The Poems of Ossian Volume I.* London: Lackington, Allen, and Co., 1803.

Macrae, Norman, ed, *Highland Second-Sight.* Dingwall: G. Souter, 1909.

Madigan, Kevin, and Carolyn Osiek. *Ordained Women in the Early Church: A Documentary History.* Baltimore: Johns Hopkins University Press, 2005.

Malcolm, L. W. G. "Notes on the Religious Beliefs of the Eghap, Central Cameroon." *Folklore* 32–3 (1900): 354–79.

Malinowski, Bronislaw. *Magic, Science and Religion: And Other Essays.* Garden City, NY: Doubleday, 1954.

———. *The Sexual Life of Savages in North-Western Melanesia.* London: Routledge and Sons, Ltd. 1929.

Malory, Thomas. *Le Morte d'Arthur.* London: Cassell, 2000.

Mango, Cyril. *Byzantium: The Empire of New Rome.* New York: Scribner, 1980.

Maori, Pakeha. *Old New Zealand.* Auckland, NZ: Whitcombe & Tombs Limited, 1922.

Martin, Martin. *A Description of the Western Islands of Scotland.* London: Printed for Andrew Bell, at the Cross-Keys and Bible in Cornhill, Near Stocks-Market, 1703.

Martin, Rafe. *Mysterious Tales of Japan.* New York: G.P. Putnam's Sons, 1996.

Marwick, Ernest. *The Folklore of Orkney and Shetland.* London: B. T. Batsford, 1986.

Mason, Arthur. *The Historic Martyrs of the Primitive Church.* London: Longmans, Green & Co., 1905.

Mason Neale, John. *The Unseen World.* London: James Burns, 1847.

Massam, J. A. *The Cliff Dwellers of Kenya.* London: Frank Cass & Co. Ltd., 1968.

Masters, Anthony. *The Natural History of the Vampire.* New York: Putnam, 1972.

Matthews, Janet. *The Two Worlds of Jimmie Barker: The Life of an Australian Aboriginal 1900–1972 as told to Janet Matthews.* Canberra: Australian Institute of Aboriginal Studies, 1977.

Mayer, Elizabeth Lloyd. *Extraordinary Knowing: Science, Skepticism, and the Inexplicable Powers of the Human Mind.* New York: Bantam Books, 2007.

McClenon, James. *Wondrous Events: Foundations of Religious Belief.* Philadelphia: University of Pennsylvania Press, 1994.

———. "Kongo Near-Death Experiences: Cross-Cultural Patterns." *Journal of Near-Death Studies* 25/1 (2006): 21–34.

McClintock, Walter. *Old Indian Trails.* Boston: Houghton Mifflin, 1923.

McGovern, William. *Jungle Paths and Inca Ruins.* London: Hutchinson & Co. Ltd., 1927.

McNamara, Jo Ann, John Halborg, and Gordon Whatley, eds and trans. *Sainted*

Women of the Dark Ages. Durham: Duke University Press, 1992.

Melland, Frank. *In Witch-Bound Africa: An Account of the Primitive Kaonde Tribe.* Philadelphia: J. B. Lippincott Company, 1923.

Meltzer, David. *Birth, An Anthology of Ancient Texts, Songs, Prayers, and Stories.* San Francisco: North Point Press, 1981.

Merton, Thomas. *What are These Wounds? The Life of a Cistercian Mystic, Saint Lutgarde of Aywieres.* Milwaukee: Bruce, 1950.

Meseguer, Pedro. *The Secret of Dreams.* Westminster, MD: Newman Press, 1960.

Michael the Syrian. *The 7th Through Mid-9th Centuries from Michael Rabo's Chronicle.* Translated by Matti Moosa. Teaneck, NJ: Syriac Orthodox Church, 2014.

Minov, Sergey. *The Marvels Found in the Great Cities and in the Seas and on the Islands Vol. 6.* Cambridge: Open Book Publishers, 2021.

Moldenke, Charles. *The Tale of the Two Brothers: A Fairy Tale of Ancient Egypt.* Watchtung, NJ: The Elsinore Press, 1898.

Moncrieff, William. *Old Booty! A Serio-Comic Sailor's Tale.* London: William Kidd, 1830.

Moosa, Matti. *Crusades: Conflict Between Christendom and Islam.* Piscataway, NJ: Gorgias Press, 2008.

———. *Ghulat Beliefs.* Syracuse, NY: Syracuse University Press, 1988.

Moreira, Isabel. *Dreams, Visions, and Spiritual Authority in Merovingian Gaul.* Ithaca: Cornell University Press, 2000.

Moreman, Christopher. *Beyond the Threshold: Afterlife Beliefs and Experiences in World Religions.* Lanham, MD: Rowman & Littlefield Pub., 2008.

Morgan, Alison. *Talking to the Dead.* London: Magpie, 2010.

Morrison, James Horne. *Streams in the Desert.* London: Hodder & Stoughton, 1919.

Morse, Melvin. *Parting Visions: An Exploration of Pre-Death Psychic and Spiritual Experiences.* New York: Villard Books, 1995.

Morse, Melvin, and Paul Perry. *Closer to the Light: Learning from Children's Near-Death Experiences.* London: Souvenir, 1990.

Morton, Lisa. *Ghosts: A Haunted History.* London: Reaktion Books, 2015. Kindle.

Moss, Robert. *The Secret History of Dreaming.* Novato, CA: New World Library, 2009.

Mukerji, S. *Mr. Mukerji's Ghosts: Supernatural Tales from the British Raj Period by India's Ghost Story "collector."* n.p.: Leonaur, 2006.

Murphy, Todd. "Near-Death Experiences in Thailand." *Journal of Near-Death Studies* 19 (2001): 161–178.

Musick, Ruth. *The Telltale Lilac Bush and Other West Virginia Ghost Tales.* Lexington: University Press of Kentucky, 1965.

Musorillo, Herbert, ed. *The Acts of the Christian Martyrs.* Oxford: Clarendon Press, 1972.

Myers, John. *Voices from the Edge of Eternity.* New York: Pyramid Books, 1971.

Nelson, Edward. *The Eskimo about Bering Strait.* Washington, D.C.: U.S. Government Printing Office, 1900.

Neumann, J. "Near-Death Experiences in Judaic Literature." *Journal of Psychology and Judaism* 14/4 (1990): 225–36.

Neusner, Jacob. *The Tosefta: An Introduction.* Atlanta: Scholars Press, 1992.

———. *The Tosefta: Translated from the Hebrew Third Division.* New York, Ktav Publishing House Inc., 1979.

Newell, W. "Current Superstitions: Omens of Death" *The Journal of American Folklore* 2/4 (1889): 20.

Newton, Henry. *In Far New Guinea.* Philadelphia: J. B. Lippincott Company, 1914.

Nicholson, Reynold. *Studies in Islamic Mysticism.* Cambridge: At The University Press, 1921.

Norman. "Balder's Dream," *The Norse Gods* website, September 11, 2013.

Normann, Regine. "Norwegian Folktales: Translations of Folklore from Norway." *Norwegian Folktales* website, 2017.

Oakley, E. S., and Tara Gairola. *Himalayan Folklore.* Haryana, India: Vintage Books, 1988.

Oberg, Kalervo. *Indian Tribes of the Northern Mato Grosso, Brazil.* Washington, D.C.: U.S. Government Printing Office, 1953.

Obeyesekere, Gananath. *The Awakened Ones: Phenomenology of Visionary Experience.* New York: Columbia University Press, 2012.

O'Donnell, Elliot. *The Meaning of Dreams.* London: Eveleigh Nash, 1911.

Ogden, Daniel. *Greek and Roman Necromancy.* Princeton: Princeton University Press, 2001.

O'Grady, Standish. *Silva Gadelica (I-XXXI): A Collection of Tales in Irish with Extracts Illustrating Persons and Places.* London: Williams & Norgate, 1892.

O'Hanlon, John. *Lives of the Irish Saints: With Special Festivals, and the Commemorations of Holy Persons.* Dublin: J. Duffy, 1875.

Oliver, Douglas. *A Solomon Island Society.* Boston: Beacon Press, 1967.

Oliver, William. *The Mystery of Dreams*. New York: Dodd, Mead & Company, 1949.

Olson, Ronald. *The Quinault Indians*. Seattle: University of Washington Press, 1967.

———. *Social Structure and Social Life of the Tlingit in Alaska*. Millwood, NY: Kraus, 1976.

Ong, Roberto Keh. "The Interpretation of Dreams in Ancient China." PhD diss., the University of British Colombia, 1981.

Opier, Morris. *Myths and Legends of the Apache Indians*. New York: Kraus Reprint, 1940.

Osis, Karlis, and Erlendur Haraldsson. *At the Hour of Death*. Mamaroneck, NY: Distributed by Publishers Group West, 1986.

Ottway, Thomas. *News from the Invisible World*. London: Published by the Bookseller, 1853.

Owen, Robert. *Footfalls on the Boundary of Another World*. Philadelphia: J. B. Lippincott & Co., 1868.

Owen, Roy. *The Legend of Roland: A Pageant of the Middle Ages*. London: Phaidon, 1973.

Owen, Stephen. *The End of the Chinese 'Middle Ages': Essays in Mid-Tang Literary Culture*. Stanford, CA: Stanford University Press, 1996.

Palmer, Frederic. *Heretics, Saints and Martyrs*. Cambridge: Harvard University Press, 1925. Britannica, T. Editors of Encyclopaedia. "Pan." *Encyclopedia Britannica*, April 10, 2024.

Paris, Matthew. *Matthew Paris's English History Vol III: From the Year 1235 to 1273*. Translated by John Giles. London: H.G. Bohn, 1852.

Parker, Katie. *Australian Legendary Tales: Folklore of the Noongahburrahs as Told to the Picaninnies*. London: D. Nutt, 1896.

———. *The Euahlayi Tribe: A Study of Aboriginal Life in Australia*. London: A Constable & Company, Ltd., 1905.

Parrinder, Geoffrey. *African Traditional Religion*. London: S.P.C.K. Publishing, 1962.

———. *West African Psychology: A Comparative Study of Psychological and Religious Thought*. London: Lutterworth Press, 1951.

Parsons, Elsie. *Taos Tales*. New York: Dover, 1996.

Pasricha, Satwant. "Near-Death Experiences in India: Prevalence and New Features." *Journal of Near-Death Studies* 26/4 (2008): 267–282.

Patch, Howard. *The Other World*. Cambridge: Harvard University Press, 1950.

Paterson, James. *Curiousities of Christian History Prior to the Reformation.* London: Methuen, 1892.

Pearson, Patricia. *Opening Heaven's Door.* London: Simon & Schuster UK, 2014. Kindle.

Pearson, Patricia, Julia Mossbridge, and Julie Beischel. *Crisis Impressions: A Historical and Conceptual Review of the Literature.* n.p.: Windbridge Research Center, 2023.

Pedroso, Consiglieri, and Henriquetta Monteiro. *Portuguese Folktales.* London: Elliot Stock, 1882.

Peebles, Bernard. "Sulpicius Severus Writings." In *The Fathers of the Church: A New Translation Vol. 7., edited by Joseph Deferrari et al., 79–252.* New York: Fathers of the Church, 1949.

Peers, Gertrude. *The Early Northern Paintings: Studies in the National Gallery.* London: Medici Society, 1922.

Percy, Thomas. *Reliques of Ancient English Poetry Vol. III.* London: F. & C. Rivington, 1794.

Perera, Arthur. *Sinhalese Folklore Notes: Ceylon.* Bombay: British India Press, 1917.

Peters, Edward. *Monks, Bishops, and Pagans.* Philadelphia: University of Pennsylvania Press, 1975.

Peters, William. *At Heaven's Door.* New York: Simon & Schuster, 2022.

Petit, Francois. *The Spirituality of the Premonstratensians in the Twelfth and Thirteenth Centuries.* Translated by Victor Szczurek. Waterloo, ON: Arouca Press, 2020.

Petrovitch, Woislav. *Hero Tales and Legends of the Serbians.* London: G. G Harrap, 1921.

Piccinini, G. M., and G. M. Rinaldi. *Fantasmi die Morenti: Inchiesta su una Credenzia.* n.p.: Viareggio, Il, 1989.

Pinch, Geraldine. *Magic in Ancient Egypt.* Austin: University of Texas Press, 2009.

Pliny. *The Natural History Vol, 2.* Translated by John Bostock and H. T. Riley. London: H. G. Bohn, 1855.

———. *Natural History, Vol. 2, books 3–7.* Translated by Harris Rackham. Cambridge, MA: Harvard University Press, 1942.

Plutarch. *Plutarch's Morals: Ethical Essays Translated with Note and Index by Arthur Richard Shiletto.* London: George Bell & Sons, 1888.

———. *Plutarch's Morals. Translated from the Greek by Several Hands.* Corrected and revised by William Goodwin. Boston: Little, Brown, & Company, 1874.

Podmore, Frank. *Apparitions and Thought-Transference.* London: W. Scott, Ltd., 1902.

Poignant, Roslyn. *Oceanic Mythology: The Myths of Polynesia, Micronesia, Melanesia, Australia.* London: Hamlyn, 1967.

Powers, Stephen. *Tribes of California.* Berkeley: University of California Press, 1976.

Prince, Walter Franklin. *Noted Witnesses for Psychic Occurrences.* New Hyde Park, NY: University Books, 1963.

Proctor, John. *Short Lives of the Dominican Saints by a Sister of the Congregation of St. Catharine of Siena.* London: Kegan Paul, Trench, Trubner, 1901.

Punzak, Daniel. *A Spiritual Hypothesis.* Bloomington, IN: AuthorHouse, 2017. Kindle.

Radcliffe, John. *Fiends, Ghosts, and Spirits.* London: R. Bentley, 1854.

Rafy, Mrs. *Folk-Tales of the Khasis.* London: Macmillan & Co., Ltd., 1920.

Rahner, Karl. *Visions and Prophecies.* Freiburg: Herder, 1963.

Ramsay, Sterling. *Folklore, Prince Edward Island.* Charlottetown, P.E.I.: Square Deal Publications, 1970.

Randolph, Vance. *Ozark Superstitions.* New York: Dover Publications, 1964.

Rasmussen, Knud. *Across Arctic America.* London: G.P. Putnam's Sons, 1927.

———. *The People of the Polar North. Compiled from the Danish Originals and Edited by G. Herring.* Philadelphia: J. B. Lippincott Company, 1908.

Rawlings, Maurice. *Beyond Death's Door.* Nashville, NY: Thomas Nelson, 1978.

Redesdale, John. *Tales of Old Japan.* London: Macmillan & Co., 1890.

Reed, Adam. *Papua New Guinea's Last Place: Experiences of Constraint in a Postcolonial Prison.* New York: Berghahn Books, 2004.

Reichard, Gladys. *An Analysis of Coeur d'Alene Indian Myths.* Philadelphia: American Folklore Society, 1947.

Reichel-Dolmatoff, Gerardo and Alicia Reichel-Dolmatoff. *The People of Aritama.* London: Routledge & Kegan Paul, 1961.

Rhine, Joseph. *New Frontiers of the Mind: The Story of The Duke Experiments.* New York: Farrar & Rinehart, 1937.

Rhine, Louisa. *Hidden Channels of the Mind.* New York: W. Sloane Associates, 1961.

Rickert, Edith. *Early English Romances in Verse.* London: Chatto & Windus, 1908.

Rieti, Ubaldus da. *Life of St. Anthony of Padau.* Boston: Angel Guardian Press, 1895.

Rink, Hinrich. *Tales and Traditions of the Eskimo*. Edinburgh: W. Blackwood & Sons, 1875.

Riordan, James. *A World of Folk Tales*. London: Hamlyn, 1981.

Ritter, Hellmut. *The Ocean of the Soul: Men, the World and God in the Stories of Farid al-Din Atar*. Translated by John O'Kane. Leiden: Brill, 2003.

Robe, Stanley. *Hispanic Legends from New Mexico*. Berkeley: University of California Press, 1980.

———. *Index of Mexican Folktales, Including Narrative Texts from Mexico, Central America, and the Hispanic United States*. Berkeley: University of California Press, 1973.

Roberts, Nancy. *Ghosts of the Southern Mountains and Appalachia*. Columbia, SC: University of South Carolina Press, 1988.

Rogers, Edmund. "A Deathbed Vision." *Light: A Journal of Psychical, Occult, and Mystical Research* 23/13 (1906): 186.

———. *New Guinea: Big Man Island*. Toronto: Royal Ontario Museum, 1970.

Rogers, Louis. *Dreams and Premonitions*. Los Angeles: Theosophical Book Concern, 1916.

Rose, Ronald. *Living Magic: The Realities Underlying the Psychical Practices and Beliefs of Australian Aborigines*. New York: Rand McNally, 1956.

Rose, Stewart. *St. Ignatius Loyola and the Early Jesuits*. London: Burns & Oates, 1891.

Ross, Mabel, and Barbara Walker. *On Another Day: Tales Told Among the Nkundo of Zaire*. Hamden, CT: Archon Books, 1979.

Routledge, Katherine. *The Mystery of Easter Island*. Kempton, IL: Adventures Unlimited Press, 1998.

Roy, Sarat, and Ramesh Roy. "Man in India Office," *Kharias Vol 2*. Ranchi, 1937.

Ruby, Robert, and John Brown. *Dreamer-Prophets of the Columbia Plateau: Smohalla and Skolaskin*. Norman, OK: University of Oklahoma Press, 1969.

Russell, Norman, trans. *The Lives of the Desert Fathers: The Historia Monachorum in Aegypto*. London: Mowbray, 1981.

Sacheverell, William. *An Account of the Isle of Man*. Douglas, Isle of Man: Printed for the Manx Society, 1859.

Sartori, Penny. *The Wisdom of Near-Death Experiences*. London: Watkins Publishing Limited, 2014.

Savage, Minot. *Life Beyond Death*. New York: G. P. Putnam's Sons, 1899.

Say, Thomas. *Short Compilation of the Extraordinary Life and Writings of Thomas Say*. New York: John Langdon, 1805.

Sayers, William. "Gunnarr, his Irish Wolfhound Sámr, and the Passing of the Old Heroic Order in Njáls saga." *Arkiv För Nordisk Filologi* 112 (1997): 43–66.

Schmied-Knittel, I., and M. T. Schetsche. "Everyday Miracles: Results of a Representative Survey in Germany." *European Journal of Parapsychology* 20/1 (2005): 3–21.

Schouppe, Francois. *Purgatory: Illustrated by the Lives and Legends of the Saints.* Rockford, IL: Tan Books, 1973.

Schwab, George. "Bulu Folk-Tales." *Journal of American Folk-Lore* 27 (1914): 266–88.

———. *Tribes of the Liberian Hinterland.* Cambridge, MA: Published by the Museum, 1947.

Schwarz, Hans. *Beyond the Gates of Death: A Biblical Examination of Evidence for Life After Death.* Minneapolis: Augsburg Publishing House, 1981.

Schwarz, Herbert. *Tales from the Smokehouse.* Edmonton: Hurtig, 1976.

Schwartz, Howard. *Lilith's Cave: Jewish Tales of the Supernatural.* New York: Harper & Row, 1988.

———. *Tree of Souls: The Mythology of Judaism.* Oxford, NY: Oxford University Press, 2004.

Scott, Walter. *The Minstrelsy of the Scottish Border.* London: Andrew Melrose, 1908.

———. *Tales from French History.* Philadelphia: H. T. Coates & Co., 1900.

Segal, Alan. *Life after Death: A History of the Afterlife in the Religions of the West.* New York: Doubleday, 2004.

Seibold, David, and Charles Adams. *Shipwrecks Near Barnegat Inlet.* Barnegat Light, NJ: D. J. Seibold, 1984.

Sels, Nadia. "Ambiguity and Mythic Imagery in Homer: Rhesus' Lethal Nightmare." *The Classical World* 106/4 (2013): 555–70.

Senungetuk, Vivian. *Wise Words of Paul Tiulana: An Inupiat Alaskan's Life.* New York: Franklin Watts, 1998.

Seuse, Heinrich. *The Life of Blessed Henry Suso.* London: Burns, Lambert & Oates, 1865.

Sevcenko, Nancy P. "Canon and Calendar: The Role of Ninth-Century Hymnographers in Shaping The Celebration of The Saints." In *The Celebration of The Saints in Byzantine Art and Liturgy*, edited by Nancy Sevcenko, 101–104. London: Routledge, 2013.

Seyed-Gohrab, Ali Asghar. *Layli and Majnun: Love Madness and Mystic Longing in Nizami's Eic Romance.* London: Brill, 2003.

Seymour, St. John, and Harry Neligan. *True Irish Ghost Stories.* Dublin: Hodges, Figgis & Co., Ltd., 1914.

Shakespeare, William. *Macbeth: Told by a Popular Novelist.* n.p.: Greening & Company, 1914.

Sharma, Jayantakumar, and Chirom Singh. *Folktales of Manipur.* Translated by Kamaljit Chriom. Khurai Lamlong: Cultural Research Centre Manipur, 2014.

Shirokogorov, Sergei. *Psychomental Complex of the Tungus.* London: Kegan, Paul, Trench, Trubner, 1935.

Shortland, Edward. *Traditions and Superstitions of the New Zealanders.* London: Longman, Brown, Green, Longmans & Roberts, 1856.

Shushan, Gregory. "The Harrowing of Hell: Did Jesus Have a Near-Death Experience?" Medium website, 2022.

Simpson, Jacqueline. *The Northmen Talk.* London: Phoenix House, 1965.

Sinel, Joseph. *The Sixth Sense. London:* T. Werner Laurie Limited, 1927.

Skeat, Walter. *Malay Magic.* London: Macmillan & Co., Ltd., London, 1900.

Skylitzes, John. *The Chronicle of John Skylitzes: A Synopsis of Byzantine History.* Translated by John Wortley. Cambridge, NY: Cambridge University Press, 2010.

Smartt, Lisa. *Words at the Threshold.* Novato, CA: New World Library, 2017.

Smith, Richard Gordon. *Ancient Tales and Folklore of Japan.* London: A. & C. Black, 1908.

Smith, Susy. *Life is Forever.* Lincoln, NE: toExcel Press, Inc., 1999.

Snorasson, Oddr. *The Sagas of Olaf Tryggvason and of Harald the Tyrant.* Translated by Ethel H. Hearn. Williams and Norgate, 1911.

Songling, Pu. *Strange Stories from a Chinese Studio.* Translated by Herbert Giles. London: T. Werner Laurie, 1909.

Sotah 33a: The William Davidson Talmud. Sefaria website, n.d.

Southwell, Robert. *A Short Rule of Good Life to Direct the Devout Christian in a Regular and Orderly Course.* At S. Omers: By [C. Boscard for] Iohn Heigham, An. 1622.

Sozomen, Philostorgius, and Photius I. *The Ecclesiastical History of Sozomen: Comprising a History of the Church from A. D. 324 to A. D. 440.* Translated by Edward Walford. London: Bohn, 1885.

Spence, Lewis. *Legends and Romances of Spain.* London: G. G. Harrap & Company Ltd., 1920.

Spencer, John. *The Encyclopedia of Ghosts and Spirits*. London: Headline Books, 1992.

Spier, Leslie, ed. *The Sinkaietk or Southern Okanagon*. Menasha, WI: George Banta Publishing Company, 1938.

Spinka, Matthew, and Robert Downey. *The Chronicle of John Malalas Books VIII–XVIII*. Chicago: University of Chicago Press, 1940.

St. Clair, Harry, and Leo Frachtenberg. "Traditions of the Coos Indians of Oregon." *The Journal of American Folklore* 22/83, (1909): 25–41.

St. Clair, Sheila. *Unexplained Encounters: Exploring The Paranormal in Ulster*. Belfast: White Row Press, 2001.

Steel, Flora Annie. *Tales of the Punjab Told by the People*. London: Macmillan & Co., 1894.

Steele, Robert, ed. *The Russian Garland, Being Russian Folk Tales*. London: A. M. Philpot, 1921.

Steiger, Brad, and Sherry Steiger. *Children of the Light: The Startling and Inspiring Truth About Children's Near-Death Experiences and How They Illuminate the Beyond*. New York: Signet-Penguin, 1995.

Stevenson, Ian. *Telepathic Impressions: A Review and Report of Thirty-Five New Cases*. New York: American Society for Physical Research, 1970.

Steward, Julian. *Northern and Gosiute Shoshone*. Berkeley: University of California Press, 1943.

St. Lys, Odette. *From a Vanished German Colony: A Collection of Folklore, Folk Tales and Proverbs from South-West-Africa*. London: Gypsy Press, 1916.

Stokes, Margaret. *Six Months in the Apennines; Or, A Pilgrimage in Search of Vestiges of the Irish Saints in Italy*. London: George Bell & Sons, 1892.

Stokes, Whitley. *Lives of Saints, from the Book of Lismore*. Oxford: Clarendon Press, 1890.

———. "The Voyage of the Hui Corra." *Revue Celtique* 14 (1893): 22–69.

Strauss, Marjory. "The Death of Meleager in the Mid-Sixteenth Century." In *Renaissance Papers 1973*, edited by Dennis G. Donovan and A Leigh Deneef, 23–36. Javea, Valencia: Southeastern Renaissance Conference, 1973.

Stroebe, Clara. *The Swedish Fairy Book*. Translated by Frederick Herman Martens. New York; Frederick A. Stokes, 1921.

Sturluson, Snorri. *Heimskringla, or The Lives of the Norse Kings*. Translated by Erling Monsen and Albert Hugh Smith. New York: Dover, 1990.

———. *The Elder Edda of Saemund Sigfusson*. Translated by I. A. Blackwell. London: Norroena Society, 1907.

———. *Anglo-Saxon and Norse Poems*. Translated by Ethel H. Hearn. London: Williams & Norgate, 1911.

Summers, Montague. *The Physical Phenomena of Mysticism*. New York: Barnes & Noble Inc., 1950.

———. *The Vampire in Europe*. Whitefish, MT: Kessinger Publishing, 2003.

Tabor, Margaret. *The Saints in Art: With Their Attributes and Symbols Alphabetically Arranged*. New York: E.P. Dutton, 1913.

Taillepied, Noel. *A Treatise of Ghosts*. Translated by Montague Summers. Plymouth, UK: Fortune Press, 1933.

Talayesva, Don. *Sun Chief: The Autobiography of a Hopi Indian*. New Haven, CT: Yale University Press.

Talbot, Percy. *In the Shadows of the Bush*. New York: G. H. Doran, 1912.

———. *Tribes of the Niger Delta*. New York: Barnes & Noble, 1967.

Teeter, Emily. *Religion and Ritual in Ancient Egypt*. Cambridge: Cambridge University Press, 2011.

Teit, James. *Traditions of the Thompson River Indians of British Columbia*. Boston: For the American Folk-Lore Society by Houghton, Mifflin & Company, 1898.

Temperley, Alan. *Tales of Galloway*. Edinburgh: Mainstream, 1986.

Terada, Alice. *The Magic Crocodile and Other Folktales from Indonesia*. Honolulu: University of Hawaii Press, 1994.

Teran, Buenaventura. "Jaguar-Man." In *Folk Literature of the Mocovi Indians*, edited by Johannes Wilbert and Karin Simoneau, 253–255. Los Angeles: UCLA Latin American Center Publications, University of California, 1988.

Terkel, Studs. *Will the Circle Be Unbroken? Reflections on Death and Dignity*. New York: The New Press, 2001.

Terry, Richard. *The Shanty Book: Sailor Shanties*. London: J. Curwen & Sons, 1921.

Theal, George. *Kaffir Folk-Lore*. London: W. Swan Sonnenschein, 1882.

———. *The Yellow and Dark-Skinned People of Africa South of the Zambesi*. London: S. Sonnenschein & Co., 1910.

Thompson, Charles. *The Mystery and Lore of Apparitions*. London: H. Shaylor, 1930.

Thrum, Thomas. *Hawaiian Folk Tales*. Chicago: McClurg & Co., 1907.

Toelken, Barre. "The Moccasin Telegraph and Other Improbabilities: A Personal Essay." In *Out of the Ordinary: Folklore and the Supernatural,* edited by Barbara Walker, 46–58. Logan: Utah State University Press, 1995.

Tong, Diane. *Gypsy Folk Tales*. San Diego: Harcourt Brace Jovanovic, 1989.

Tremearne, Arthur. *The Ban of the Bori; Demons and Demon-Dancing in West and North Africa*. London: Heath, Cranton & Ouseley Ltd., 1914.

Trevelyan, George. *Garibaldi and the Thousand*. London: Longmans, Green & Co., 1912.

Truss. David G. "The Psychic Story of a Parson." *Psychic Science* 18 (1939): 61–71.

Turner, Victor. *Revelation and Divination in Ndembu Ritual*. Ithaca, NY: Cornell University Press, 1975.

Tyler, Royall. *Japanese Tales*. New York: Pantheon Books, 1987.

Tylor, Edward. *Primitive Culture: Researches into the Development of Mythology, Philosophy, Religion, Art, and Custom*. London: Murray, 1920.

Tyrrell, George. *Science and Psychical Phenomena and Apparitions, in One Volume*. New Hyde Park, NY: University Books, 1962.

Ury, Marion. *Tales of Times Now Past: Sixty-Two Stories from a Medieval Japanese Collection*. Berkeley: University of California Press for the Center for Japanese and Korean Studies, University of California, 1979.

Văcărescu, Helene. *Songs of the Valiant Voivode, and Other Strange Folk-Lore*. New York: C. Scribner's Sons, 1905.

Van Bronkhorst, Jeanne. *Dreams at the Threshold*. Woodbury, MN: Llewellyn Publications, 2015.

van der Post, Laurens. *The Lost World of the Kalahari*. London: The Hogarth Press, 1918.

van Diemerbroeck, Ysbrand. *Tractatus de Peste*. Amstelaedami: Joannis Blaev, 1665.

Velimirovic, Nikolaj. *Stories of Saints from the Prologue: Based on the Prologue from Ohrid by Bishop Nikolai Velimirovich*. Compiled and adapted by Johanna Manley. Libertyville, IL: Bishop Nikolai Resource Center, St. Sava Serbian Orthodox Monastery, 1998.

Velimirovic, Nikolaj. *The Prologue From Ohrid*. n.a. n.a., 1926.

Vickers, William. "Cultural Adaptation to Amazonian Habitats: The Siona-Secoya of Eastern Ecuador." PhD diss., University of Florida, 1976.

Vigil, Angel. *The Eagle on the Cactus: Traditional Tales from Mexico*. Englewood, CO: Libraries Unlimited, 2000.

Villa, Susie, ed. *100 Armenian Tales*. Detroit: Wayne State University Press, 1966.

Virtanen, Leea. *That Must Have Been ESP! An Examination of Psychic Experiences*. Bloomington, IN: Indiana University Press, 1990.

Virtue, Doreen. *Angel Visions*. Carlsbad, CA: Hay House, Inc, 2000.

Vitalis, Ordericus. *The Ecclesiastical History of England and Normandy Vol. II*. Translated by Thomas Forester. London: Henry G. Bohn, 1853.

von Furer-Haimendorf, Christoph. *The Konyak Nagas: An Indian Frontier Tribe*. New York: Holt, Rinehart & Winston, 1969.

von Haxthausen, August. *Transcaucasia, Sketches of the Nations and Races Between the Black Sea and the Caspian*. London: Chapman & Hall, 1854.

Vyasa. *The Mahābhārata*. Translated by John Smith. New Delhi: Penguin, 2009.

Wade, John. *Select Proverbs of All Nations*. London: Longman, Hurst, Rees, Orme, Brown, & Green, 1824.

Wallace, Ernest. *The Comanches: Lords of the South Plains*. Norman, OK: University of Oklahoma Press, 1952.

Walker, John. "A Sampling of Folklore from Rutherford County." *North Carolina Folklore* 3/2 (1955): 14–5.

Walker Jr., Deward. *Witchcraft and Sorcery of the American Native Peoples*. Moscow, ID: University of Idaho Press, 1989.

Walsh, Angela. "Rendering 20th Century Peruvian Folklore for a 21st Century Reader: ES>EN Translation and Analysis of Peruvian Folktales and Mythology." Master's thesis, Minnesota State University, Mankato, 2020. Cornerstone Library website.

Walsh, Michael. *New Dictionary of Saints: East and West*. London: Burns & Oats, 2007.

Walton, Izaak. *The Lives of Dr. John Donne, Sir Henry Wotton, Mr. Richard Hooker, Mr. George Herbert*. York: Wilson, Spence & Mawman, 1796.

Wanley, Nathaniel. *The Wonders of the Little World*. London: Printed For W. J. and J. Richardson, 1806.

Wardrop, Marjory, translator. *Georgian Folk Tales*. London: D. Nutt, 1894.

Warner, Elizabeth. *Heroes, Monsters and Other Worlds from Russian Mythology*. New York: P. Bedrick Books, 1996.

Watkins, John Elfreth. "Ghosts and Visions that People have Seen." *The Ladies Home Journal* 22/4 (1905): 6.

Watson, Robert. "Hiding from Pandemics, and from Ourselves: The Case of Ben Jonson," *Los Angeles Review of Books* website, May 5, 2020.

Webster, Wentworth. *Basque Legends*. London: Griffith and Farran, 1879.

Wells, Michael. *Untold Stories and Unknown Saints*. Littleton, CO: Abiding Life Press, 2008.

Welsch, Roger. *A Treasury of Nebraska Pioneer Folklore*. Lincoln, NE: University of Nebraska Press, 1984.

Westervelt, William Drake. *Hawaiian Legends of Ghosts and Ghost-Gods*. Boston: Ellis Press, 1916.

Westwood, Jennifer. *The Penguin Book of Ghosts: The Spectres, Apparitions and Phantoms That Haunt the Lore of the Land.* London: Allen Lane, 2008.

Wheeler, Post. *Albanian Wonder Tales.* Garden City, NY: Doubleday, Doran & Company Inc., 1936.

White, Patrick. *Comala Or The Irish Princess: A Dramatic Poem Founded Upon an Ancient Irish Legend.* Wateford: J. H. McGrath, 1870.

White, R. A. "An Analysis of ESP Phenomena in the Saints." *Parapsychology Review* 13/1 (1982): 15–18.

White, William. *Life of Emanuel Swedenborg.* Philadelphia: J. B. Lippincott & Co., 1866.

Whitlock, Ralph. *The Folklore of Wiltshire.* Totowa, NJ: Rowman & Littlefield, 1976.

Wiebe, Phillip. *God and Other Spirits.* Oxford, NY: Oxford University Press, 2004.

Wilberforce, Bertrand. *Devotions to Saint Dominic.* North Guildford, CT: Our Lady of Grace Monastery, 1957.

"William." "Dream Meeting with his Dead Friend." All About Heaven website, November 2, 2002.

Wilson, Christopher. "The Dissemination of Visions of the Otherworld in England and Northern France c.1150–c.1321." PhD diss., Exeter University, 2012.

Wimberly, Lowry. *Death and Burial Lore in the English and Scottish Popular Ballads.* Lincoln, NE: University of Nebraska, 1927.

Windham, Joan, and Renee George. *Sixty Saints for Girls.* Westminster, MD: Christian Classics, 1990.

Winters, Riley. "The Saga of Norna-Gest: Does Man Control His Destiny?" *Ancient Origins* website, March, 31, 2015.

Wodrow, Robert. *Analecta.* Glasgow: Printed for the Maitland Club, 1842.

Woodyard, Chris. "Tokens of Death: Owls, Cats, and Phantom Funerals," *Haunted Ohio* website, November 27, 2012.

Work, Henry. *Songs of Henry Clay Work.* Compiled by Bertram G. Work. New York: Press of J.J. Little & Ives Co., 1920.

Yanagita, Kunio. *The Legends of Tono.* Translated by Ronald Morse. Lanham, MD: Lexington Books, 2008.

Zaleski, Carol. *Otherworld Journeys: Accounts of Near-Death Experience in Medieval and Modern Times.* New York: Oxford University Press, 1987.

Zerffi, Gustavus. *Spiritualism and Animal Magnetism.* London: Robert Hardwicke, 1871.

Zupitza, Julius. *The Romance of Guy of Warwick.* London: N. Trubner & Co., 1966.

Zur, Judith. *Violent Memories: Mayan War Widows.* Boulder: Westview Press, 1998.

Index

symbolic visions, 92
waking visions, 74
watery graves, 186–87
Green, Lawrence George, 58
Gregory, William, 190
Gregory the Great, 76, 93, 174, 199, 211
Grettir's Saga, 160
Grey, Margot, 218–19, 220–21
Greyson, Dr. Bruce, 207
grief, 23, 76
Grose, Francis, 106–7
Gros Ventre Indians, 70
Guala of Bergamo, 101–2
Guatemalan tales, 16, 23
Guggenheim, Bill and Judy, 136, 162
Guingamor, 206
Gundrun's vision, 188–89
Gunnlaug, 172, 191
Gun-nop-do-yah, 21–22
Gurney, Edmund, 4
Guy of Warwick, 83, 85

Haggard, Rider, 129
hagiographers, 62
Hamilton, Allan, 214
Hamundarson, Gunnar, 129
Haraldsson, Erlendur, 175–76, 192
Hardy, Alister, x, xi
Harrison, William Henry, 69
Hawaiian tales, 22, 70, 122–23, 138
health, life tokens and, 106–12
Hedin, Sven, 57–58
Henderson, William, 96, 113
Herod the Great, 44
Hildebrand, 204
Himalayan legend, 111
Hind Horn, 114
HMS *Beagle*, 117–18

Hoffman, Luellen, 31
Hopi Indian tales, 132
Hosmer, Harriet, 4–5
Hufford, David, 7
Hurly, Berta, 72
Hyatt, Harry Middleton, 178

Ibn Abi al-Dunya, 129
Ibn al-Farid, 147
Icelandic stories
  apparition appearance at death, 190–91, 194
  collective apparitions, 175
  crisis apparitions, 14
  locating the lost, 55
  out-of-body journeys, 200–201
  symbolic dreams and visions, 89
  veridical voices, 143
  watery graves, 189
Ichiko, 61
Ilatsiak, 100
Iliad, death scenes, 42–43
Indian's telegram, 59
Indian tales, 12, 46–47, 49, 101, 104, 109, 167
Indonesian tale, 18
Inglis, Brian, 150
Inupiat tales, 110–11, 155
Iphigenia at Aulis, 92–93
Irish banshee, 120
Irish tales
  apparition appearance at death, 194–95
  life tokens, 111
  on-the-nose death imagery, 98–99
  simultaneous visions, 166–67
Iroquois legend, 21–22
Islamic vision, 41